CHARMING
SMALL HOTEL
GUIDES

France

CHARMING SMALL HOTEL GUIDES

France

Edited by Chris Gill

DUNCAN PETERSEN

HUNTER
PUBLISHING INC

300 Raritan Center Parkway,
CN 94, Edison, N.J. 08818

Copyright © Chris Gill 1996
        © Duncan Petersen Publishing Ltd 1996

Conceived, designed and produced by
Duncan Petersen Publishing Ltd,
Edited by Fox and Partners, The Old Forge,
Norton St Philip, Bath, U.K.

Editor	Chris Gill
Revisions editor	Nicola Davies
Art director	Mel Petersen
Editorial director	Andrew Duncan

This edition published in the UK and Commonwealth 1996 by
Duncan Petersen Publishing Ltd,
31 Ceylon Road, London W14 OYP

Sales representation in the U.K. and Ireland by
World Leisure Marketing,
Downing Road,
West Meadows Industrial Estate
Derby DE21 6HA
Tel: 01332 343 332

Distributed by Grantham Book Services

ISBN 1 872576 60 5

A CIP catalogue record for this book is available
from the British Library

AND

Published in the USA 1995 by
Hunter Publishing Inc.,
300 Raritan Center Parkway, CN 94, Edison, N.J. 08818.
Tel (908) 225 1900 Fax (908) 417 0482

ISBN 1-55650-734-8

Typeset by Duncan Petersen Publishing Ltd
Printed by G. Canale & Co SpA, Turin

Contents

Readers' reports

Reports from readers are of enormous help to us in keeping up to date with the hotels in the guide – and other hotels that should be in it. The most helpful reporters are invited to join our Travellers' Panel, and to stay in listed hotels at little or no cost. More information on p11.

Introduction

The best hotels in France

It's eight years now since we first set out to identify the hotels that help to make travelling in France such a special experience. Then, we were looking for the 300 most captivating auberges, châteaux, moulins and chalets in the land. After our recent major overhaul of the guide, we now have an expanded coverage of over 360 hotels, with photographs of more than 120. We've achieved this by organising the book differently, as explained on page 8.

This expansion could not have come at a better time. The country hotel scene in France seems to us to be more vigorous than ever. There are more small hotels opening, few closing, and lots continuing to invest in improvements. With confidence returning in the UK after the recession, and the Channel tunnel at last delivering its long-awaited stimulus to cross-Channel travel, those French hotels with a significant British trade, at least, can look forward to a period of prosperity.

To create the expanded edition, we threw the net wide, and gathered information on many more hotels than we could accommodate. As a result, we have a long list of hotels that failed to make an entry, but which might well make one next year. These include hotels that readers have written in about; hotels that produce an impressive brochure, but about which we at present know little else; hotels highly recommended in other guides.

It seemed to us that readers might like to know of these hotels. Certainly, we'd like to encourage readers to try them out and report back. So we're including lists of these 'Contenders' at the start of each section of the book. Do bear these hotels in mind when looking for somewhere to stay. Naturally, you're likely to want to look before you book, but we've included phone numbers so that you can at least find out what's available.

We are, naturally, enthusiastic about French hotels in general. But we are not blind to their faults. Here is a list of our current pet hates.

The 'confused' booking You make a booking, even send a deposit, and on arrival find that you're not expected. If you can't be accommodated and are put up in some other house in the village, there is the teeniest suspicion that what is at work is not confusion but greed.

The soggy bed As we've observed in our British edition, it's the easiest thing in the world to fail to spot the gradual decay of a bed unless you take the precaution of occasionally testing every one in the house.

The dreary breakfast We know that the French aren't very keen on breakfast, but hoteliers ought to be aware that many other people are – especially when travelling, and a good start to the day is important.

Introduction

The second-class pensionnaires' meals If you're tempted to stay on pension or demi-pension terms, be sure you know what choice of dishes will be open. There may be none at all; or you may be confined to the cheapest menu.

The windowless garden room Quite a few French country hotels accommodate some or all of their guests in single-storey outbuildings with glazed doors opening on to the garden or the pool. And quite a few provide no ventilation other than those doors, which most travellers would naturally be reluctant to leave open at night.

The rough deal for vegetarians The acceptance of vegetarianism in France is still very limited, and progressing very slowly. Too many cooks, waiters and proprietors of small hotels find it hard to conceal the fact that they think vegetarians are mad, and a great nuisance.

For new readers

This guide is part of a series also covering Italy, Spain, the British Isles, Germany, Austria, Switzerland, New England, Tuscany and Umbria and (autumn 1996) Florida. There is also a companion volume focusing on bed-and-breakfast accommodation in France.

We aim to include only those hotels and guest-houses which are in some way captivating, and which offer truly personal service, usually from the owner. In France, most of our recommendations have fewer than 20 rooms.

Our ideal hotel has a peaceful, pretty setting; the building itself is either handsome or historic, or at least has a distinct character. The rooms are spacious. The decorations and furnishings are harmonious, comfortable and impeccably maintained, and include antique pieces that are meant to be used, not revered. The proprietors and staff are dedicated, thoughtful and sensitive – friendly and welcoming without being intrusive. Last but not least, the food, whether simple or elaborate, is fresh, interesting and carefully prepared.

Our entries employ words, not symbols. They are written by people with something to say, not a bureaucracy which has long since lost the ability to distinguish the praiseworthy from the mediocre. Every entry aims to give a definite feel of what it is actually like to stay in that place. The editorial team is small and highly experienced at assessing hotels. Although we place great emphasis on consistency, we have made use of reports from readers, and would welcome more of them (see box on page 11).

The guide contains colour photographs of about one-third of the entries – usually the more attractive ones; the entries are presented in clear geographical groups; and each entry is categorized by the type of accommodation (for example, country inn).

Introduction

How to find an entry

In this guide, the entries are arranged in geographical groups. First, the whole country is divided into three major sections; we start with Northern France and proceed to Central and finally Southern France. Within these sections, the entries are dealt with in regions consisting of groups of départements. The Contents page lists the regions we have used.

Each regional section follows a set sequence:

> • First comes an Area introduction – an overview of that region, incorporating (if there's space) a summary of the tourist highlights. Under the heading 'Contenders', we list hotels that have failed to make an entry this year, but which we believe to be strong candidates for an entry in future. These listings may be useful if recommended hotels are full, or if there are no recommendations in a particular area. We particularly welcome reports on these hotels.

> • Then come the main, full-page entries for that region, arranged in alphabetical order by town. These are generally the hotels that we judge most attractive.

> • Finally come the shorter, quarter-page entries for that region, similarly arranged alphabetically by town. These are generally not as special as the hotels given a full-page entry; but don't disregard them – they are still hotels we would happily stay at, and many are clear candidates for 'promotion' in later editions.

To find a hotel in a particular area, simply browse through the headings at the top of the pages until you find that area – or use the maps following this introduction to locate the appropriate pages. The maps show not only the place-name under which each hotel appears, but also the page number of the entry.

To locate a specific hotel or a hotel in a specific place, use the indexes at the back, which list the entries alphabetically, first by name and then by place-name.

How to read an entry

At the top of each entry is a coloured bar highlighting the name of the town or village where the establishment is located, along with a categorization which gives some clue to its character.

Fact boxes

The fact box given for each hotel follows a standard pattern; the explanation that follows is for full entries – short, quarter-page entries have less detailed fact boxes.

Under **Tel** we give the telephone number, starting with (1) if the hotel is in the Paris area; if dialling such a number within Paris, you should omit the (1). When dialling Paris from the provinces, or vice versa, you must preface the whole number with 16. When dialling a provincial number in the provinces, the eight digits we give are all you need to dial. We now also give **Fax** numbers where appropriate.

Under Location we give information on the setting of the hotel and on its car parking arrangements, as well as pointers to help you find it. It is worth bearing in mind that many of our hotels are in remote spots where a large-scale road map is more-or-less essential for reliable route-finding.

Under **Meals** we list the meals available.

The basic **Prices** in this volume – unlike our volume on Britain and Ireland – are **per room**. We normally give the range of prices you can expect to pay for a room – from the cost of the cheapest single room in low season to the cost of the dearest double in high season. If the room price we give includes breakfast, we say so; otherwise, space permitting, we normally give the price of breakfast separately; where it is not given, allow 40F to 70F, according to the room price. We then give the prices of other meals, concentrating on fixed-price menus, or of prices for a room plus meals – either for dinner, bed and breakfast (DB&B), or for full board (FB) – all meals included. All these meal-inclusive prices are **per person**. Prices includes tax and service.

Wherever possible we have given prices for 1995, but for many hotels these were not available when the guide was prepared. Bear in mind also that proprietors may change their prices from one year to another by more than the rate of inflation, particularly if the hotel has been upgraded in some important respect. Always check when booking.

Introduction

Under **Rooms** we summarize the number and style of bedrooms available. Our lists of facilities in bedrooms cover only mechanical gadgets, and not ornaments such as flowers or consumables such as toiletries or free drinks.

Under **Facilities** we list public rooms and then outdoor and sporting facilities which are either part of the hotel or immediately on hand; facilities in the vicinity of the hotel but not directly connected with it (for example, a nearby golf course) are not listed here, though they sometimes feature at the end of the main description in the **Nearby** section, which presents interesting things to see or do in the locality.

We use the following abbreviations for **Credit cards:**

AE American Express
DC Diners Club
MC MasterCard (Access/Eurocard)
V   Visa (Barclaycard/Bank Americard/Carte Bleue etc)

The final entry in a fact box is normally the name of the proprietor(s); but where the hotel is run by a manager we give his or her name instead.

Reporting to the guides

Please write and tell us about your experiences of small hotels, guest-houses and inns, whether good or bad, whether listed in this edition or not. As well as hotels in France, we are interested in hotels in Britain and Ireland, Italy, Spain, Austria, Germany, Switzerland and the USA. We assume that reporters have no objections to our publishing their views unpaid, either verbatim or in edited form.

Readers whose reports prove particularly helpful may be invited to join our Reporters' Register; this means that you receive a free copy of the new edition of the guide in the winter, preceded by a newsletter in the autumn and followed by another in the spring. In return, we hope to receive further reports.

Register members who report regularly and reliably may be invited to join our Travellers' Panel. Members give us notice of their own travel plans; we suggest hotels that they might inspect, and contribute to the cost of accommodation.

The address to write to is:

Duncan Petersen Publishing Ltd
31 Ceylon Road, London W14 0YP, England.

Checklist
Please use a separate sheet of paper for each report; include your name and address on each report.

Your reports will be received with particular pleasure if they are typed, and if they are organized under the following headings:

Name of establishment
Town or village it is in, or nearest
Full address, including post code
Date and duration of visit
The building and setting
The public rooms
The bedrooms and bathrooms
Comfort (chairs, beds, heat, light, hot water)
Standards of maintenance and housekeeping
Atmosphere, welcome and service
Food
Value for money

Barfleur **37**

Cherbourg ○

St-Vaast-
la-Hougue
32

Trelly **44**

Perros-Guirec **41**   Tréguier **44**

Trébeurden **34 44**   Paimpol **41**

Le Mont-St-
Michel **41**

Pléhédel **42**

St-Malo **30**

Ducey
25

Dinard **39**

Ste-Anne-la-
Palud **33**

Rennes ○

Trégunc **44**

Hennebont **39**

Raguenês-Plage **42**   Moëlan-
sur-Mer **40**

La Roche-
Bernard
42 43

Nantes ○

Belle-Ile-en-Mer **38**

Marans **95**

La Rochelle **87**

Tonnay-
Boutonne **91**

Dieppe

Martin-Église **40**

Etretat **26**

Le Havre
Honfleur **40**
St-André-d'Hébertot **29**

Caudebec-
en-Caux **39**
La Bouille **39**
Rouen **43**

Bayeux **37**

Beuzeville **38**
Campigny **22**
Pont-Audemer **28**

Le Bec-Hellouin **38**
Louviers **40**
St-Pierre-du-Vauvray **31**
Verneuil-sur-Avre **35**

Les Andelys **37**
Gisors **27**

Clécy **23**

Sourdeval **43**

Bagnoles-de-
l'Orne **21 37**

PARIS

Villeray **36**

Cloyes-sur-
le-Loir **24**

Le Mans

Orléans
Olivet **96**

Châteauneuf-
sur-Sarthe **93**

Tavers **90**
Beaugency **92**
Gien **95**
Souvigny-en-Sologne **99**

Briollay **82**
Angers

Ouchamps **97**
Chaumont-
sur-Tharonne **93**

Les Rosiers-
sur-Loire **88**
St-Patrice **98**

Amboise **92**
Fondettes **94**
Tours
Cangey **83**
Montrichard **96**

Brinon-sur-
Sauldre **93**

Chinon **84**
Bléré **92**
Chenonceaux **94**

St-Hilaire-de-Court **98**

Loches **95**

Thouars **99**

Buzançais **93**

Bourges

Bannegon **81**

Angles-sur-
l'Anglin **92**
Poitiers

Châteauroux
Fontgombault **94**
St-Chartier **89**

St-Maixent-
l'Ecole **98**

Lusignan **95**

Coulon **94**

Nieuil **86**

St-Martin-
du-Fault **98**

Bassac **92**

La Roche-
l'Abeille **97**
Limoges

Pons **97**
Angoulême
Mosnac **96**

Montbron **85**

Dunkerque

Calais

Boulogne-sur-Mer **75**

Hesdin-
L'Abbé **70**

Lille

Lumbres **78**

Valenciennes

Aire-sur-la-Lys **69**
Montreuil-sur-Mer
72 73 78

Doullens **76**

Amiens

Etréaupont **76**

Vervins **79**

Rouen

Ermenonville
76

Courcelles-sur-
Vesle **75**

Reims
74

PARIS
47-67

Sept-Saulx **79**

Senlisse
58

Châlons-sur-
Marne **75**

L'Épine **76**

Chartres

Fontenay-
Trésigny **59**

Barbizon **59**

Troyes

Flagy **46**

14

Dordogne
Beynac **143**
Buisson-de-Cadouin **127**
Domme **144**
Eyzies-de-Tayac **130 144**
Floriment-Gaumier **131**
Lalinde **145**
Razac d'Eymet **147**
St-Cyprien **148**
Sarlat **149**
Trémolat **142**
Vézac **150**

Angoulême

St-Saud-en-Périgord **140**

Vieux-Mareuil **150**
Champagnac-de-Belair **128**
Brantôme **125 126**
Ribérac **147**
Périgueux
Coly **129**

Pauillac **135**

Bordeaux
St-Émilion **148**

Dégagnac **143**
Touzac **149**
Mauroux **133**

Sauternes **149**

Mimizan **134**
Puymirol **146**
Poudenas **146**

Sabres **147**

Condom **143**

Soustons **149**
Hossegor **145**

Plaisance **146**

Montfort-en-Chalosse **146**
Auch

Escos **144**
St-Jean-de-Luz **148**
Pau
Sare **141**
Aïnhoa **124**
St-Etienne-de-Baïgorry **139**
Lestelle-Bétharram **145**

Coulandon **155**

Target **162**

Clermont-Ferrand

Ydes **163**

St-Martin-
Valmeroux **160**

Lacave
132 145

Le Puy

Carennac
143

Moudeyres
157

Gluges **144**

Vitrac **165**

Rocamadour
136 137

Montsalvy
164

Conques **153**

St-Cirq-Lapopie
138 147

La Malène **164**

Najac **158 165**

Rodez

Castelpers **152**

Cordes **154 164**

St-Sernin-sur-
Rance **161**

St-Jean-du-Bruel **159**

Cuq-Toulza **164**

Pont-de-
L'Arn **165**

Lacabarède **156**

Toulouse

St-Félix-
Lauragais **148**

Côte d'Or
Aloxe-Corton **101**
Arnay-le-Duc **114**
Châteauneuf **117**
Curtil-Vergy **118**
Gevrey-Chambertin **107**
Meursault **120**

Chatillon-sur-Seine **117**

St-Florentin **121**

La Celle-St-Cyr **115**
Chablis **115**

Auxerre **103**
Chassignelles **116**

Tonnerre **121**

Mailly-le-Château **108**

Vézelay **113**

Val-Suzon **122**

Avallon **104 114**

Chagny **115 116**

Mercurey **111**
Givry **119**

Charolles **116**
Fleurville **119**

Cluny **118**
Igé **119**
Maçon

Marcigny **110**

Bagnols **114**

Clermont-Ferrand

Chonas-l'Amballan **117**

Condrieu **118**

Valence **213**
Lamastre **206**

Baix **204**
Rochegude **209**
St-Restitut **212**

Vallon-Pont-d'Arc **201**

Villeneuve-lès-Avignon **202 214**

La Favède **177**

Tavel **213**
Les Angles **203**

Madières **185**

Noves

Montpellier

Le Pontet **190**

Olargues **208**

Toulouse

Carcassonne **204**

Narbonne

Les Stes-Maries-de-la-Mer **197**

Ornaisons **208**

Perpignan

St-Pierre-dels-Forcats **211**
Céret **172 205**

Angelès-sur-Mer **203**

Llo **184**

Dijon

Levernois **120**
Goumois **119**
Bonnevaux-le-Prieuré **115**
Chaublanc **106**
Passenans **112**

Annecy-le-Vieux **102**
Manigod **109**
Pérouges **120**
Veyrier-du-Lac **122**
Doussard **118**
Chamonix **105 116**
Lyon
Val-Thorens **122**
St-Lattier **121**
Grenoble

Mirmande **207**
Dieulefit **175**
Crillon-le-Brave **174**
Séguret **212**
Le Barroux **169**
Vénasque **214**
Gordes **206**
Les Beaumettes **171**
Gigondas
205
Chateau-Arnoux **173**
Roussillon **193**
Reillanne **191**
Fayence **178**
Vence **214**
St-Paul-de-Vence **194 210**
Peillon **188**
Èze **205**
St-Jean-Cap-Ferrat **210**
Haut-de-Cagnes **183**
Roquefort-les-Pins **192**
Cap d'Antibes **204**
Mougins **186 208**
Trigance **200**
Seillans **199**
Montferrat **207**
Cotignac **205**
Tourtour **213**
Les Baux-de-Provence **170 204**
Les Arcs **203**
Gémenos **180**
Marseille
Nans-les-Pins **208**
Pégomas **209**
Auribeau **203**
Plan-de-la-Tour **189**
St-Tropez **196 212**
Grimaud **181 182**
St-Clair **209**
Le Lavandou **207**
Ile de Port-Cros **209**
Aix-en-Provence **167 168**
Salon-de-Provence **198**
Eygalières **176**
Maussane-les-Alpilles **207**
St-Rémy-de-Provence **195 211 212**
Fontvieille **179**

Barcaggio **215**
Bastia
Calvi **215**
Monticello **215**

19

The North-west

The North-west is familiar territory to many British visitors. Lush Normandy, full of apple orchards and contented cows, is close enough to be convenient for a weekend break, and many people who live in the west of Britain prefer to use the Normandy ports when aiming further south. Further to the west, Brittany is bucket-and-spade country, and has much in common with Cornwall – a dramatic coastline, and a vigorous climate. On the border between the two regions is the most popular tourist sight in France: Mont St Michel.

Contenders in the North-west

Agneaux, Château d'Agneaux 33.57.65.88 Severe-looking little manor house, immaculately furnished.

Balisne, Moulin de Balisne 32.32.03.48 'Well-restored water mill' with good furnishings and extensive lawn.

Bazouges, Hostellerie de Mirwault 43.07.13.17 'Relaxing' English-run Logis with gardens overlooking the Mayenne.

Bénouville, La Pommeraie 31.44.62.43 Renowned restaurant with modern bedrooms in new building in grounds.

Brélidy, Château de Brélidy 96.95.69.38 Stern little stone manor house in peaceful setting.

Concarneau, Le Galion 98.97.30.16 Cosily beamed restaurant with rooms in old town, with neat modern rooms across the way.

Creully, Hostellerie Saint Martin 31.80.10.11 Shuttered Logis on village square with charming vaulted restaurant serving good-value menus.

Honfleur, Hostellerie Lechat 31.89.23.85 Smartly renovated inn, with bold colour schemes; central – parking not easy.

Lisieux, La Ferme des Poiriers Roses 31.64.72.14 Superbly furnished timbered house in a beautiful garden doing bed and wonderful breakfast.

Mür-de-Bretagne, Auberge Grand'Maison 96.28.51.10 One-star restaurant with rooms – some quite swish, though winning no prizes for taste.

Percy, La Voisinière 33.61.18.47 A pair of rustic cottages with prettily furnished rooms, in a beautiful flowery garden with pond.

Pleugueneuc, Château de la Motte Beaumanoir 99.69.46.01 Elegantly decorated 15thC château in ornamental grounds.

Plouharnel, Les Ajoncs d'Or 97.52.32.02 Cottagey stone-built Logis in shady, flowery garden.

Plozevet, Moulin de Brenizenec 98.91.30.33 Traditionally furnished old water mill in wooded grounds.

Pluherlin, Château de Talhouet 97.43.34.72 Slightly severe 16th/17thC château in grassy grounds, tastefully furnished and run as a B&B.

Pornichet, Hôtel Sud Bretagne 40.11.65.00 Smooth, luxurious seaside hotel (close to beach) with attractive garden.

Roscoff, Le Brittany 98.69.70.78 Neatly furnished stone manor house with particularly attractive restaurant, and indoor pool.

St-Briac-sur-Mer, Manoir de la Duchée 99.88.00.02 Little manor house B&B deep in countryside, handsomely furnished.

St-Pierre-de-Plesguen, Le Petit Moulin du Rouvre 99.73.85.84 Neatly restored 17thC water mill by a small lake.

The North-west

Manoir du Lys

The addition of 12 extra bedrooms a few years ago has not diminished our enthusiasm for this typically Norman half-timbered hunting lodge, with geraniums at its foot and dripping from its balconies. It was reopened as a hotel by the Quintons in 1985 after a long period of disuse, and many improvements have been introduced. The new building is harmonious, and the bedrooms are very attractive – all spacious and well equipped, with stylish furnishings far removed from the French norm. Most have balconies overlooking the gardens.

Marie-France oversees the smart dining-rooms (also overlooking the gardens, through floor-to-ceiling windows) where you can enjoy her son Franck's delicious cuisine, which is rooted in local tradition but acknowledges modern preferences. In good weather you can dine outside. There is also a polished little bar/sitting-room with a huge open fire and a grand piano (played on Friday nights).

The Quintons organise popular educational 'mushroom' weekends, during which up to 120 varieties may be picked in the surrounding woods; English-language tuition can be laid on.

Nearby Andaines forest – walking, riding, cycling.

La Croix Gauthier, Route de Juvigny, 61140 Bagnoles-de-l'Orne **Tel** 33.37.80.69 **Fax** 33.30.05.80
Location in middle of countryside in forest of Andaines; with car parking
Meals breakfast, lunch, dinner
Prices rooms 300F-780F; menus 130F-260F
Rooms 20 double, 19 with bath, one with shower; 3 suites; all have phone, TV, minibar
Facilities dining-room, sitting-room/bar, billiards; tennis court
Credit cards AE, DC, MC, V
Children welcome; special menu 85F
Disabled 1 bedroom
Pets dogs accepted in bedrooms only 35F
Closed 6 Jan to 12 Feb; Sun evening and Mon from Nov to Easter
Proprietor Marie-France and Paul Quinton

The North-west

Le Petit Coq aux Champs

A thatched house with its own heliport – it sounds unlikely, but convention counts for little at this smart, secluded retreat, amid rolling meadows and sweeping forests in the Risle valley. Le Petit Coq offers an intriguing mixture of the rustic, the sophisticated and the downright idiosyncratic – a cocktail that may be too heady for some, to judge by our empty postbag.

The building, mostly 19th century, has two main wings with a spacious, airy, modern extension in between. The style varies considerably – modern cane furniture in the large sitting-room, while antiques predominate in the restaurant, which has a huge open fireplace at one end. An intimate piano bar has been squeezed into the new building. The bedrooms are all furnished and arranged in different ways, some brightly coloured, others more restrained; none is particularly large.

Jean-Marie Huard, who has returned to his Norman roots after some years in highly reputed restaurants in Paris, pays serious attention to detail, presentation and local tradition in his cooking – with impressive results.

Nearby fishing, golf; Pont-Audemer – half-timbered houses, church of Saint-Ouen; Honfleur (30 km) – old port.

Campigny 27500 Pont-Audemer
Tel 32.41.04.19
Fax 32.56.06.25
Location in countryside, 6 km S of Pont-Audemer; in gardens with ample car parking
Meals breakfast, lunch, dinner
Prices rooms 440F-790F; breakfast 55F; menus 180F-300F
Rooms 12 double (4 twin), one family room, one suite, all with bath; all rooms have central heating, phone
Facilities sitting-room, 4 dining-rooms, bar; swimming-pool
Credit cards AE, DC, MC, V
Children very welcome
Disabled dining-rooms and 8 bedrooms are on ground floor
Pets welcome
Closed January
Proprietors Fabienne Desmonts and Jean-Marie Huard

The North-west

Converted mill, Clécy

Hostellerie du Moulin du Vey

Just when we were beginning to wonder about this old, creeper-clad water-mill, a burst of readers' reports reassures us about its continuing appeal. 'Very pleasing,' says one. 'Bright, tastefully decorated rooms, excellent restaurant, friendly service.'

The Moulin is at the heart of some of the best scenery in the region, where the river Orne has carved a majestic valley between green, rolling hills. It is within easy driving distance of the ferry at Caen, and makes an attractive first- or last-night stop.

Both the buildings and the gardens are beautifully kept, and there is a pleasant waterside terrace for eating and drinking, with a garden beyond. Food in the half-timbered, rather barn-like restaurant, just across the courtyard from the main building, is carefully prepared and served, and the less expensive menus are sound value. Bedrooms are comfortable, furnished simply but with touches of style, and reasonably priced. Some rooms are in annexes: the Manoir de Placy, 400 metres away, and the Relais de Surosne, 3 km away on the other side of the village – a peaceful, small Gothic-style house with a lush garden.

Nearby Suisse Normande region; Thury-Harcourt (10 km) – ruined château; Falaise (30 km) – castle.

Le Vey 14570 Clécy
Tel 31.69.71.08
Fax 31.69.14.14
Location 2 km E of Clécy and 35 kms S of Caen; with river terrace and car parking
Meals breakfast, lunch, dinner **Prices** rooms 380F-500F; menus 135F-350F
Rooms 17 double (7 twin) all with bath; 2 family rooms, one with bath, one with shower; all rooms have central heating, phone, colour TV

Facilities dining-room, banqueting-room, conference room
Credit cards AE, DC, MC, V
Children accepted
Disabled no special facilities
Pets accepted but not in dining-room
Closed Dec
Proprietor Denise Leduc

The North-west

Le St-Jacques

Has this old coaching inn, for some years now enjoying a new lease of life as an *étape gastronomique*, lost its way? It has certainly lost its Michelin star – as predicted by a reader who ate there before the event. He also records a poor reception, and a mediocre bedroom. But other reporters have been much happier, and we retain a soft spot for the place. For the moment, look before you book – and let us know your conclusions.

The dining-room, looking out over the garden, is pleasantly intimate. But in good weather meals are served in the shade of the trees in the garden, which is a lush expanse leading down to the banks of the little Loir. The bedrooms (at the back, looking over the garden) have been smartly done out in designer fabrics and cherry-wood reproduction antiques.

Nearby Châteaudun (10 km) – feudal château; Vendôme – la Trinité, Porte St Georges; Beaugency (45 km) – bridge, keep.

Place du Marché aux Oeufs
28220 Cloyes-sur-le-Loir
Tel 37.98.40.08
Fax 37.98.32.63
Location in village, 28 km NE of Vendôme; with garden and car parking
Meals breakfast, lunch, dinner
Prices rooms 360F-480F; suite 680F; breakfast 50F; menus 170F
Rooms 22 double, 18 with bath, 4 with shower (5 twin); one family room; all rooms have central heating, phone, TV
Facilities dining-room, sitting-room, bar
Credit cards MC, V
Children welcome
Disabled lift/elevator
Pets accepted in room and dining-room
Closed Nov to Mar
Proprietor Eric Thureau

The North-west

Village hotel, Ducey

Auberge de la Sélune

We have nothing but positive reports on file for this splendid small hotel, which has undergone extensive improvements recently. It offers excellent value for money and tends to be pretty busy in high season. But do give it a try.

It is difficult to decide whether the housekeeping or the food earns the prize, as both are first-class. The whole place is pleasantly decorated – mainly in bright and stylish prints – and spotlessly kept; there are fluffy towels and endless hot water, crisp linen and sound beds. Jean-Pierre Girres's cooking is excellent; his fish, seafood and *pâtisserie* are particularly well regarded; crab pie is one of his noted specialities. There are now two dining-rooms, though eating here is popular with locals, and dinner can take some time to serve – but there is not much else to occupy your time in the evening here. Breakfast is above average, too. Josette Girres is not a chatty hostess, but her welcome is warm. The hotel fronts directly on to the street, so parking is awkward. To compensate, there is a little garden at the back beside the Sélune.

Nearby Salmon fishing (river Sélune); Avranches (10 km) – museum; Le Mont-St-Michel (15 km) – fortified abbey on island.

2 Rue St-Germain 50220 Ducey
Tel 33.48.53.62
Fax 33.48.90.30
Location by river in village, on N176 11 km SE of Avranches; with small garden and some car parking
Meals breakfast, lunch, dinner
Prices rooms 260F-280F; breakfast 40F; menus 78F-120F
Rooms 19 double, all with bath (5 twin); one single; one family room with bath; all rooms have central heating, phone; TV on request
Facilities sitting-room, bar, conference room; salmon fishing
Credit cards DC, MC, V
Children accepted
Disabled no special facilities
Pets not accepted
Closed mid-Jan to mid-Feb
Proprietor Jean-Pierre Girres

The North-west

Le Donjon

After a recent inspection, this extraordinary little hotel remains one of our favourite places for a short break on the Norman coast, and is worth bearing in mind for the first or last night of a longer trip (it's only half an hour from Le Havre).

It is a former hilltop castle, with venerable origins and secret subterranean channel to the sea, now safely surrounded by the leafy suburbs of Etretat. Inside, all is bright and light, decorated with a Parisian sophistication by Madame Abo-Dib. The dining-room, candle-lit and mirrored, is wonderfully atmospheric; the cocktail bar overlooks Etretat's famous cliffs; and there is an impeccably kept small swimming pool surrounded by sunshades and loungers. But it is perhaps the eight bedrooms which best show off Madame Abo-Dib's creative skills: all are different, and immensely stylish. The largest, almost circular, has an Eastern theme, with black chintz drapes and gigantic mirror; another is in bright Impressionist hues, and one has a large fireplace for real log fires. Bathrooms, some in the turrets, are spacious and elegant in pure white; five have whirlpool baths.

The menu offers rather more possibilities for *pensionnaires* than many, with the option of choosing dishes from the *carte*, as well as an excellent four-course *menu du Gentleman*.

Nearby Etretat − cliffs; Fécamp (17km) − Benedictine distillery.

Chemin de Saint Clair
76790 Etretat
Tel 35.27.08.23
Fax 35.29.92.24
Location on hill behind resort, 28 km N of Le Havre; with garden and car parking
Meals breakfast, lunch, dinner
Prices DB&B 600F-800F; menus 130F- 260F
Rooms 10 double, 9 with bath, one with shower (5 with whirlpool baths); all have central heating, phone, TV
Facilities dining-room, sitting-room; swimming-pool
Credit cards AE, V
Children accepted
Pets accepted
Disabled access difficult
Closed never
Proprietor Mme Abo-Dib

The North-west

Château hotel, Gisors

Château de la Râpée

'A comfortable stay, although we found the decoration, with carpets for wallcoverings, rather idiosyncratic,' says our most recent reporter on this 19th-century Gothic mansion. Well, yes: perhaps we should have warned about the carpet; but it is more-or-less confined (along with the antlers) to the reception area. The rest of this grandly conceived but small-scale period piece is less eccentric.

The château lies in a peaceful setting at the end of a long, rutted forest track from Bazincourt. Inside, original features have been carefully preserved and, although the public areas are rather dark in places, the house has been pleasantly furnished with antiques and reproductions. Some of the spacious, calm bedrooms are quite stately, with fine country views, plenty of antiques and creaky wooden floors; others verge on the eccentric (but are antler-free). Immediately next to the house is a small, pleasant flower-garden.

Pascal and Philippe Bergeron take their cooking seriously – classic dishes, with some regional influences and occasional original flourishes.

Nearby Gisors – castle; Jouy-sous-Thelle (25 km) – church.

Bazincourt-sur-Epte 27140 Gisors
Tel 32.55.11.61
Location in countryside 4 km NW of Gisors; in small park with ample car parking
Meals breakfast, lunch, dinner
Prices rooms 405F-525F; apartment 720F; menus 160F-205F
Rooms 13 double, 11 with bath, 2 with shower (5 twin); 2 rooms form an apartment; all rooms have central heating, phone
Facilities sitting-room, 2 dining-rooms, bar, banqueting-room; riding stables next door
Credit cards AE, DC, V
Children by arrangement
Disabled no special facilities
Pets small ones accepted
Closed Feb and mid to end Aug; restaurant Wed
Proprietors M. and Mme Bergeron

The North-west

Auberge du Vieux Puits

Our latest report on this wonderful, half-timbered, 17thC building is short and to the point: 'Excellent.' It might equally well have said: 'Unchanging'.

Although war-damaged Pont-Audemer still has a charming historic centre, it is rather dwarfed by the nondescript suburbs which have grown up around it. The Vieux Puits shines out like a beacon – all crooked beams and leaded windows. The inside is a medievalist's dream, with its twisting wooden staircases and dark beams hung with shining copper and ancient pewter.

Jacques Foltz and his charming wife bring out the best in the building, by keeping the style simple and restrained. The small, intimate salon and dining-rooms are carefully furnished with antiques, and are decorated with fresh flowers. Three of the bedrooms in the old building have been converted into a family apartment; the other three are quite small but full of character. Across the peaceful, flowery courtyard a new wing provides six bedrooms – smarter and well equipped, but in keeping.

M. Foltz sees the *auberge* very much as a restaurant with rooms, and those who want to stay are encouraged to have dinner. To do so is hardly a penance, given the kitchen's high standards and the interesting dishes on the rarely changing menus and *carte*.

Nearby Half-timbered houses, church of St-Ouen, the canalised Risle; Honfleur (25 km)

6 Rue Notre-Dame-du-Pré
27500 Pont-Audemer
Tel 32.41.01.48
Location near middle of town; with small garden and car parking
Meals breakfast, lunch, dinner
Prices rooms 270F-420F; menus, 195F-300F
Rooms 12 double (4 twin), 7 with bath, 4 with shower; 11 have phone
Facilities dining-rooms, bar/sitting-area
Credit cards MC, V
Children welome; special meals on request
Disabled 2 ground-floor rooms, specially equipped
Pets accepted in dining-room
Closed mid-Dec to late Jan; Mon evening, Tue in low season
Proprietors Jacques and Hélène Foltz

The North-west

Country hotel, St-André-d'Hébertot

Auberge du Prieuré

We continue to keep our fingers crossed for the Millets. Perhaps they don't need good luck, but they have improved and extended their country home so vigorously over the last few years that we can't help worrying. Will they go too far? Will they spoil their retreat simply by being too enterprising?

The former rectory, built of pale stone beneath a steep slate roof, has made a delicious little hotel. Inside, it is all beams, stone walls, country antiques and earthy colours. There is a surprisingly big dining-room, with stone-flagged floor and heavy wood tables gleaming with polish. At one end, there are easy chairs before an open fire. On the first floor, a cosy sitting-room offers books and board games; next door is a billiard room. Bedrooms in the main house are full of character, and attic rooms are no less spacious than those on the first floor, although rather dark. A new but harmonious annexe accommodates about half the rooms. Outside, a lush garden is surrounded by Norman orchards, and features one of the Millets' earliest improvements – a neat heated pool. Traditional food is offered – one mid-priced menu and a more expansive *carte*.

Nearby Pont-l'Évêque; Honfleur (15 km); Deauville (20 km).

St-André-d'Hébertot 14130
Pont-l'Évêque
Tel 31.64.03.03
Fax 31.64.16.66
Location by church in village, S of N175 7 km E of Pont-l'Évêque; in gardens with some private car parking
Meals breakfast, lunch, dinner
Prices rooms 310F-980F; breakfast 45F, meals 145F-320F
Rooms 13 double (5 twin), 11 with bath; all rooms have central heating, phone, TV, radio, hairdrier
Facilities billiard room, library; swimming-pool
Credit cards MC, V
Children welcome; special meals
Disabled ground-floor rooms
Pets 30F supplement
Closed restaurant only, Wed
Proprietors M. and Mme Millet

The North-west

La Korrigane

Jean-Maurice Marchon took over this handsome, turn-of-the-century mansion in late 1992, but its appeal remains unchanged: it is an elegantly furnished home, which you feel privileged to share. The bedrooms are individually decorated, and have comfortable armchairs, beautiful lamps and mirrors, and antique paintings dotted about. There are two harmonious sitting-rooms; you can have your breakfast in the small, pretty garden. An excellent place for a romantic short break without the children but note that there is no restaurant at present.

Nearby Emerald Coast; Château du Bosq (10 km); Dinan

39 Rue Le Pomellec 35400 St-Malo
Tel 99.81.65.85
Fax 99.82.23.89
Location in S part of town, near harbour; with gardens and car parking
Meals breakfast
Prices rooms 450F-800F; breakfast 55F
Rooms 10 double/twin, all with bath or shower; all rooms have central heating, phone, TV

Facilities 2 sitting-rooms, bar
Credit cards AE, DC, MC, V
Children accepted
Disabled no special facilities
Pets dogs accepted (50F)
Closed never
Proprietor Jean-Maurice Marchon

The North-west

Hostellerie St-Pierre

'Perfect for a short break,' says our latest report on this unusual hotel on the banks of the Seine. Could be; we've always seen it as an ideal stopover – reliably well run, and located only a short drive from the Paris-Rouen motorway. It is a bizarre concoction: a modern building, triangular in plan with a turret on one corner, half-timbered like a traditional Norman manor-house. It sounds naff, but don't dismiss it.

Not the least of the attractions is the cuisine – classical in style but inventive and light in approach, and of excellent quality, with the emphasis on fish and seafood – witness the enormous tank of langoustes and other consumables dominating the heavily decorated dining-room (which has big picture windows looking on to the river). The hotel's other public areas are limited, and solid rather than elegant – the baroque/rococo decoration does not suit all tastes – but the bedrooms are comfortable and well equipped, and many have balconies overlooking the river. (For the full flavour of this eccentric establishment, opt for the top room in the turret, with exposed beams and token four-poster.) The garden, which stretches down to the water's edge, is a relaxing place to sit. The hotel is family-run; service is friendly.

Nearby Louviers – church of Notre-Dame; Acquigny (10 km) – château; Gaillon (15 km) – château.; Giverny (30 km)

Chemin des Amoureux 27430 St-Pierre-du-Vauvray
Tel 32.59.93.29
Fax 32.59.41.93
Location on edge of village 8 km E of Louviers, beside Seine; with gardens and car parking
Meals breakfast, lunch, dinner
Prices DB&B 550F-645F; menus 195F-295F
Rooms 14 double (4 twin), all with bath; all rooms have central heating, phone, TV; most have minibar
Facilities dining-room, sitting-room
Credit cards V
Children accepted
Disabled lift/elevator
Pets accepted at extra charge
Closed mid-Nov to mid-Mar; restaurant only, Tue, and Wed lunch
Proprietors Potier family

The North-west

Seaside town hotel, St-Vaast-la-Hougue

Hotel de France et des Fuchsias

'The garden is still in good order, as are the fuschias, and the conservatory where we ate a memorable, beautifully presented meal is very enticing; friendly and efficient staff.' So says a reporter, confirming that the essential attractions of this perennially popular halt for Cherbourg ferry passengers (French and British alike) are unchanged.

The emphasis is on the restaurant; and the expressions of delight at the superb seafood platters, or the wonderfully presented produce from the Brix family farm, prove that the customers are happy. The wine list offers plenty of half-bottles and good-value options, the service is friendly and efficient, the atmosphere warm – whether in the cosy dining-room or in the conservatory, recently redecorated by a local *décorateur anglais*.

At the far end of the delightful English-style garden, where free chamber music concerts are held on the last ten days of August, is the hotel's annexe. Here bedrooms are more spacious and decoration more sophisticated than in the fairly simple ones in the main part of the hotel. A suite sleeping two or three people and a ground-floor bedroom have been created.

Nearby museum, fortifications; Normandy beaches.

18 rue Marechal Foch
50550 Saint-Vaast-la-Hougue
Tel 33.54.42.26
Fax 33.43.46.79
Location in quiet street near fishing port and marina; with garden
Meals breakfast, lunch, dinner
Prices rooms 145F-500F; menus 76F (weekdays only), 118F-245F (weekends)
Rooms 33 double, 28 with bath, 2 with shower; all rooms have central heating, phone; almost all have TV
Facilities dining-room, sitting-room
Credit cards AE, DC, MC, V
Children welcome; special menu available
Disabled access only to dining-room
Pets tolerated
Closed early Jan to late Feb; Mon, mid-May to mid-Sep
Proprietor Mme Brix

The North-west

Hôtel de la Plage

A seaside hotel indeed – yards from the shore, with a vast strand of pale sand just next door. But this is far from being a bucket-and-spade holiday hotel. Although prices are not high by the elevated standards of fellow Relais & Châteaux members, they are high by summer-fortnight-with-the-kids standards. And although children are welcome, as usual in France, there are no special facilities for them.

It's as a place for relaxing, pampering breaks with an outdoors element that the Plage wins a place here. The hotel combines its splendid, peaceful seaside setting – plus attractive pool and tennis court – with one of the best kitchens in Brittany (special-ising, of course, in seafood), which earns a star from Michelin and two toques from Gault-Millau. Within the manicured grounds is a bar in a separate thatched cottage. Mme Le Coz and her staff generate a welcoming atmosphere; service is sometimes a little slow but always friendly, and details are not overlooked. Bedrooms are comfortable, even if they do tend towards traditional French styles of decoration, and some have stunning views (worth booking ahead).

Nearby Beach; Locronan (10 km) – town square; Quimper.

Ste-Anne-la-Palud 29127
Plonévez-Porzay
Tel 98.92.50.12
Fax 98.92.56.54
Location in countryside 4 km W of Plonévez and 25 km NW of Quimper; with garden and ample car parking
Meals breakfast, lunch, dinner **Prices** rooms 750F-1350F; breakfast 70F
Rooms 20 double (10 twin), 2 single, 4 family rooms, all with bath; all rooms have central heating, TV, phone, minibar
Facilities sitting-room, dining-room, bar, conference room
Credit cards AE, DC, MC, V
Children welcome
Disabled lift/elevator
Pets accepted but not in dining-room
Closed mid-Oct to Apr
Proprietor M. Le Coz

The North-west

Ti Al-Lannec

Happy reports about this handsome house on the 'pink granite' coast of Brittany suggest that the hotel manages to pamper while at the same time coping with the families who are drawn to this seaside holiday area.

The house stands high above the sea with a path down to the beach; its south-facing terrace has a splendid view over the bay of Lannion. It is a supremely comfortable hotel, with that elusive private-house feel. Bedrooms are thoughtfully decorated, light and airy but cosy, with fresh flowers and books, small tables and table lamps liberally used. Some have terraces or verandas. The dining-room has the sea view, and is crisp and fresh with rich drapes and old stone walls. Antique and modern furnishings mix well in the comfortable sitting-room, dotted with pot plants.

The house was completely renovated and opened as a hotel in 1978 by Gérard and Danielle Jouanny, and is run by them with a convincing blend of charm, taste and efficiency. Danielle's food is 'consistently delicious', the service 'five-star' and the welcome for children genuine – witness the swing and seesaw on the lawn.
Nearby Perros-Guirec (15 km) – large resort; Tréguier (30 km).

Allée de Mezo-Guen, BP 3
22560 Trébeurden
Tel 96.23.57.26
Fax 96.23.62.14
Location in wooded grounds above resort, 10 km NW of Lannion; with car parking
Meals breakfast, lunch, dinner
Prices rooms 630F-1,050F; lunch 130F, dinner menus 180F-390F, children's 90F
Rooms 20 double, 2 single, 8 family rooms, all with bath; all rooms have phone, TV

Facilities dining-room, 2 sitting-rooms, bar, billiards room, play room, fitness centre, sauna, jacuzzi
Credit cards AE, MC, V
Children welcome; early meals, baby-sitting available
Disabled lift/elevator; some bedrooms and WCs suitable
Pets accepted in bedrooms at extra charge
Closed mid-Nov to mid-Mar
Proprietors Danielle and Gérard Jouanny

The North-west

Le Clos

Le Clos remains one of our favourite upmarket French hotels – partly because it remains just affordable by ordinary mortals, but also because it avoids the pretension and vulgarity that afflict so many château-style places.

The hotel is on the edge of the pleasant little country town of Verneuil, in a quiet back street – though with a busy bypass visible (and just audible) in the background. It is a rather comical turn-of-the-century building of highly patterned brickwork, with a mock-medieval tower, set in well-kept leafy grounds with lawns and creeping willows that are overlooked by a large terrace. Inside, everything is of the highest quality: smart, antique-style cane chairs, heavy linen tablecloths and huge bunches of flowers in the dining-room, neat reproduction armchairs in the salon, chintzy drapes in the bedrooms, deep pile carpets everywhere – even in the luxurious bathrooms. The bedrooms are light and airy, and furnished in individual style. The kitchen wins no awards, but produces a range of classical dishes with absolute professionalism and finesse.

Nearby Church of la Madeleine (flamboyant tower); Château de Pin au Haras (40 km) – stud farm; Chartres – cathedral.

98 Rue de la Ferté-Vidame
27130 Verneuil-sur-Avre
Tel 32.32.21.81
Fax 32.32.21.36
Location on edge of town, 56 km NW of Chartres and 39 km SW of Evreux; with gardens and car parking
Meals breakfast, lunch, dinner
Prices rooms 600F-780F, suites 780F-880F; apartments 950F-1,100F; DB&B 775F-925F; breakfast 80F
Rooms 6 double, 2 suites, all with bath; 3 apartments with bath/jacuzzi; all rooms have central heating, phone, TV
Facilities 2 dining-rooms, sitting-room, bar; tennis court, jacuzzi
Credit cards AE, DC, MC, V
Children welcome
Disabled 3 rooms in garden on ground floor **Pets** accepted
Closed mid-Dec to mid-Jan; restaurant Mon, except holiday periods **Proprietors** Patrick and Colette Simon

The North-west

Converted mill, Villeray

Moulin de Villeray

This grand old mill – restored from dereliction and gradually improved over a 20-year period (a heated outdoor swimming-pool is the most recent addition) – was taken over by the Eelsens in 1992. It remains one of our favourite ports of call in southern Normandy, and worth the detour from the A11 Nantes-Paris *autoroute.*

It is no longer what you would call a simple rustic retreat; but the mill-wheel is still there, and the setting is delectable – beside the rushing river Huisne, on the edge of a neat village of red-roofed stone houses, in rolling, wooded farmland on the fringe of the distinctive Perche region. Its membership of the Relais du Silence group is justified, even if prices are approaching Relais & Chateaux levels.

Much of the tall, white-painted mill has been rebuilt rather than restored, but its main focus, the restaurant, is thoroughly traditional, retaining old beams and a huge fireplace – and giving a view of the mill-wheel. The 'excellent' food is more than a match for the surroundings. Guests gather for drinks in the salon. Bedrooms are very comfortable and newly refurbished. Outside there is a pleasant terrace, a large, relaxing and informal garden bordering the river and, beyond that, countryside.

Nearby Nogent – Gothic and Renaissance buildings; Chartres (55 km) – cathedral; Alençon (55 km) – lace- making.

Villeray 61110 Condeau
Tel 33.73.30.22
Fax 33.73.38.28
Location at foot of village, 10 km N of Nogent; with garden and car parking
Meals breakfast, lunch, dinner
Prices rooms 480F-740F, suite 1,150F; menus 130F-300F
Rooms 16 double, all with bath and shower (3 twin); 2 suites; all rooms have phone, minibar

Facilities sitting-room, dining-room, bar; helipad; swimming-pool
Credit cards AE, DC, V
Children accepted
Disabled access to restaurant
Pets accepted (must be kept on lead)
Closed never
Proprietors Christian and Muriel Eelsen

The North-west

Hôtel de la Chaîne d'Or

This old inn, superbly set beside the Seine, has jumped upmarket since it was dropped from the guide some years ago. Bedrooms vary in size and style, but many share the restaurant's river views. Not the least of the improvements is in the food, which is now seriously good.

■ 27 Rue Grande, 27700 Les Andelys (Eure) **Tel** 32.54.00.31 **Fax** 32.54.05.68 **Meals** breakfast, lunch, dinner **Prices** rooms 395F-740F; breakfast 65F, lunch 135F, menus 225F-295F **Rooms** 11, all with bath, central heating, phone, TV **Credit cards** AE, MC, V **Closed** early Jan to early Feb; restaurant only, last week of Aug

---

Bois Joli

The Gattis, who took over this upright little 19thC building about seven years ago, are now well into their stride, to judge by our most recent report – 'pretty, airy bedroom; very good dinner; excellent service; excellent value.' There is a pleasant garden, leading into the forest. Sauna and solarium.

■ 12 Avenue Philippe du Rozier, 61140 Bagnoles-de-l'Orne (Orne) **Tel** 33.37.92.77 **Meals** breakfast, lunch, dinner **Prices** rooms 195F-495F; menus 115F-295F **Rooms** 20, all with bath, central heating, phone; TV on request **Credit cards** AE, DC, MC, V **Closed** never

---

Le Conquérant

A shell's throw from the port, this fine grey-stone 17thC building offers a peaceful halt for travellers, and is inviting enough for a longer stay, with its spacious garden and modest but comfortable bedrooms. Delicious crêpes in the *salon de thé*.

■ 16-18 Rue St-Thomas Becket, 50760 Barfleur (Manche) **Tel** 33.54.00.82 **Fax** 33.54.65 .25 **Meals** breakfast, tea, light suppers **Prices** rooms 160F-350F; breakfast 36F-45F, supper 75F-98F **Rooms** 16, all with bath or shower, phone; some have satellite TV **Credit cards** MC, V **Closed** mid-N ov to mid-Dec, Jan

---

Hôtel d'Argouges

'Comfortable, quiet, helpful people,' runs the latest telegraphic report on this 18thC house. There is a rather formal sitting-room and a small garden; bedrooms vary in size and are traditionally furnished; some are in an annexe across the courtyard. No restaurant.

■ 21 Rue St-Patrice, 14400 Bayeux (Calvados) **Tel** 31.92.88.86 **Fax** 31.92.69.16 **Meals** breakfast **Prices** rooms 260F-395F, suites 480F; breakfast 38F **Rooms** 25, all with bath or shower, central heating, phone, minibar **Credit cards** AE, DC, MC, V **Closed** never

The North-west

Village inn, Le Bec-Hellouin

Auberge de l'Abbaye

The archetypal atmospheric Norman inn, simple and welcoming, with tiled floors, rough stone walls and gleaming furniture. Bedrooms are cheerful and rustic, meals are typical of the region – with apples, cider and quantities of cream.

■ Le Bec-Hellouin, 27800 Brionne (Eure) **Tel** 32.44.86.02 **Fax** 32.46.32.23 **Meals** breakfast, lunch, dinner **Prices** rooms 360F-400F; breakfast 40F, menus 130F-250F **Rooms** 11, all with bath, central heating, phone **Credit cards** MC, V **Closed** restaurant only, Mon evening and Tue Nov to Apr

---

Seaside hotel, Belle-Ile-en-Mer

Le Clos Fleuri

A new and stylishly simple hotel in grassy grounds 600m from the main port of Le Palais on Belle-Ile, 45 minutes by ferry from Quiberon. The catering is as fresh as the decoration, with meals tailored to guests' requirements, and the option of a substantial brunch instead of standard breakfast.

■ Bellevue, Route de Sauzon, Le Palais, 56360 Belle-Ile-en-Mer (Morbihan) **Tel** 97.31.45.45 **Fax** 97.31.45.57 **Meals** breakfast or brunch, lunch, dinner **Prices** rooms 400F-500F; suites 580F; breakfast 40F, brunch 70F; menu around 150F **Rooms** 20, all with bath, central heating, phone, cable TV **Credit cards** AE, DC, MC, V **Closed** never

---

Country hotel, Belle-Ile-en-Mer

La Désirade

La Désirade, drawn to our attention by a satisfied reader, calls itself a 'hôtel-village'; it is an unusual creation – a grouping of new, traditional-style houses around a neat heated pool (beside which you can have breakfast in good weather). Stylishly simple furnishing in the rooms.

■ 56360 Belle-Ile-en-Mer (Morbihan) **Tel** 97.31.70.70 **Fax** 97.31.89.63 **Meals** breakfast, lunch, dinner **Prices** rooms 430F-550F; breakfast 60F, menu 200F **Rooms** 26, all with bath, central heating, phone, TV, hairdrier **Credit cards** AE, DC, MC, V **Closed** Jan, Feb

---

Town hotel, Beuzeville

Cochon d'Or et Petit Castel

Two small hotels on opposite sides of the main street and under the same ownership. The Petit Castel offers simple, pleasant modern-style bedrooms; the Cochon d'Or has cheaper, rather more old-fashioned bedrooms with fewer facilities. The food is above average and excellent value.

■ Place du General-de-Gaulle, 27210 Beuzeville (Eure) **Tel** 32.57.70.46 (Cochon) 32.57.76.08.(Peti t Castel) **Fax** 32.42.25.70 **Meals** breakfast, lunch, dinner **Prices** rooms 175F-325F; breakfast 32F, menus 82F-225F **Rooms** 21, all with bath or shower, central heating, phone; some have TV **Credit cards** MC, V **Closed** mid-Dec to mid-Jan

The North-west

Restaurant with rooms, La Bouille

Le Saint-Pierre

Smart, thriving restaurant-with-rooms by the Seine. Showy modern decoration dominates, especially in the airy riverside restaurant; cooking is professional and inventive; bedrooms mostly overlook the river. More reports welcome.

■ La Bouille, 76530 Grand Couronne (Seine-Maritime)
Tel 35.18.01.01 **Fax** 35.18.12.7 6 **Meals** breakfast, lunch, dinner
Prices rooms 280F-350F; menus 160F-260F **Rooms** 7, all with bath or shower, central heating, phone, TV **Credit cards** AE, DC, MC, V
Closed Jan; Mon, Nov to end May; Sun eve

Riverside hotel, Caudebec-en-Caux

Le Normandie

A friendly and well-cared-for hotel, if uninspiring in style, in a good position on the Seine. Bedrooms are simple but comfortable, many with river views. Food is carefully prepared and sound value - typical of a two-fireplace Logis.

■ 19 Quai Guilbaud, 76490 Caudebec-en-Caux (Seine-Maritime)
Tel 35.96.25.11 **Fax** 35 .96.68.15 **Meals** breakfast, lunch, dinner
Prices rooms 210F-360F; breakfast 35F; menus 59F-180F **Rooms** 16, all with bath or shower, central heating, phone, TV **Credit cards** AE, DC, MC, V **Closed** Feb

---

Seaside hotel, Dinard

Roche Corneille

A tall château-style building in the middle of Dinard, recently renovated in a crisp and confident style by new owners, and run with clear attention to detail – fresh flowers, fluffy towels, impeccable housekeeping. A gastronomic restaurant has just been opened, with weekly changing menus.

■ 4 Rue G Clemenceau, 35800 Dinard (Ille-et-Vilaine)
Tel 99.46.14.47 **Fax** 99.46.40. 80 **Meals** breakfast **Prices** rooms 280F-440F; breakfast 50F; menus 93F-240F **Rooms** 28, all with bath, central heating, phone, TV **Credit cards** AE, MC, V **Closed** mid-Nov to mid-Mar

---

Château hotel, Hennebont

Château de Locguénolé

A Dutch reader writes to recommend inclusion of this refined country house looking down on the estuary of Le Blavet. Splendid spacious bedrooms, plentiful sitting-rooms, very good (Michelin-starred) food. Lots of ways to mitigate the damage – walks, tennis, bikes as well as a good-sized pool.

■ Route de Port-Louis en Kervignac, 56700 Hennebont (Morbihan)
Tel 97.76.29.04 **Fax** 97.76.82.35 **Meals** breakfast, lunch, dinner
Prices rooms 660F-1,480F; breakfast 82F, menus 190F-480F **Rooms** 22, all with bath, central heating, phone, TV; most have hairdriers
Credit cards AE, DC, MC, V **Closed** early Jan to early Feb

The North-west

Country hotel, Honfleur

La Chaumière

Set peacefully in an orchard garden with the sea in view (and direct access to the shore), this typically Norman timbered building offers deeply comfortable, relaxing accommodation. The bedrooms are decorated with flair and taste, and warmly furnished. Serious cooking of regionally-based dishes.

■ Route du Littoral, Vasouy, 14600 Honfleur (Calvados) **Tel** 31.81.63.20 **Fax** 31.89.5 9.23 **Meals** breakfast, lunch, dinner **Prices** rooms 990F-1,350F; breakfast 75F, menus 180F-380F **Rooms** 9, all with bath, central heating, phone, TV, minibar, hairdrier **Credit cards** AE, MC, V **Closed** never; restaurant only, Tue, and Wed lunch

---

Country hotel, Honfleur

La Ferme Saint-Siméon

The Boelen family wrote to tell us about their second hotel in Honfleur – they also own La Chaumière (above). This fine old farmhouse used to be a favourite haunt of the Impressionist painters, and is still a tranquil spot. Rustic beams and furniture combine with modern luxuries, including an indoor heated swimming-pool, sauna, steam room and solarium. Cooking blends bold innovation with the traditional. Extensive wine list. Reports please.

Rue Adolphe-Marais, 14600 Honfleur (Calvados) **Tel** 33.31.89.23.61 **Fax** 33.31.89.48.48 **Meals** breakfast, lunch, dinner **Prices** rooms 990F-1,970F; apartments 2,300F-3,510F; menus 240F-550F **Rooms** 26, apartments 16, all with bath or shower, central heating, phone **Credit cards** AE, MC, V **Closed** never

---

Country hotel, Louviers

La Haye-le-Comte

There's an energetic air about this pleasant little country house with golf, tennis, table-tennis, mountain bikes and local walks on offer. Bedrooms are are neat and airy. Food is quite wide-ranging, with as much seafood as meat in evidence. Reports welcome.

■ 4 Route de la Haye-le-Comte, 27400 Louviers (Eure) **Tel** 32.40.00.40 **Fax** 32.25.03. 85 **Meals** breakfast, lunch, dinner **Prices** rooms 250F-470F; breakfast 45F, menus 110F-180F, children's 70F ; 10% reduction for 3 nights **Rooms** 16, all with bath, central heating, phone, satellite TV **Credit cards** AE, DC, MC, V **Closed** mid-Dec to end March; restaurant only, Mon and Tues lunch

---

Village inn, Martin-Église

Auberge du Clos Normand

A simple old auberge built of patterned brick and timber with a flowery garden and stream behind. Bedrooms in a converted outb uilding are attractive and comfortable. Food is classically Norman, involving much cholesterol and alcohol.

■ 22 Rue Henri IV, Martin-Église, 76370 Neuville-les-Dieppe (Seine-Maritime) **Tel** 35.04.40.34 **Fax** 35.04.48.49 **Meals** breakfast, lunch, dinner **Prices** rooms 300F-470F; breakfast 38F; DB&B 35 0F-445F **Rooms** 8, all with bath or shower, central heating, phone, TV **Credit cards** AE, MC, V **Closed** mid-Nov to mid-Dec; Mon, Tue

The North-west

Converted mill, Moëlan-sur-Mer

Les Moulins du Duc

The main building of this unusual hotel is a former mill but the spacious and well equipped accommodation is in two-storey cottages scattered around the secluded grounds. Breakfast can be had on the terrace by the pond. A reporter rates the food 'totally delicious'. Indoor swimming-pool.

■ 29116 Moëlan-sur-Mer (Finistère) **Tel** 98.39.60.73 **Fax** 98.39.75.56 **Meals** breakfast, lunch, dinner **Prices** rooms 440F-805F, suites 1,100F-1,300F; breakfast 55F, menus150F-350F, children's 60F **Rooms** 27, all with bath or shower, phone, TV, minibar **Credit cards** AE, DC, MC, V **Closed** mid-Jan to Mar

---

Town hotel, Le Mont-St-Michel

Hôtel Saint-Pierre

The Saint-Pierre is the pick of the hostelries that line the main street at the foot of France's premier tourist attraction. Its dining-rooms are satisfyingly rustic, its bedrooms (half in an annexe up many steps) tastefully decorated and comfortable. Efficient service, good plain food.

■ BP16, 50116 Le Mont-St-Michel (Manche) **Tel** 33.60.14.03 **Fax** 33.48.59.82 **Meals** breakfast, lunch, dinner **Prices** rooms 450F-850F; breakfast 50F, dinner 120F-180F **Rooms** 20, all with bath or shower, central heating, phone, TV, hairdrier **Credit cards** AE, V **Closed** Dec to Feb

---

Quayside hotel, Paimpol

Le Repaire de Kerroc'h

Set in an enviable position right on the quay, this handsome 18thC house has been beautifully restored. Bedrooms are well furnished and equipped. Excellent breakfasts. In the guide since our first edition, but we get few reports. Why?

■ 29 Quai Morand, Port de Plaisance, 22500 Paimpol (Côtes-d'Armor) **Tel** 96.20.50.13 **Fax** 96.22.07.46 **Meals** breakfast, lunch, dinner **Prices** rooms 250F-490F; breakfast 45F, menus 135F-350F **Rooms** 13, all with bath, phone, TV, minibar **Credit cards** MC, V **Closed** Jan to mid-Feb

---

Seaside villa, Perros-Guirec

Le Sphinx

There are splendid sea views from this tall house atop low cliffs on the 'pink granite coast' – both from the dining-room and the best of the spacious, tastefully decorated bedrooms. Service is friendly, food reliably good and night-time silence absolute .

■ Chemin de la Messe, 22700 Perros-Guirec (Côtes-d'Armor) **Tel** 96.23.25.42 **Fax** 96.9 1.26.13 **Meals** breakfast, lunch, dinner **Prices** rooms F470-F550; breakfast F45; menus F125-F265 **Rooms** 20, all with bath or shower, central heating, phone, alarm, TV **Credit cards** AE, MC, V **Closed** Jan to mid-Feb

The North-west

Château hotel, Pléhédel

Château de Coatguélen

This fine 19thC château, set in a large park, has a relaxed and friendly atmosphere. Families are well catered for – playroom, good sports facilities (including its own golf course) and a network of 'bush trails'. In the guide since the beginning; more reports welcome.

■ Pléhédel, 22290 Lanvollon (Côtes-d'Armor) **Tel** 96.55.33.40 **Fax** 96.22.37.67 **Meals** breakfast, lunch, dinner **Prices** rooms 450F-950F; breakfast 55F, menus 150F-380F **Rooms** 17, (14 with bath, 3 with shower), central heating, TV **Credit cards** AE, DC, V **Closed** never

---

Seaside hotel, Raguenès-Plage

Chez Pierre

A family seaside Logis completely without pretension and offering reliably good, traditional, sea-based cooking. 'Superb' family rooms in the modern annexe (2 suitable for the disabled) next to the turn-of-the-century main house have single beds upstairs and doubles downstairs. Big garden, early meals for kids.

■ Raguenès-Plage, 29920 Nevez (Finistère) **Tel** 98.06.81.06 **Fax** 98.06.62.09 **Meals** breakfast, lunch, dinner **Prices** rooms 185F-410F; breakfast 32F, menus 100F-270F, children's 75F **Rooms** 35, all with phone **Credit cards** MC, V **Closed** Oct to May

---

Country inn, La Roche-Bernard

Auberge Bretonne

Food takes pride of place at this small, welcoming auberge; people come from far afield for Jacques Thorel's cooking (two Michelin stars). There is a formidable cellar, too. Bedrooms are prettily furnished in rural Breton style; the rustic dining-room surrounds the vegetable garden.

■ 2 Place Duguesclin, 56130 La Roche-Bernard (Morbihan) **Tel** 99.90.60.28 **Fax** 99.90 .85.00 **Meals** breakfast, lunch, dinner **Prices** rooms 480F-1400F; breakfast 80F, menus 150F-450F **Rooms** 8, all with central heating **Credit cards** AE, MC, V **Closed** mid-Nov to early Dec; 2 weeks in Jan

---

Town hotel, La Roche-Bernard

Auberge des Deux Magots

A warm welcome awaits inside this prim-looking 17thC stone house. The furniture in the elegant dining-rooms and bedrooms may be reproduction, but it is all part of a careful, fresh decorative scheme. Good-value menus concentrate on traditional regional dishes.

■ 1 Place du Bouffay, 56130 La Roche-Bernard (Morbihan) **Tel** 99.90.60.75 **Fax** 99.90. 87.87 **Meals** breakfast, lunch, dinner **Prices** rooms 280F-320F; family rooms 380F-460F; breakfast 35F, menus 80F-320F, children's 50F **Rooms** 14, all with bath or shower, phone, satellite TV **Credit cards** MC, V **Closed** restaurant only, Mon; Sun eve and Mon out of season

The North-west

Manor house hotel, La Roche-Bernard

Manoir du Rodoir

This plain-looking house, recently taken over by a new owner, attracts golfing guests, who enjoy discounts at some of the excellent courses in southern Brittany. But with its peaceful wooded setting, relaxed ambience and tasteful decoration it also appeals to many others. Reports welcome.

■ Rte de Nantes, 56130 La Roche-Bernard (Morbihan) **Tel** 99.90.82.68 **Fax** 99.90.76.22 **Meals** breakfast, lunch, dinner **Prices** rooms 280F-555F; suites 690F-1,000F; breakfast 52F; DB&B 385F-415F; menus 125F-230F **Rooms** 26, all with bath or shower, central heating, phone, TV **Credit cards** AE, MC, V **Closed** Jan

---

Town hotel, Rouen

Hôtel de la Cathédrale

This ancient, rambling, half-timbered hotel is tucked away down a pedestrian street, only yards from the cathedral. Most of the chintzy bedrooms have been renovated over recent years. Delightful courtyard with a mass of flowers. No restaurant but plenty of choice nearby. 'Friendly service'.

■ 12 Rue St-Romain, 76000 Rouen (Seine-Maritime) **Tel** 35.71.57.95 **Fax** 35.70.15.54 **Meals** breakfast **Prices** rooms 270F-355F; breakfast 35F **Rooms** 24, all with bath or shower, central heating, phone, TV **Credit cards** MC, V **Closed** never

---

Bed and breakfast guest-house, Sourdeval

La Maurandière

A chambres d'hôtes establishment, where you share the sitting and dining room of Mme Dupart. Her lovely stone farmhouse, in an idyllic setting, was beautifully restored about ten years ago. The bedrooms are spacious and delightful. Breakfast can be served in the garden in summer.

■ 50150 Sourdeval (Manche) **Tel** 33.59.65.44 **Meals** breakfast **Prices** ro oms 200F with breakfast **Rooms** 4, all with bath or shower, central heating **Credit cards** MC **Closed** never

---

Manor house hotel, Trébeurden

Manoir de Lan-Kerellec

A member of the Relais & Châteaux group, but one of the least pretentious and most captivating, this handsome and unusual family house stands in trees high above the rocky shore, with splendid sea views from all rooms. Very relaxing and welcoming.

■ 22560 Trébeurden (Côtes-d'Armor) **Tel** 96.23.50.09 **Fax** 96.23.66.88 **Meals** breakfast, lunch, dinner **Prices** rooms 500F-2,000F; breakfast 70F, menus 140F-350F **Rooms** 20, all with bath, central heating, phone, TV **Credit cards** AE, DC, MC, V **Closed** mid-Nov to mid-Mar; restaurant only, Mon (and Tue lunch in low season)

The North-west

Manor house hotel, Tréguier

Kastell Dinec'h

We have received enthusiastic reports in the past on this 'oasis' – a
handsome old farmhouse, tucked away in lush wooded gardens.
Bedrooms are smallish – beware the stable block – but comfortable
and stylishly decorated. Food rated 'good' to 'excellent'. Neat
heated pool.

■ Rte de Lannion, 22220 Tréguier (Côtes-d'Armor) **Tel** 96.92.49.39
Fax 96.92.34.02 **Meals** breakfast, dinner **Prices** rooms 400F-450F;
breakfast 62F, menus 120F-300F **Rooms** 14, all with central heating,
phone **Credit cards** MC, V **Closed** Jan to mid-Mar, 2 weeks end of Oct;
Tue evening and Wed out of season

Country hotel, Trégunc

Les Grandes Roches

From the roadside this looks much like any other simple Logis,
but in the extensive flowery grounds are charmingly restored
farm buildings containing some of the bedrooms. 'Comfortable,
peaceful, friendly, good value.' What more could you ask?

■ Route des Grandes Roches, 29910 Trégunc (Finistère)
Tel 98.97.29.97 **Fax** 98.50 29 .19 **Meals** breakfast, dinner; lunch
weekends and holidays **Prices** rooms 250F-550F; breakfast 45F; DB&B
285-440F; menus 98F-250F **Rooms** 21, all with bath or shower, central
heating, phone **Credit cards** MC, V **Closed** mid-Dec to mid-Mar, Feb
holidays; restaurant only mid-Nov to mid-Mar

Country inn, Trelly

La Verte Campagne

Pascal Bernou has won the Michelin star he set his sights on when
he bought this 18thC farmhouse from his former employer.
Reporters agree that the food is delicious, but service can be slow.
Bedrooms in the main building are delightful but vary widely in
size; the annexe suite is less comfortable.

■ Hameau Chevalier, 50660 Trelly (Manche) **Tel** 33.47.65.33
Fax 33.47.38.03 **Meals** breakfast, lunch, dinner **Prices** rooms 260F-380F;
menus 135F-350F **Rooms** 9, all with central heating, phone
Credit cards MC, V **Closed** 3 weeks in Jan; restaurant Sun dinner
and Mon out of season

Ile-de-France

We've lumped together Paris and the surrounding *départements* of Ile de France because for many visitors they are sensible alternatives. If you're passing through the area and need a stopover, your instinct will probably be to stay out of the city; and if you're bent on a sightseeing holiday or a romantic break you'll probably want to be in the heart of things. But it's not necessa rily so: an overnight stop in Paris can work perfectly well, and a rural base for city sightseeing can be very restful.

Paris is a compact city – much more so than London, for example – and for many visitors choice of location is not very important (from the convenience point of view) unless you intend to spend a lot of time in one place (the Louvre, say). From the point of view of atmosphere and charm, location can make a deal of difference. It pays to know something about the districts (*arrondisements*) that make up the city. The one-digit or two-digit number at the end of Paris postcodes is the number of the *arrondisement*. Thus 75006 is the 6th, for example.

The *arrondisements* are numbered in a clockwise spiral starting in the centre on the Right Bank of the Seine (the northern bank). You'll mainly be interested in the first turn of the spiral.

The 1st is an upmarket area extending from the Place de la Concorde past the Louvre to Les Halles; we have a few entries here. We have only one (Gaillon Opéra) in the 2nd, to the north, away from the river, and none in the 3rd to the east. But the spiral then turns back towards the Seine, and we have a number of entries in the 4th – in the revitalised Marais, east of the Pompidou centre, and around Notre Dame. Across the river, the 5th, 6th and 7th make up the Left Bank, with the Boulevard St-Germain its main axi s. Between the Jardin des Plantes in the east and the Eiffel Tower in the west, there are more Charming Small Hotels here than anywhere else. The spiral crosses the river again to the 8th, and the Champs Elysées area, where we have a couple of entries. Outside this first central spiral, all our entries are to the north, in the 9th, 17th and 18th (Montmartre).

Paris phone numbers
If dialling a Paris number from elsewhere in Paris, omit the (1) at the beginning of the number. When dialling from elsewhere, you need the whole number, including the (1). And if dialling from provincial France, you must first of all dial 16. Similarly, when dialling provincial France from Paris, you must dial 16.

Contenders in Paris
Paris, Relais Christine (1) 43.26.71.80 Pricey and comfortable place in old abbey; courtyard and garden.
Paris, Hôtel Left Bank (1) 43.54.01.70 Cosy, beamed, antique-filled place in excellent position.
Paris, Hôtel Lido (1) 42.66.27.37 Comfortable, richly decorated place near the Madeleine.
Paris, Hôtel du Panthéon (1) 43.54.32.95 Classical glossy lobby, vaulted breakfast room, neat bedrooms, some with beams.
Paris, Pavillon de la Reine (1) 42.77.96.40 Comfortable and highly atmospheric old house in excellent position.
Paris, Hôtel Pergolèse (1) 40.67.96.77 Ultra-modern designer interior behind an austere classical façade.

Ile-de-France

Converted mill, Flagy

Hostellerie du Moulin

Over the years since its inclusion in our first edition, we have received a steady flow of readers' reports approving of this imaginatively converted flour mill an hour from Paris.

The setting, with tables in the grassy garden beside the stream that still gently turns the mill wheel, is idyllic. Beyond the neat gardens you look out on to cultivated fields which until the 1950s supplied the grain that was milled here. The heavy beams, wheels and pulleys of the mill dominate the cosy sitting-room, and the bedrooms, named after cereals, are as quirkily captivating as you would hope in a building of this character; space is at a premium, and low beams lead some guests to move about with a permanent stoop.

The cooking is satisfying and mildly adventurous, though our most recent report is less enthusiastic than usual. The menu and carte have English translations, underlining the Moulin's popularity with British travellers. Claude Scheidecker is a charming and friendly host who gives his little hotel an exceptionally welcoming atmosphere. And he still manages to keep his prices admirably low.

Nearby Fontainbleau Château; Sens (40 km) – cathedral.

2 Rue du Moulin 77940 Flagy
Tel (1) 60.96.67.89
Fax (1) 60.96.69.51
Location in village, 23 km SE of Fontainebleau, 10 km W of Montereau; with car parking
Meals breakfast, lunch, dinner
Prices rooms 240F-500F; breakfast 45F; menus 170F-220F
Rooms 7 double, 3 family rooms, all with bath; all rooms have phone

Facilities dining-room, bar, sitting-room; fishing
Credit cards AE, DC, MC, V
Children accepted
Disabled access to dining-room, not to bedrooms
Pets accepted
Closed late Sep, Christmas and early Jan; Sun evening and Mon (except some public hols: closed Mon evening and Tue)
Proprietor Claude Scheidecker

Ile-de-France

Town hotel, Paris

Hôtel de Banville

This 1930s hotel north of the Etoile, offers an attractive combination of style, comfort and middle-of-the-road prices. Convenient, too, at least for motorists: finding your way from the Périphérique to the Boulevard Berthier is easy, and parking here does not pose an insoluble problem.

With its flower-filled window boxes, the airy art deco building – the work of a celebrated architect, we are told – looks promising, and does not disappoint. Inside, all is tastefully decorated and comfortable, bordering on the luxurious. There is an elegantly furnished sitting-area in reception, and another welcoming sitting-room (with antique pieces as well as comfy sofas) that puts the Banville comfortably ahead of the Parisian norm in this important respect.

Murals create a garden effect in the breakfast room. In the bedrooms, several of which have just been renovated in individual styles, light furniture and decorations create a spacious feel; antiques are dotted throughout, and flower arrangements add a reassuring personal touch. Peace is ensured by the efficient sound-proofing. Friendly staff.

Nearby Arc de Triomphe, Champs-Elysées, Palais des Congrès.

166 Blvd Berthier 75017 Paris
Tel (1) 42.67.70.16
Fax (1) 44.40.42.77
Location on service road off major boulevard, N of Arc de Triomphe; with garage and roadside car parking nearby
Meals breakfast
Prices rooms 625F-740F; breakfast 45F
Rooms 39 double, 33 with bath, 6 with shower (13 twin); 4 family rooms, all with bath, one with shower; all rooms have central heating, phone, satellite TV, radio
Facilities sitting- room, small dining- room
Credit cards AE, MC, V
Children welcome; baby-sitting available
Disabled no special facilities
Pets accepted
Closed never
Proprietor Mme Lambert

Ile-de-France

Hôtel de la Bretonnerie

'Most certainly deserves its entry: for character and welcome, you could hardly do better,' says a reporter of this very distinctive 17th-century townhouse – echoing our own view.

The Bretonnerie is set in the middle of the picturesque, convenient and (now) fashionable Marais district, and has been converted with a good deal of sympathy and style. The exposed beams in the public areas and the upper bedrooms are echoed throughout the house by the sturdy hardwood furniture (some antique, some reproduction). The small basement breakfast- and sitting-rooms have a medieval feel, with pale stone vaulted ceilings, iron light fittings, richly coloured fabrics and polished tiled floors. Bedrooms are comfortable and pretty, and every room is different; some are arranged with the beds on a mezzanine floor and the 'downstairs' used as a small sitting-area. All have a glossy modern bathroom and guests will not find any lack of comfort.
Nearby Hôtel de Ville; Pompidou Centre; Les Halles.

22 Rue Ste-Croix-de-la-Bretonnerie 75004 Paris
Tel (1) 48.87.77.63
Fax (1) 42.77.26.78
Location in Marais district, off the Rue du Temple, near Hôtel de Ville; with garage car parking nearby
Meals breakfast
Prices rooms 620F-900F; breakfast 45F
Rooms 28 double (10 twin), 2 suites, all with bath; all have central heating, phone, TV, minibar, safe
Facilities cellar sitting-room/breakfast room
Credit cards MC, V
Children welcome
Disabled lift/elevator but access difficult
Pets not accepted
Closed Aug
Proprietor M. P Sagot

Ile-de-France

Hôtel des Deux Iles

As Roland Buffat's converted townhouse approaches its 20th year as an archetypal charming small hotel, the operation seems as satisfactory as ever – though to be frank we should welcome more reports from readers.

The enchanting Ile-St-Louis is one of the most desirable addresses in the city and has long been a popular residential area for wealthy and well-known Parisians (Pompidou among them). So it's no surprise that the Deux Iles is popular, particularly among those looking for a prime location, combined with charm and individuality. Rooms need to be booked several weeks in advance – and that applies all year round. It is a far from spacious hotel, but imaginative decoration (M. Buffat is an interior designer by trade) and the private-house atmosphere make up for the smallish size of the rooms. Reception and lounge are particularly attractive. The bedrooms (and matching bathrooms) are often decorated in blue and white, and furnished with bamboo and Provençal fabrics.

Nearby Church of St-Louis-en-L'Ile; Boulevard Saint-Germain; Ile de la Cité – Notre Dame; Rue de Rivoli.

59 Rue St-Louis-en-l'Ile 75004 Paris
Tel (1) 43.26.13.35
Fax (1) 43.29.60.25
Location on island in the Seine; car parking nearby
Meals breakfast
Prices rooms 720F-830F; breakfast 45F
Rooms 13 double, 8 with bath, 5 with shower (4 twin); 4 single, all with shower; all rooms have phone, TV
Facilities sitting-rooms

Credit cards not accepted
Children accepted
Disabled no special facilities
Pets accepted
Closed never
Proprietor Roland Buffat

Ile-de-France

Town hotel, Paris

Hôtel Duc de St-Simon

If we have a reservation about this stylish hotel on a stylish street, just off the Boulevard St-Germain, it is the obvious one; the prices are high. Are they *too* high? More reports from readers would be welcome.

First glimpsed through two pairs of French windows which lie beyond a pretty little courtyard, the interior of the Duc de St-Simon looks wonderfully inviting; and so it is – there is a warm, beautifully furnished salon with the distinctly private-house feel that the proprietor seeks to maintain, and elegant yet cosy bedrooms, all individually decorated with not a jarring note. The twin bedrooms are more spacious than those with double beds.

The white-painted 19thC house backs on to a 18thC building behind, also part of the hotel, with a tiny secret garden wedged in between. Breakfasts can be taken here, or in the intimate cellar bar; service is smiling and courteous. But as the hotel's own brochure points out, there are two famous cafés (the Deux Magots and the Flore) only a few yards away.

Nearby Hôtel des Invalides, Musée d'Orsay, church of St-Germain-des-Prés, Rodin Museum.

14 Rue de St-Simon 75007 Paris
Tel (1) 44.39.20.20
Fax (1) 45.48.68.25
Location St-Germain-des-Prés
Meals breakfast, light meals
Prices rooms 1,025F-1,425F; suites 1,800F-1850F
Rooms 29 double, 28 with bath, one with shower (10 twin); 5 suites, with bath; all have central heating, phone, safe; TV on request; some rooms have air-conditioning

Facilities 2 sitting-rooms, bar
Credit cards not accepted
Children accepted
Disabled no special facilities
Pets not accepted
Closed never
Proprietor M. G Lindqvist

Ile-de-France

Hôtel Eber

Jean-Marc Eber remains as committed as ever to the little hotel he took over in the late 1980s after more than a decade practising his hotelkeeping in four-star Paris hotels.

The turn-of-the-century house is in a quiet residential area of Paris, not far from the Champs Elysées and near the Parc Monceau (the hotel used to be called the Monceau Lenox), and is well served by the metro and bus networks. It was thoroughly refurbished a few years ago, and is now prettily furnished and decorated, and feels cared for.

M. Eber and his pleasant staff strive to lift the place out of the rut in several ways. Breakfast is notably good, involving 15 sorts of *confiture* and 3 sorts of tea; it may be served in the small but pretty courtyard – some of the bedrooms lead on to it – or in the bedrooms, or in the small beamed sitting-area off reception that also serves as a bar. There is no dining-room, but light meals can be brought in and served in the bedrooms; full meals are available at a nearby restaurant. The house rule is to 'make yourself at home' – after a hard day's sightseeing, an inviting prospect.

Nearby Parc Monceau, Arc du Triomphe, Champs Elysées.

18 Rue Léon Jost 75017 Paris
Tel (1) 46.22.60.70
Fax (1) 47.63.01.01
Location in residential area, close to Champs Elysées; with public car parking nearby
Meals breakfast
Prices rooms 610F-660F, suites 1,000F-1,300F; breakfast 50F
Rooms 18 double (3 twin), all with bath; all rooms have central heating, cable TV, phone, minibar

Facilities some rooms have private sitting-area
Credit cards AE, DC, MC, V
Children accepted
Disabled no special facilities
Pets not accepted
Closed never
Proprietor Jean Marc Eber

Ile-de-France

L'Hôtel

Here's an exercise in guide-book democracy for you. Since we've at last got a picture of this extraordinary little hotel, we're keeping it in the guide for the moment. But it's years since we had a report from a reader, which leads us to think that L'Hôtel is just too expensive. Tell us we're wrong, or out it goes.

The Rue des Beaux-Arts, in the heart of St-Germain-des-Prés, has been the home of many artists and writers. L'Hôtel's claim to fame is that Oscar Wilde 'died here beyond his means'. Then a local hotel of no real distinction, it is now the most lavish establishment on the Left Bank. Film stars and politicians figure on the guest list, along with the merely super-rich.

Bedrooms are sumptuous. All thick-pile carpets, Venetian marble bathrooms and antiques, they are the ultimate in luxury – although only the Penthouse (which takes up to five) could be described as spacious. Public rooms are equally extravagant. The winter garden has been converted into a glamorous piano bar/restaurant with fountain, goldfish and exotic plants. Both bar and restaurant are open until the early hours.

Nearby Palais du Louvre; Saint Germain-des-Prés; Delacroix museum; Rue de Buci and Rue de Seine – food-market.

13 Rue des Beaux Arts 75006 Paris
Tel (1) 43.25.27.22
Fax (1) 43.25.64.81
Location in Saint-Germain-des-Prés
Meals breakfast, lunch, dinner
Prices rooms 950F-2,300F, suites 2,800F-3,800F; breakfast 90F, lunch 120F-170F, dinner 180F
Rooms 23 double, 13 with bath, 10 with shower (15 twin); 3 suites; one single with bath; all rooms have central heating, air-conditioning, phone, TV, video, radio, minibar
Facilities 2 restaurants (winter garden, cellar bar)
Credit cards AE, DC, MC, V
Children accepted
Disabled no special facilities
Pets accepted
Closed never
Manager Alain-Philippe Feutré

Ile-de-France

Hôtel St-Dominique

M. Tible writes to inform us that much improvement and redecoration has taken place recently. So the scene above, pleasant though it is, doesn't accurately portray the hotel as you'll find it now. We trust that you will simply find a refreshed version of the original, rather than marble reception desks and wall-to-wall mirrors.

These latest improvements, coming hard on the heels of a much-needed refurbishment of the bedrooms and bathrooms in 1993, should restore the reputation of the St-Dominique, which had been flagging a little of late. The reception-cum-sitting-room has always been part of the appeal of the place – a pleasant, comfortable spot in which to meet or wait a while. Wooden stairs lead down to a little breakfast room – a white-painted stone vault with comfy banquette seats and Lloyd loom chairs. Bedrooms are small but well equipped. The 1993 refurbishment was done in confidently colourful style, retaining predominantly pine furniture. Breakfasts are generous and beautifully presented, and drinks can be had in the flowery little courtyard.

Nearby Invalides, Rodin Museum, Musée d'Orsay, Blvd-St-Germain, church of St-Germain, Place de la Concorde, Tuileries.

62 Rue St-Dominique 75007 Paris
Tel (1) 47.05.51.44
Fax (1) 47.05.81.28
Location on busy street between Les Invalides and the Eiffel Tower; with patio, and car parking nearby
Meals breakfast
Prices rooms 475F-610F, extra child's bed 90F; breakfast 40F
Rooms 34 double (10 twin), 14 with bath, 20 with shower; all rooms have central heating, phone, TV, minibar
Facilities sitting-room, breakfast room
Credit cards AE, DC, MC, V
Children accepted
Disabled lift/elevator
Pets accepted
Closed never
Proprietors M. Antoine Tible and Mme Michèle Petit

Ile-de-France

Hôtel St-Merry

If there is a more distinctive small hotel in Paris than this, we haven't found it – and since some of the smaller rooms were knocked together and refurbished it has become recommendable on the grounds of comfort as well as novelty. Its location, in an area revitalised by the Pompidou centre, is attractive too.

This former presbytery of the church of St-Merry, next door, became a private residence after the 1789 revolution, and served as a brothel before it was rescued from decay in the 1960s and converted to a hotel by Christian Crabbe. It is famous for room 9, where the spectacular flying buttresses of the next-door church form an alarmingly low stone canopy over the bed. But the whole hotel has a church-like, Gothic style. Rooms 12 and 17 have remarkable Gothic bedheads. Pale stone, wrought iron fitting and dark carved wood predominate, with muted fabrics and oriental rugs, and stained glass windows reinforcing the medieval atmosphere.

There are no public areas to speak of; breakfast is prepared in a galley squeezed behind the reception, and brought to your room. M. Crabbe is a charming and attentive host.

Nearby Ile de la Cité – Notre Dame; Pompidou centre.

78 Rue de la Verrerie 75004 Paris
Tel (1) 42.78.14.15
Fax (1) 40.29.06.82
Location in the Marais, close to Rue de Rivoli; with public car parking nearby
Meals breakfast
Prices rooms 400F-1200F; breakfast 45F
Rooms 11 double, 2 with bath, 7 with shower (4 twin); 2 family rooms, both with shower; all rooms have central heating, phone
Facilities bar beneath hotel
Credit cards not accepted
Children accepted
Disabled no special facilities
Pets accepted
Closed never
Proprietor Christian Crabbe

Ile-de-France

Hôtel le Sainte-Beuve

Our most recent reporter was unimpressed by this exceptionally tasteful establishment – basically a bed-and-breakfast place, but with extra services as well as extra style – and for very good reason. She found the bedrooms tiny and afflicted by street noise, though we have been told that double glazing has been installed. Other reporters have been luckier in both respects, but these are points to bear in mind. All is discretion and understatement: light, plain walls; restrained patterns in the rich fabrics; beds draped in white; sparse furnishing, mixing antiques with modern designs; fresh flowers strategically placed. A log fire burns in the little classically-styled salon – not a place to while away evenings, but a civilized meeting-place. Cold meals are served in the bedrooms at any time; an excellent breakfast arrives on a tray beautifully laid with English porcelain. Friendly and welcoming service.
Nearby Montparnasse; Postal Museum; Jardin du Luxembourg; Blvd St-Germain within easy walking distance.

9 Rue Ste-Beuve 75006 Paris
Tel (1) 45.48.20.07
Fax (1) 45.48.67.52
Location between Blvd Montparnasse and Jardin du Luxembourg; car parking in Blvd Montparnasse
Meals breakfast; cold dishes available at all times
Prices rooms 700F-1,300F
Rooms 22 double (9 twin), all with bath; all rooms have phone, TV
Facilities sitting-room

Credit cards AE, MC, V
Children accepted
Disabled no special facilities
Pets small dogs accepted
Closed never
Manager Bobette Compagnon

Ile-de-France

Town hotel, Paris

Hôtel des Tuileries

A recent inspection visit convinced us that this attractive 18thC mansion with revolutionary associations deserved a full entry, offering as it does a pleasant combination of a quiet but convenient setting, comfortable accommodation and – perhaps most important in a town where you can't count on it – a genuinely warm welcome.

The hotel is very well placed both for sightseeing and shopping – close to the beautiful Place Vendôme and the exclusive shops of the Rue du Faubourg St-Honoré. It has two small salons with velvet seats, paintings and tapestries on plain walls, and a breakfast room in the basement, where there is a better-than-average buffet, with cheeses and yoghurt – and decent coffee. Bedrooms are prettily and individually decorated – one with a sky-and-clouds theme, another in Japanese style, another with a four-poster and yellow drapes; antique, reproduction and modern furniture is successfully mixed. Front rooms are the most elegant and spacious, and street noise should not be a problem. Bathrooms may be small but are very smart, with much use of marble.

Nearby Tuileries, Louvre, Opéra, Rue de Rivoli.

10 Rue St-Hyacinthe 75001 Paris
Tel (1) 42.61.04.17
Fax (1) 49.27.91.56
Location in middle of city, N of Tuileries; with public car parking nearby Place du Marché Saint Honoré or Place Vendome
Meals breakfast
Prices rooms 690F-1,200F; breakfast 60F
Rooms 26 double (12 twin), 4 suites, all with bath; all rooms have central heating, air conditioning, phone, minibar, hairdrier, safe, satellite TV
Facilities breakfast room, bar
Credit cards AE, DC, V
Children accepted
Disabled no special facilities
Pets accepted
Closed never
Proprietors Poulle-Vidal family

Ile-de-France

Hôtel Verneuil-St-Germain

A change of ownership a few years ago resulted in a move upmarket for this old townhouse between the Blvd St-Germain and the river, not far from the marvellous Musée d'Orsay – since when readers seem to have been leaving the place well alone. But the new prices don't seem unreasonable, for what you get.

The lobby makes a great impression, with its classical statues on a polished wooden floor reflected in a wall of mirrored glass, contrasting with other walls of bare stone and a ceiling of exposed beams. Furnishings are imaginative, with richly striped curtains, and attractive sofas and armchairs in spotted and Paisley prints. The bedrooms fulfil the promise of the stylish ground floor, done out in designer fabrics; it pays to ask for a good-sized room when booking – they vary widely, some being very small. The marble-tiled bathrooms are well equipped. In the basement there is an attractive stone-walled breakfast room, with appropriately traditional-style furniture; breakfast is copious, including croissants.

Nearby Musée d'Orsay, Tuileries, Louvre, Ile de la Cité, Notre Dame, St-Germain-des-Prés.

8 Rue de Verneuil 75007 Paris
Tel (1) 42.60.82.14
Fax (1) 42.61.40.38
Location in middle of St-Germain-des-Prés; in quiet street with public car parking nearby
Meals breakfast
Prices rooms 650F-950F; breakfast 50F
Rooms 22 double (4 twin), all with bath; all rooms have central heating, phone, TV, radio, alarm

Facilities breakfast room, 2 sitting-rooms
Credit cards AE, DC, MC,V
Children welcome; baby-sitting available
Disabled no special facilities
Pets welcome if well behaved
Closed never
Proprietor M Le Boudec

Ile-de-France

Auberge du Gros Marronnier

Mme Trochon advises us of further improvements to this rustic little inn, which have been going on steadily since we first encountered the place in 1990. Much of the older parts of the interior have been renovated, the sitting-room has been smartened up, and a new glass veranda with lovely views over the valley has become the restaurant.

The Gros Marronier is tucked away next door to the church (it used to be the presbytery) in an affluent residential village. It's a captivating place for a night or two when passing through the Paris area – close enough to the metropolis for sightseeing expeditions, and handily placed for the Normandy ferry ports. The bedrooms are spacious and prettily decorated, and the food, served on a flowery terrace overlooking the informal grassy garden, is interesting, excellent and well presented. The staff are smiling and helpful, but not over-numerous; the pace of service at dinner is elegantly described by one reporter as 'a good tempo for digestion and civilized discourse'. More reports please.

Nearby Versailles (15 km); Paris (35 km).

3 Place de l'Église, 75720 Senlisse
Tel (1) 30.52.51.69
Fax (1) 30.52.55.91
Location in heart of village, next to church, 12 km NE of Rambouillet on D91; with garden and limited car parking
Meals breakfast, lunch, dinner
Prices rooms 280F-375F; breakfast 45F, menus 155F-295F
Rooms 15 double, one single, 4 family rooms, 12 with bath, 8 with shower; all rooms have central heating, phone
Facilities dining-room, TV room, bar, terrace
Credit cards AE, V
Children welcome
Disabled no special facilities
Pets accepted
Closed one week at Christmas
Proprietor Mme Trochon

Ile-de-France

Inn, Barbizon

Hôtellerie du Bas-Breau

Half of Europe's political grandees have been guests at this handsome and luxurious (Relais & Châteaux) inn. The best rooms are in the inn itself; but the majority are in a modern chalet set amid the beautifully tended flower gardens. Excellent food. Swimming-pool.

■ 22 Rue Grande, 77630 Barbizon (Seine-et-Marne)
Tel (1) 60.66.40.05 **Fax** (1) 60.69.22.89 **Meals** breakfast, lunch, dinner **Prices** rooms 950F-2,800F; breakfast 90F, dinner from 500F **Rooms** 20, all with bath, central heating, phone, TV, hairdrier **Credit cards** AE, MC, V **Closed** never

---

Restaurant with rooms, Barbizon

Hostellerie de la Clé d'Or

The key attraction is the shady courtyard where meals (well cooked, ample portions) are served in summer. Bedrooms are in a handsome single-storey extension. Smart dining-room with an open fireplace and walls covered in daubs by local artists. Delightful garden.

■ 73 Grande Rue, 77630 Barbizon (Seine-et-Marne)
Tel (1) 60.66.40.96 **Fax** (1) 60.66.42.71 **Meals** breakfast, lunch, dinner **Prices** rooms 290F-850F; menus 160F-230F, children's 75F **Rooms**16, all with bath or shower, central heating, phone, TV, minibar **Credit cards** AE, DC, MC, V **Closed** never

---

Manor house hotel, Fontenay-Trésigny

Le Manoir

From the outside, this half-timbered turn-of-the-century mansion in gloriously spacious gardens (with pool) looks English. But its interior is distinctively French – rich and ornate and occasionally gloomy. Bedrooms differ widely in style. Good classic cooking.

■ 77610 Fontenay-Trésigny (Seine-et-Marne) **Tel** (1) 64.25.91.17 **Fax** (1) 64.25.95. 49 **Meals** breakfast, lunch, dinner **Prices** rooms 830F-1,190F, breakfast 70F; menus 240F-350F **Rooms** 20, all with bath, phone, TV, minibar **Credit cards** AE, DC, MC, V **Closed** never

---

Town hotel, Paris

Hôtel de l'Abbaye

This elegant 18thC town house has been tastefully and comfortably refurbished over the last couple of years. Bedrooms overlook the lush garden or the courtyard where breakfast is served in fine weather. Exceptionally inviting sitting-rooms.

■ 10, Rue Cassette, 75006 Paris **Tel** (1) 45.44.38.11 **Fax** (1) 45.48.07.86 **Meals** breakfast **Prices** rooms 980F-1,600F with breakfast; suites 1,915F-2,000F **Rooms** 46, all with bath, central heating, air conditioning, phone, TV, radio, hairdrier **Credit cards** AE, MC, V **Closed** never

Ile-de-France

Town hotel, Paris

Hôtel Agora

Hard to beat for a simple base in an ideal area. It contrives to be old-fashioned with its flowery entrance and lacy curtains, yet in other ways it seems modern and even slightly chic, and practical necessities are well looked after.

■ 7 Rue de la Cossonerie, 75001 Paris **Tel** (1) 42.33.46.02 **Fax** (1) 42.33.80.99 **Meals** breakfast **Prices** rooms 350F-595F; breakfast 35F **Rooms** 29, all with bath or shower, central heating, phone, TV **Credit cards** AE, MC, V **Closed** never

---

Town hotel, Paris

Hôtel d'Angleterre

Once the British Embassy, this 18thC building still has something faintly British about it. The location is something else – in a lively area of the Left Bank; but the bedrooms are peaceful, some overlooking a delightful white courtyard with fountain. Pricey, but worth it.

■ 44 Rue Jacob, 75006 Paris **Tel** (1) 42.60.34.72 **Fax** (1) 42.60.16.93 **Meals** breakfast **Prices** rooms 600F-1,250F; breakfast 50F **Rooms** 24, 3 suites, all with bath or shower, central heating, phone, TV **Credit cards** AE, DC, MC, V **Closed** never

---

Town hotel, Paris

Hôtel Beaubourg

Although this six-storey town house dates back to the 1600s, the hotel is not lacking in modern comforts; bedrooms and public rooms are pleasantly furnished and effectively lit. Some bedrooms overlook the courtyard garden, full of trailing plants.

■ 11 Rue Simon Lefranc, 75004 Paris **Tel** (1) 42.74.34.24 **Fax** (1) 42.78.68.11 **Meals** breakfast **Prices** rooms 490F-580F (extra bed 150F); breakfast 40F **Rooms** 28, all with bath or shower, central heating, phone, TV, radio, minibar **Credit cards** AE, DC, MC, V **Closed** never

---

Town hotel, Paris

Hôtel Bersoly's Saint-Germain

On a quiet street in the administrative heart of Paris, this 17thC former convent makes an excellent sightseeing base. Each of the bedrooms – generally on the small side – has been thoughtfully done out in a favourite colour of the impressionist painter it is named after. Reports welcome.

■ 28 Rue de Lille, 75007 Paris **Tel** (1) 42.60.73.79 **Fax** (1) 49.27.05.55 **Meals** breakfast, snacks **Prices** rooms 580F-680F; breakfast 50F **Rooms** 16, all with bath or shower, central heating, phone, TV, radio, hairdrier, safe **Credit cards** MC, V **Closed** 2 weeks in Aug

Ile-de-France

Town hotel, Paris

Hôtel Danemark

Everything about this smart hotel is deliberately stylish: the triple-arched frontage, the striking modern art, the shiny chairs, low glass tables and slick black, green and blue furniture. Bedrooms are refreshingly simple and recently refurbished.

■ 21 Rue Vavin, 75006 Paris **Tel** (1) 43.26.93.78 **Fax** (1) 46.34.66.06 **Meals** breakfast **Prices** rooms 590F-790F; breakfast 50F **Rooms** 15, all with bath, central heating, phone, T V, minibar, hairdrier **Credit cards** AE, DC, V **Closed** never

---

Town guest-house, Paris

Hôtel Esmeralda

A small hotel of great character, occupying a quaint 16thC building in a superb position (great views of Notre Dame) and steadily upgraded over many years by the present ageing owner. Objets d'art are scattered throughout, mixing well with the old beams, stone walls and quarry-tiled floors. Avoid the annexe, unless it has been redecorated.

■ 4 Rue St-Julien-le-Pauvre, 75005 Paris **Tel** (1) 43.54.19.20 **Fax** 20(1) 40.51.00.68 **Meals** breakfast **Prices** rooms 160F-490F; breakfast 40F **Rooms** 20, all with central heating, phone **Credit cards** not accepted **Closed** never

---

Town hotel, Paris

Hôtel Étoile Péreire

Well placed for motorists and air travellers, this hotel has been smartly done out in a restrained modern style. Some of the rooms are split-level, with living as well as sleeping space. Breakfast is an à la carte affair – a treat, but not cheap.

■ 146 Blvd Pereire, 75017 Paris **Tel** 20(1) 42.67.60.00. **Fax** 20(1) 42.67.02.90 **Meals** breakfast **Prices** rooms 566F-1,012F; breakfast 54F **Rooms** 26, all with bath or shower, central heating, phone, satellite TV, minibar, hairdrier **Credit cards** AE, DC, MC, V **Closed** never

---

Town hotel, Paris

Hôtel Gaillon Opéra

There is a rustic feel about this well established, popular hotel in the heart of the Right Bank shopping district; bedrooms are neither light nor spacious, but they are warmly and tastefully furnished, and bathrooms are modern and well equipped. Not cheap, but not expensive for the area.

■ 9 Rue Gaillon, 75002 Paris **Tel** (1) 47.42.47.74 **Fax** (1) 47.42.01.23 **Meals** breakfast **Prices** rooms 500F-850F; breakfast 35F **Rooms** 26, all with bath, central heating, phone, TV, minibar, safe **Credit cards** AE, DC, MC, V **Closed** never

Ile-de-France

Bed and breakfast guest-house, Paris

Hôtel des Grandes Écoles

The name refers to the Sorbonne, next door; the far-from-grand hotel retains the ambience of a country house, aided by its court-yard-garden. Bedrooms are modestly furnished and some have thin walls; but a recent visitor was very pleased, especially by Mme LeFoch's 'cheerful disposition'.

■ 75 Rue de Cardinal Lemoine, 75005 Paris **Tel** (1) 43.26.79.23 **Fax** 20(1)_2043.25.28.1 5 **Meals** breakfast **Prices** rooms 350F-650F; breakfast 40F **Rooms** 36, all with central heating , phone **Credit cards** MC, V **Closed** never

---

Town hotel, Paris

Hôtel des Grands Hommes

Conflicting views on this handsome and well placed hotel, named after the artists and writers who used it in the past, the critics taking the view that prices are rather high for what you get. More reports would be welcome. If you opt for a view of the Panthéon, be prepared for a little street noise.

■ 17 Place du Panthéon, 75005 Paris **Tel** (1) 46.34.19.60 **Fax** (1)43.26.67.32 **Meals** breakfast **Prices** rooms 606F-792F **Rooms** 32, all with bath or shower, central heating, air-conditioning, cable TV, radio, minibar, hairdrier **Credit cards** AE, DC, MC, V **Closed** never

---

Town hotel, Paris

Le Jardin des Plantes

Situated directly opposite the botanical gardens, this bright little hotel has floral decorative themes for each of its five floors. Rooms on the top floor have the best views and some open on to the roof terrace. Breakfast can be served here, or in a café-style room.

■ 5 Rue Linné, 75005 Paris **Tel** (1) 47.07.06.20 **Fax** (1) 47.07.62.74 **Meals** breakfast, lunch **Prices** rooms 420F-640F; breakfast 40F, lunch 55F-90F **Rooms** 33, all with bath or shower, central heating, phone, TV, minibar, hairdrier **Credit cards** DC, MC, V **Closed** restaurant only, Aug

---

Town hotel, Paris

Jeu de Paume

A bold conversion of a 17thC real tennis court, with what must be the greatest array of exposed beams in Paris, married to high-tech gadgets such as a glass lift. Bedrooms have recently been redecorated in soft shades. There are several salons, and a little garden.

■ 54 Rue St-Louis-en-l'Ile, 75004 Paris **Tel** (1) 43.26.14.18 **Fax** (1) 40.46.02.76 **Meals** breakfast **Prices** rooms 795F-1,250F; breakfast 75F **Rooms** 32, all with bath, central heating, phone, TV, radio, minibar, hairdrier **Credit cards** AE, DC, MC, V **Closed** never

Ile-de-France

Town hotel, Paris

Hôtel Lenox

The more central of a pair of polished sister hotels, both marked out by smoothly traditional furnishings. The Lenox started life at the turn of the century as a pension, but is now quite a suave hotel, with a clubby bar. Notably tasteful decoration in the bedrooms.

■ 9 Rue de l'Université, 75007 Paris **Tel** (1) 42.96.10.95 **Fax** (1) 42.61.52.83 **Meals** breakfast **Prices** rooms 590F-960F; breakfast 45F **Rooms** 34, all with bath or shower, cent ral heating, phone, TV **Credit cards** AE, DC, MC, V **Closed** never

---

Town hotel, Paris

Résidence Lord Byron

In an area of grand hotels, the Lord Byron stands out for its personal service and (by local standards) reasonable prices. Bedrooms tend to be smallish, but are modern and comfortable, with a mix of old and new furnishings. There is a little courtyard garden.

■ 5 Rue de Chateaubriand, 75008 Paris **Tel** (1) 43.59.89.98 **Fax** (1) 42.89.46.04 **Meals** breakfast **Prices** rooms 700F-1,300F; breakfast 55F **Rooms** 31, all with bath or shower, central heating, phone, TV, minibar, hairdrier, safe **Credit cards** AE, MC, V **Closed** never

---

Town hotel, Paris

Hôtel de Lutèce

Sister hotel to the Deux-Iles (just along the street), this converted townhouse has the feel of the Provençal countryside, with a tiled floor and a stone fireplace. Rooms are pretty, but quite small. The location, superb for sightseeing, does have drawbacks – some noise at night, and car parking problems. Friendly staff.

■ 65 Rue St-Louis-en-l'Ile, 75004 Paris **Tel** (1) 43.26.23.52 **Fax** 20(1) 2043.29.60.25 **Meals** breakfast **Prices** rooms 836F; breakfast 45F **Rooms** 23, all with bath or shower, cable TV, phone, hairdrier **Credit cards** not accepted **Closed** never

---

Town hotel, Paris

Hôtel des Marronniers

Birds and leaves decorate every available surface of this tall, gracious, country-style hotel in the heart of bustling St-Germain. Bedrooms are brightly decorated but varied in size; the stone-vaulted cellars form the cosy breakfast room and sitting-room. Reports welcome.

■ 21 Rue Jacob, 75006 Paris **Tel** (1) 43.25.30.60 **Fax** (1) 40.46.83.56 **Meals** breakfast **Prices** rooms 700F-800F; breakfast 45F **Rooms** 37, all with bath or shower, central heating, phone **Credit cards** not accepted **Closed** never

Ile-de-France

Town hotel, Paris

Hôtel Mayflower

In the same ownership as the Lord Byron and right next door to it, the Mayflower shares the same refined but relaxed atmosphere and is similarly well run. Bedrooms are pretty and calm, and mainly spacious. Elegant and comfortable sitting-room.

■ 3 Rue de Chateaubriand, 75008 Paris **Tel** (1) 45.62.57.46
Fax (1) 42.56.32.38 **Meals** breakfast **Prices** rooms 650F-950F; breakfast 50F **Rooms** 24, all with bath, central heating, phone, satellite TV, minibar **Credit cards** MC, V **Closed** never

---

Town hotel, Paris

Le Relais Medicis

If you can afford it, this glorious little hotel – opened in 1992 by the proprietors of the Relais St-Germain – is one of the most compelling places to stay in Paris. Its 16 beamed bedrooms,around a pretty courtyard, are designer-decorated with tremendous flair.

■ 23 Rue Racine, 75006 Paris **Tel** (1) 43.26.00.60 **Fax** (1) 40.46.83.39 **Meals** breakfast **Prices** rooms 930F-1,495F with breakfast **Rooms** 16, all with bath, central heating, air conditioning, phone, TV, radio, minibar, hairdrier **Credit cards** AE, DC, MC, V
Closed never

Town hotel, Paris

Hôtel de la Place des Vosges

Set in a quiet street only 25 metres from one of the loveliest squares in Paris, this 17thC house is entirely in harmony with the surrounding area. The salon is suitably traditional and rustic in style; bedrooms have less character but are well kept – and reasonably priced.

■ 12 Rue de Birague, 75004 Paris **Tel** (1) 42.72.60.46
Fax (1) 42.72.02.64 **Meals** breakfast **Prices** rooms 315F-460F; breakfast 30F; children under 2 free **Rooms** 16, all with bath or shower, central heating, phone **Credit cards** DC, MC, V **Closed** never

---

Town hotel, Paris

Hôtel Prima-Lepic

Set in bustling Montmartre, this is a cheerful bed and breakfast place. The ground floor is done out as an indoor courtyard giving an airy and peaceful effect; bedrooms are individually and well decorated, though not over-spacious. Breakfast is buffet-style.

■ 29 Rue Lepic, 75018 Paris **Tel** (1) 46.06.44.64 **Fax** (1) 46.06.66.11 **Meals** breakfast **Prices** rooms 350F-700F; breakfast 40F **Rooms** 38, all with bath or shower, central heating, phone, TV, hairdrier **Credit cards** MC, V **Closed** never

Ile-de-France

Town hotel, Paris

Hôtel Prince Albert

Reasonably priced hotels of any comfort are hard to come by in the 1er arondissement; the Prince Albert – well placed for culture, entertainment and shopping alike – is an exception. The corridors upstairs are rather dim, but lead to bedrooms that are well cared for and comfortable; we hear that renovation, maintaining the same style of the hotel, is under way.

■ 5 Rue St-Hyacinthe, 75001 Paris **Tel** (1) 42.61.58.36
Fax (1) 42.60.04.06 **Meals** breakfast **Prices** rooms 430F-580F, extra bed 160F; breakfast 35F **Rooms** 30, all with bath or shower, central heating, phone, TV, minibar, safe **Credit cards** AE, MC, V **Closed** never

Town hotel, Paris

Hôtel Récamier

Cheap and cheerful – sober-looking from the outside but welcoming within. Bedrooms are small and modern, and all have been recently redecorated. All in all, a sensible choice as a quiet, central and reasonably priced base.

■ 3 bis Place St-Sulpice, 75006 Paris **Tel** (1) 43.26.04.89
Meals breakfast **Prices** rooms 390F-620F **Rooms** 30, all with central heating, phone **Credit cards** MC, V **Closed** never

Town hotel, Paris

La Régence Etoile

This 'listed' 1875 house is furnished in suitably traditional style. The bedrooms are mostly spacious and comfortable with smart bathrooms – and there is more space for sitting than is common in Parisian bed-and-breakfast places.

■ 24 Ave Carnot, 75017 Paris **Tel** (1) 43.80.75.60 **Fax** (1) 47.66.78.86
Meals breakfast **Prices** rooms 420F-700F **Rooms** 38, all with bath or shower, central heating, phone, TV, minibar, hairdrier **Credit cards** AE, MC, V **Closed** never

Town hotel, Paris

Hôtel Riboutté Lafayette

Not one of the most conspicuous of the city's charming small hotels, but a reasonably priced and cheerful base. Bedrooms are small, friendly and individual; all rooms are quiet, whether overlooking the courtyard or the street.

■ 5 Rue Riboutté, 75009 Paris **Tel** (1) 47.70.62.36 **Fax** (1) 48.00.91.50
Meals breakfast **Prices** rooms 370F-460F; breakfast 30F **Rooms** 24, all with bath or shower, phone, satellite TV **Credit cards** AE, MC, V **Closed** never

Ile-de-France

Town hotel, Paris

Le Relais St-Germain

Irresistible, if you can afford it: a sumptuous 17thC house filled with stunning antiques and period furniture. The enormous beamed bedrooms have retained their 'olde worlde' charm, but now have every modern convenience, including large marble bathrooms. Four rooms have self-catering facilities. All staff speak English.

■ 9 Carrefour de l'Odéon, 75006 Paris **Tel** (1) 43.29.12.05 **Fax** (1) 46.33.45.30 **Meals** breakfast **Prices** rooms 1,260F-1,650F with breakfast; suites 1,900F **Rooms** 22, all with bath, central heating, air-conditioning, phone, cable TV, radio, minibar, hairdrier **Credit cards** AE, DC, V **Closed** never

---

Town hotel, Paris

Hôtel Saint-Germain-des-Prés

This small Left Bank hotel stands out for charm and individuality, if not for notably good taste or coherence of interior design – its bedrooms are all furnished in different styles and colours. Large salon-cum-breakfast-room.

■ 36 Rue Bonaparte, 75006 Paris **Tel** (1) 43.26.00.19 **Fax** (1) 40.46.83.63 **Meals** breakfast **Prices** rooms 750F-1,600F **Rooms** 30, all with bath or shower, central heating, phone , TV, radio, minibar; some have air-conditioning **Credit cards** MC, V **Closed** never

---

Town hotel, Paris

Le Saint-Grégoire

Confidently designer-decorated in neo-classical style, this tall 18thC town house makes an exceptionally warm and sleek hotel, though not a cheap one. It has a tiny enclosed garden, full of ferns and flowers, and two of the bedrooms have their own terrace/gardens. Neat stone vault for breakfast.

■ 43 Rue de l'Abbé Gregoire, 75006 Paris **Tel** (1) 45.48.23.23 **Fax** (1) 45.48.33.95 **Meals** breakfast **Prices** rooms 790F-1,390F; breakfast 60F **Rooms** 20, all with bath, central heating, phone, TV, radio, hairdrier **Credit cards** AE, DC, MC, V **Closed** never

---

Bed and breakfast guest-house, Paris

Hôtel Saint-Louis

The simplest and cheapest of three sister hotels on a busy street on the Ile-St-Louis. The welcoming atmosphere and its ideal location for sightseeing make up for any lack of facilities (only one public room) and the small size of the bedrooms.

■ 75 Rue St-Louis-en-l'Ile, 75004 Paris **Tel** (1) 46.34.04.80 **Fax** (1) 46.34.02.13 **Meals** breakfast **Prices** rooms 685F-785F; breakfast 45F **Rooms** 21, all with bath or shower, phone **Credit cards** MC,V **Closed** never

Ile-de-France

Town guest-house, Paris

Hôtel Saint-Louis Marais

A sound, friendly choice if you are looking for a peaceful, reasonably priced base close to the Bastille. The beamed bedrooms are far from spacious, but are prettily decorated with antiques, wall hangings and fresh flowers.

■ 1 Rue Charles V, 75004 Paris **Tel** (1) 48.87.87.04 **Fax** (1) 48.87.33.26 **Meals** breakfast **Prices** rooms 510F-710F; breakfast 40F **Rooms** 15, all with bath or shower, central heating, phone **Credit cards** MC, V **Closed** never

---

Town hotel, Paris

Hôtel Solférino

The bedrooms of this family-run Left Bank bed and breakfast place are more notable for their comfort than their character. It is chiefly distinguished by its comfortable, tastefully furnished sitting room and bright café-style breakfast room.

■ 91 Rue de Lille, 75007 Paris **Tel** (1)47.05.85.54 **Fax** (1) 45.55.51.16 **Meals** breakfast **Prices** rooms 311F-737F; extra bed 169F; breakfast 38F **Rooms** 33, all with bath or shower, phone **Credit cards** MC, V **Closed** Christmas

---

Restaurant with rooms, Paris

Thoumieux

Set in the shadow of the Eiffel Tower, this efficient, friendly place revolves around its popular brasserie-style restaurant, which offers good country-style cooking and drinkable house-wine. Bedrooms are modern and comfortable, with tasteful fabrics and stylish furniture.

■ 79 Rue St-Dominique, 75007 Paris **Tel** 20(1) 47.05.49.75 **Fax** (1) 47.05.36.96 **Meals** breakfast, lunch, dinner **Prices** rooms 550F-600F; breakfast 35F, meals about 150F **Rooms** 10, all with bath, central heating, phone, TV, radio **Credit cards** MC **Closed** never

---

Town hotel, Paris

Hôtel de l'Université

This dignified town house in an area of quiet, elegant streets is not cheap, but does offer reasonable value – antiques in the beamed public areas and in the comfortable bedrooms, efficient and friendly service and breakfasts well above the Parisian norm in quality but not price.

■ 22 Rue de l'Université, 75007 Paris **Tel** (1) 42.61.09.39 **Fax** (1) 42.60.40.84 **Meals** breakfast, light snacks **Prices** rooms 650F-1,500F; breakfast 45F **Rooms** 28, all with bath or shower, air-conditioning, phone, TV **Credit cards** AE, MC, V **Closed** never

The North-east

Area introduction

Our North-east region contains some large areas with not much to offer the holidaymaker, and which contain few Charming Small Hotels; there are several *départements* with no entries at all. But this region embraces four areas worth singling out for their touristic interest and their hotels.

The hinterland of the main Channel ferry ports includes some pleasant rolling countryside, and of course proximity to those ports makes this area – particularly the *département* of Pas-de-Calais, containing Calais and Boulogne – prime territory for a quick weekend away.

The *départements* of Oise and Seine-et-Marne, respectively to the north and east of the Ile de France, contain some tourist highlights (Compiègne, Chantilly, Vaux-le-Vicomte), and some desirable hotels – though they may owe their existence more to proximity to Paris than to the demands of the local tourist trade.

More or less due east of Paris, where the motorway from Paris to Strasbourg meets that coming down from Calais, is Champagne country. Wherever there is wine there is a satisfyingly cultivated landscape, and here there is also the architectural spectacle of R eims, at the heart of the Champagne business as well as the region, of which the cathedral is only one part.

And then there is Alsace, at the far eastern end of this region, against the German border. This is another wine region – a hilly one, with some wonderful scenery. The wines and the food alike are German-influenced, as you might expect.

Contenders in the North-east

Audinghen-par-Wissant, La Maison de la Houve 21.32.97.06 Well modernised old farmhouse B&B, comfortably furnished and well run, in flowery garden.

Illhaeusern, Hôtel des Berges 89.71.87.87 Luxurious barn-style lodgings at foot of garden of one of the most celebrated restaurants in Alsace.

Langres, Le Cheval Blanc 25.87.07.00 Neat Logis in ancient town-centre building; small terrace.

Sars-Poteries, Hôtel Fleuri 27.61.62.72 Old farm building, now a prettily furnished B&B hotel, with independently run Michelin-starred restaurant (Auberge Fleurie) next door.

Reporting to the guide

We're very keen to hear from readers about their hotel-going experiences. We can't visit every hotel in the guide every year; even if we could, we wouldn't be staying in them all. And it's only when you stay in a place that you find out how the plumbing deals with the demand for hot water, what that much-vaunted 70F breakfast is really like, and what happens when you request something extraordinary like an extra pillow. So please do let us know how you get on next time you're travelling in France.

In particular, please do write when you like a small hotel, whether or not you've chosen it with our help. People are pretty good at letting us know when we've got a place wrong (usually, we hope, because the place has gone downhill). Places that come up to expectations don't always trigger a reaction.

The North-east

Hostellerie des 3 Mousquetaires

Most visitors are thoroughly well pleased by this jolly 19thC château, equidistant from the ferry ports of Boulogne, Calais and Dunkerque, although one report indicates that the service in the restaurant at the weekend is sometime overstretched. Is the place becoming too popular for its own good?

The hotel is a family-run *logis*, a world away from the classical château pattern. The charming and vigilant Mme Venet is in charge front of house, aided by her daughter-in-law, while husband Marcel and son Philippe prepare regionally based meals offering 'enormous portions' and 'astonishing value' in the spotless open-to-view kitchen. (The cheeseboard is 'magnificent'.)

The building is an eccentric mixture of stone-and-brick stripes and pseudo-timbering beneath a steep slate roof, set in a large wooded garden with ponds and streams (ducks and swans). A reader reports delightedly that children can follow the example of the owners' own children and run around without raising eyebrows. The interior is traditionally grand in style, the best of the old bedrooms (eg 'Milady') huge and elegant (though some are much smaller); those in the annexe are sumptuously decorated in various styles – one has a Japanese theme, for example. But several guests have been worried by street noise in these rooms.

Nearby Aire – Renaissance bailiff's court, collegiate church of St-Pierre; St Omer (20 km) – basilica, fine arts museum.

Château du Fort de la Redoute 62120 Aire-sur-la-Lys
Tel 21.39.01.11
Fax 21.39.50.10
Location in countryside off N43, 2km S of Aire; in parkland, with ample car parking
Meals breakfast, lunch, dinner
Prices rooms 300F-560F, suites 850F; breakfast 45F, menus 110F- (except weekends) 130F
Rooms 31 double (9 twin), 24 with bath, 2 with shower; one suite with bath; one family room with bath; all rooms have central heating, phone, TV
Facilities 2 sitting- rooms, 2 dining-rooms, bar; golf
Credit cards AE, MC, V
Children welcome; cots and special menu available
Disabled no special facilities
Pets accepted
Closed mid-Dec to mid-Jan
Proprietors M. and Mme Philippe Venet

The North-east

Country mansion, Hesdin-l'Abbé

Hôtel Cléry

We have just heard that new owners, Catherine and Didier Legros, have taken over this elegant 18th-century mansion and that renovation is already in hand. Properly called the Château d'Hesdin-l'Abbé, a dignified façade dominates the fine tree-lined approach to the house, surrounded by parkland. But there is no need to be intimidated: this is not a stuffy place. Inside, there is not an antler in sight; nor are the public rooms stiff with Louis XV chairs (although there is a very fine Louis XV wrought-iron staircase), or even laden with chintz. Here, all is bright and light in harmonious pastel tones, in understated modern style.

The hotel already has an established British trade; the excellent golf at nearby Hardelot is an attraction in addition to proximity to the Channel and the merits of the place itself. Bedrooms are well decorated, including those in the sensitively designed modern annexe. There is an attractive bar, and a log fire in the sitting-room when the weather calls for it. Dinner can now be had at Hôtel Cléry on weekday evenings, and there is also a large choice of restaurants in nearby Boulogne. We would welcome reports on the recent changes.

Nearby Hardelot, golf and beach (9km); Le Touquet (15km)

62360 Hesdin-L'Abbé
Tel 21.83.19.83
Fax 21.87.52.59
Location in tiny rural village, 9 km SE of Boulogne; with gardens and ample car parking
Meals breakfast, dinner
Prices rooms 390F-590F; menu 120F
Rooms 21 double, 12 with bath, 9 with shower (12 twin); all have central heating, phone, TV

Facilities bar, sitting-room; tennis court, table tennis, mountain bikes for hire
Credit cards AE, DC, MC, V
Children accepted
Pets not accepted
Disabled no special facilities
Closed mid-Dec to end Jan
Proprietors Catherine and Didier Legros

The North-east

Village inn, Marlenheim

Le Cerf

All the signs are that the Cerf is as compelling as ever for visitors who like the cooking of Alsace as much as its wines. Michel Husser carries on the gastronomic tradition of father Robert, who has now taken a back seat; Michelin awards two stars. Bedrooms are not particularly luxurious, but are well furnished and thoroughly comfortable. There is a cobbled courtyard for drinks and breakfast – so, when the weather is fine, the shortage of sitting space should not be a problem.

Nearby Strasbourg (20 km); wine villages.

30 Rue du Général-de-Gaulle
67520 Marlenheim
Tel 88.87.73.73
Fax 88.87.68.08
Location on main road through village, 18 km W of Strasbourg; with courtyard and car parking
Meals breakfast, lunch, dinner
Prices rooms 300F-600F; menus 250F-485F
Rooms 17 double, 8 with bath, 7 with shower (6 twin); one single with shower; 2 family rooms, both with bath; all rooms have central heating, phone
Facilities dining-room, 2 function rooms
Credit cards AE,V
Children accepted
Disabled access to dining-room; 2 ground-floor bedrooms
Pets accepted
Closed restaurant, Tue, Wed
Proprietor Robert Husser

The North-east

Auberge de la Grenouillère

We receive conflicting messages about this low Picardy-style farmhouse (known to many as the Froggery), a popular gastronomic halt with the British. Two visitors particularly commend lunch on the terrace ('most agreeable', 'delightful') while the third relates an unhappy incident concerning undrinkable wine. An isolated blip, we trust.

The spacious gravel terrace is certainly an excellent spot for leisurely lunches, rather overshadowing the gleaming brass and polished wood of the restaurant – complete with frog-motif mural (done by an Englishman, of course). And the food is excellent, too – Michelin-starred, and not wildly expensive. Bedrooms are captivating (one is very large, and eminently suitable for families), complete with well equipped and very attractive bathrooms.

If you are normally resolute about going native once on French soil, and feel you might be put off by all those other English voices, relax. You can safely resist the temptation to carry on driving: this is a serious French enterprise and M. Gauthier has not allowed the popularity of his establishment to make him complacent.

Nearby Ramparts, citadel; Le Touquet (15 km).

La Madelaine-sous-Montreuil, 62170 Montreuil-sur-Mer
Tel 21.06.07.22
Fax 21.86.36.36
Location by river at end of lane off D139, NW of Montreuil-sur-Mer; with ample car parking
Meals breakfast, lunch, dinner
Prices rooms 300F-500F; breakfast 40F; menus 150F-350F
Rooms 2 double, 1 twin, one flat; all with bath; all rooms have central heating, phone,
Facilities dining-room, small bar
Credit cards AE, DC, MC, V
Children welcome
Disabled two ground-floor room
Pets welcome
Closed mid-Dec to end Jan; Tue and Wed from Sep to Jun
Proprietor M. Gauthier

The North-east

Château de Montreuil

'Montreuil, Château de: Charming host, exceptional food, great advice on local shopping for food and wine. Comfortable, well equipped rooms. Not cheap. Wife of patron: English.' Military man, our most recent reporter; as usual, verdict spot-on; other readers concur. No doubt about it: full entry merited, as of now.

This substantial, luxurious country house, dating from the 1930s, is a well established favourite with British travellers, who make up most of the resident guests. The house is immaculately done out, with great taste throughout. Bedrooms are splendid – decorated with real flair and furnished with character; those on the top floor are very spacious, but the first floor rooms give better views of the beautiful English-style gardens. There is a snug brick-and-beams bar for an aperitif, an airy glass-fronted sitting-room and a lovely, elegant dining-room. Although you're quite close to the town centre, the setting is quiet, the gardens secluded.

Christian Germain's cooking aims high and hits the target (the restaurant does not rely on British custom but has a loyal French following); even breakfast ('home-made everything') is delicious.
Nearby Ramparts (still intact), citadel; Le Touquet (15 km).

4 Chaussée des Capucins
62170 Montreuil-sur-Mer
Tel 21.81.53.04
Fax 21.81.36.43
Location in quiet part of town, 38 km S of Boulogne, off N1; with large garden and ample car parking
Meals breakfast, lunch, dinner
Prices rooms 750F-950F, DB&B 1600F-1700F; menus 240F-390F
Rooms 11 double, 10 with bath (6 twin); 3 single; 2 family rooms all with bath or shower; all rooms have central heating, phone
Facilities sitting-room, dining-room, bar
Credit cards AE, DC, MC, V
Children welcome
Disabled 3 ground-floor bedrooms
Pets not accepted
Closed mid-Dec to end Jan
Proprietors Christian and Lindsay Germain

The North-east

Château hotel, Reims

Château des Crayères

At last! We were beginning to have doubts about our continued inclusion of this wonderful but prohibitively expensive mansion when a reporter who 'stayed in the best room and drank one of the best wines' wrote to approve of the place – singling out for praise (of all things) baby croissants that 'melt in the mouth'.

Gérard Boyer (by common consent one of the finest chefs in the land) and his wife Elyane had a good starting point: a graceful turn-of-the-century mansion (built in Louis XVI style), situated in a spacious park almost at the heart of Reims, and surrounded by the *caves* of the famous Champagne names. With Elyane's exquisite taste and skill in interior decoration, they could hardly go far wrong. There are a wonderful grand staircase, enormous windows, marble columns and tapestries; the dining-room is wood panelled and candle-lit. Bedrooms are sumptuous, individually decorated to a theme, and have views over the park; two have a large balcony.

The cooking is not merely for the benefit of Champagne grandees; it's good enough to attract businessmen from Paris. Not surprisingly, it is necessary to book well ahead.

Nearby Basilica, cathedral; Champagne Route.

64 Blvd Henry Vasnier 51100 Reims
Tel 26.82.80.80
Fax 26.82.65.52
Location on edge of city centre, near St-Remi basilica; in own grounds with ample car parking
Meals breakfast, lunch, dinner
Prices rooms 990F-1,940F; menus 510F-650F
Rooms 19 double, all with bath (15 twin); all rooms have air-conditioning, phone, TV, radio, minibar
Facilities dining-room, bar, function room; tennis, helistation
Credit cards AE, DC, MC, V
Children welcome
Disabled access possible, lift/elevator
Pets dogs welcome
Closed 3 weeks at Christmas/New Year; restaurant only, Mon and Tue lunch
Proprietor M. Boyer

The North-east

Auberge d'Artzenheim

'A beflowered oasis in the middle of nowhere,' says a recent report on this cosy auberge. Its focal point is the restaurant, all beams and polished wood, but there is a terrace for outdoor eating. Bedrooms (some small) are prettily decorated with rustic furniture and jolly fabrics.

■ 30 Rue du Sponeck, 68320 Artzenheim (Haut-Rhin) **Tel** 89.71.60.51 **Fax** 89.71.68.21 **Meals** breakfast, lunch, dinner **Prices** rooms 255F-310F; menus 165F-235F **Rooms** 10, all with bath or shower, central heating, phone, TV **Credit cards** MC, V **Closed** Feb; restaurant only, Mon dinner and Tue

---

Hôtel Métropole

A very pleasant hotel, centrally situated in one of the main shopping streets of Boulogne but with the bonus of a pretty and colourful garden. Bedrooms were rated 'surprisingly attractive for a modest town hotel' by a recent visitor. No restaurant but 'excellent' breakfasts. Private garage.

■ 51-53 Rue Thiers, 62200 Boulogne-sur-Mer (Pas-de-Calais) **Tel** 21.31.54.30 **Fax** 21. 30.45.72 **Meals** breakfast **Prices** rooms 330F-430F; breakfast 40F **Rooms** 25, all with bath or shower, central heating, phone, TV **Credit cards** AE, DC, MC, V **Closed** mid-Dec to early Jan

---

Hôtel d'Angleterre

A traditional town hotel from the outside, the Angleterre has been largely modernized inside. Subtle colour schemes predominate throughout. Smart, modern bathrooms. A recent report suggests, however, that economies may be cutting into the level of service. Breakfast is no longer an event, but now a rather scrappy buffet, and Jacky Michell, who runs the restaurant, seems less of a welcoming presence than in earlier years.

■ 19 Place Monseigneur Tissier, 51000 Châlons-sur-Marne (Marne) **Tel** 26.68.21.51 **Fax** 26.70.51.67 **Meals** breakfast, lunch, dinner **Prices** rooms 370F-490F; breakfast 60F, menus 120F-400F **Rooms** 18, all with bath, central heating, 16 with air-conditioning, phone, TV, minibar, hairdrier **Credit cards** AE, DC, MC, V **Closed** last 3 weeks in Jul; Christmas

---

Château de Courcelles

Set in a small formal park, this impressive – and expensive – 17thC château can name Napoléon and Jean-Jacques Rousseau among former visitors. Bedrooms are spacious and individually decorated, food rated 'very impressive' by a visitor. Pool, tennis.

■ 02220 Courcelles-sur-Vesle (Aisne) **Tel** 23.74.13.53 **Fax** 23.74.06.41 **Meals** breakfast, lunch, dinner **Prices** rooms 800F-1200F, suites 1,200F-1500F; breakfast 70F, menus 220F-400F **Rooms** 12, all with bath or shower, central heating, phone, TV, minibar **Credit cards** AE, MC, V **Closed** mid-Jan to mid-Feb

The North-east

Château hotel, Doullens

Château de Remaisnil

Once the residence of Laura Ashley, this 18thC rococo mansion is a gracious home rather than a hotel. Bedrooms in the château can be extremely grand; even the simplest, in the coach-house, are harmonious and comfortable. Beautiful grounds. Dinner is a fixed four-courses, for which the Doulls often join their guests.

■ Remaisnil, 80600 Doullens (Somme) **Tel** 22.77.07.47 **Fax** 22.77.41.23 **Meals** breakfast, dinner by arrangement **Prices** rooms 750F-1,600F; breakfast 75F, dinner 355F **Rooms** 17, all with bath or shower, central heating, phone, TV, minibar **Credit cards** AE, MC, V **Closed** late Feb to early Mar

---

Village hotel, L'Épine

Aux Armes de Champagne

The main attractions here are the renowned cuisine and cellar, and the hotel's refreshing lack of pretension. The modern bedrooms are comfortable and impeccable; sixteen of the rooms are in an annexe 200 metres down the road, away from the traffic noise that afflicts the main building.

■ Avenue du Luxembourg, 51460 L'Épine (Marne) **Tel** 26.69.30.30 **Fax** 26.66.92.31 **Meals** breakfast, lunch, dinner **Prices** rooms 380F-780F; breakfast 55F, menus 100F-480F **Rooms** 37, all with bath or shower, central heating, phone, TV, minibar **Credit cards** DC, MC, V **Closed** Sun eve and Mon, Nov to Mar

---

Village bed-and-breakfast, Ermenonville

Hôtel le Prieuré

We await reader reaction to this polished little B&B place, introduced to the guide a couple of years ago. The former vicarage is beautifully furnished with antiques and decorated with unusual style, with exposed beams in the attic rooms. There is a neat breakfast room and an immaculate 'English' garden.

■ Chevet de l'Eglise, 60950 Ermenonville (Oise) **Tel** 44.54.00.44 **Fax** 44.54.02.21 **Meals** breakfast **Prices** rooms 450F-600F; breakfast 50F **Rooms** 11, all with bath or shower, cen tral heating, phone, TV, minibar **Credit cards** AE, DC, MC, V **Closed** Feb

---

Town hotel, Etréaupont

Le Clos du Montvinage

This imposing, spacious red-brick building is effectively the annexe of the cheerful Auberge du Val de l'Oise. Bedrooms are well equipped; those at the back have views of the walled garden and suffer no disturbance from the busy main road.

■ RN 2, 02580 Etréaupont (Aisne) **Tel** 23.97.91.10 **Fax** 23.97.48.92 **Meals** breakfast, lunch, dinner **Prices** rooms 285F-430F; dinner 87F-230F **Rooms** 20, all with bath, central heating, air-conditioning, phone, TV, minibar, hairdrier **Credit cards** AE, DC, MC, V **Closed** Sun night; 2 weeks mid-Aug; restaurant only, Mon lunch, Sun eve

The North-east

Village hotel, Florent-en-Argonne

Le Jabloire

Recently refurbished and promoted to three-star status, this elegant little house fronting directly on to the street impressed a reader as 'an excellent staging post just off the A4 motorway'. The proprietor (formerly the local mayor) offers a warm welcome.

■ 51800 Florent-en-Argonne (Marne) **Tel** 26.60.82.03 **Fax** 26.60.85.45 **Meals** breakfast **Prices** rooms 250F-380F; breakfast 35F **Rooms** 12, all with bath or shower, heating, TV **Credit cards** AE, MC V **Closed** Feb

---

Country hotel, Futeau

A L'Orée du Bois

Surrounded by woods, this modest hotel enjoys perfect peace, although the mood is often jolly in the elegantly rustic restaurant at its heart. The cooking is excellent, with seafood very much the high-point. Madame serves, with great charm. Rooms are adequate: motel-style, in a ground-floor extension.

■ Futeau, 55120 Clermont-en-Argonne (Meuse) **Tel** 29.88.28.41 **Fax** 29.88.24.52 **Meals** breakfast, lunch, dinner **Prices** rooms 295F-360F; breakfast 48F, lunch 110F, menus 185-350F **Rooms** 7, all with bath, central heating, phone, TV, hairdrier **Credit cards** MC, V **Closed** one week Nov, Jan; restaurant only, Tue and Sun dinner out of season

---

Village inn, Kaysersberg

Hôtel Résidence Chambard

Pierre Irrmann's sober, highly traditional-looking inn is almost better thought of as a restaurant with rooms; there is sitting space, but you'll spend most of your time (when you're not out tasting Alsatian wines) in the restaurant 50 metres away and in your elegantly furnished, spacious bedroom.

■ 13 Rue de Général de Gaulle, 68240 Kaysersberg (Haut-Rhin) **Tel** 89.47.10.17 **Fax** 8 9.47.35.03 **Meals** breakfast, lunch, dinner **Prices** rooms 550F-650F, suites 750F; breakfast 60F, menus 300F -450F **Rooms** 20, all with bath or shower, phone, TV, radio **Credit cards** AE, MC, V **Closed** 3 weeks Mar; restaurant only, Mon, and Tue lunch

---

Country hotel, Lapoutroie

Les Alisiers

This simple, farmhouse-style place enjoys a splendid setting, high in the Vosges, with floor-to-ceiling windows in the dining-room to exploit the view. The rustic interior has an intimate, private-house feel, the bedrooms are small but comfortable. Alsatian specialities dominate the menus. Good value.

■ 5 Faudé, 68650 Lapoutroie (Haut-Rhin) **Tel** 89.47.52.82 **Fax** 89.47.22.38 **Meals** breakfast, lunch, dinner **Prices** rooms 250F-365F; menus 80F-155F;reductions for children sharing parents' room **Rooms** 13, all with phone **Credit cards** MC, V **Closed** Tue; Jan

The North-east

Converted mill, Lumbres

Moulin de Mombreux

An old mill, dropped from the guide four years ago but much improved, to judge by recent reports. Pleasant, compact bedrooms in a modern block built to match the mill; public rooms that are charmingly traditional or light and airy; 'deserved' Michelin star for food; friendly atmosphere.

■ Rte de Bayenghem, 62380 Lumbres (Pas-de-Calais)
Tel 21.39.62.44 **Fax** 21.93.61.34 **Meals** breakfast, lunch, dinner
Prices rooms 500F-680F; breakfast F60; menus 200F-500F
Rooms 24, all with bath or shower, central heating, TV, phone
Credit cards AE, DC, V **Closed** around Christmas

Town hotel, Montreuil-sur-Mer

Les Hauts de Montreuil

A reader who resorted to this timbered hotel near the centre of Montreuil when our recommendations in the area were closed recommends it for a combination of well-furnished rooms (some in a modern annexe), a warm welcome from the patron and his wife, 'fantastic' traditional food and 'excellent' value.

■ 21-23, Rue Pierre Ledent, 62170 Montreuil-sur-Mer (Pas-de-Calais)
Tel 21.81.95.92 **Fax** 21.86.28.83 **Meals** breakfast, lunch, dinner
Prices rooms 346F-435F; breakfast 50F, menus 145F-235F
Rooms 27, all with bath or shower, central heating, phone, TV
Credit cards AE, DC, MC, V **Closed** never

Country hotel, Ribeauvillé

Le Clos Saint-Vincent

The service at this elegant hotel is almost impossible to fault. The bedrooms are beautifully furnished, the staff friendly and the food delicious, reports a recent visitor. Although the restaurant is closed on Tuesday and Wednesday evenings, there are excellent alternatives in the town. Indoor swimming-pool.

■ Rte de Bergheim, 68150 Ribeauvillé (Haut-Rhin) **Tel** 89.73.67.65
Fax 89.73.32.20 **Meals** breakfast, lunch, dinner **Prices** rooms 700F-1,170F; menus 180F-280F **Rooms** 15, all with bath, central heating, phone, minibar; TV on request **Credit cards** MC, V **Closed** mid-Nov to mid-Mar; restaurant only, Tue and Wed

---

Restaurant with rooms, Ribeauvillé

Les Vosges

Chef-Patron Joseph Matter has moved on, so we should welcome more reports on this neat little place in the middle of one of the most attractive wine towns of Alsace. The emphasis, we presume, will remain on the restaurant; the rooms were never more than pleasantly comfortable.

■ 2 Grande Rue, 68150 Ribeauvillé (Haut-Rhin) **Tel** 89.73.61.39
Fax 89.73.34.21 **Meals** breakfast, lunch, dinner **Prices** rooms 230F-490F; breakfast 50F, menus 160F-390F **Rooms** 18, all with bath or shower, phone, TV **Credit cards** AE, DC, MC, V **Closed** Sun evening; restaurant only, mid-Nov to Apr

The North-east

Country hotel, Sept-Saulx

Le Cheval Blanc

'Excellent food and accommodation in a lovely setting,' said the reader's report that first drew our attention to this old inn, extended over the years but still blessed with a charming garden. Food is ambitious, although no longer endorsed by Michelin with a star.

■ 51400 Sept-Saulx (Marne) **Tel** 26.03.90.27 **Fax** 26.03.97.09
Meals breakfast, lunch, dinner **Prices** rooms 450F-800F, suites 980F; breakfast 50F, **Rooms** 25, all with bath or shower, phone, TV, minibar **Credit cards** AE, DC, MC, V **Closed** 3 weeks Feb

---

Town mansion, Vervins

La Tour du Roy

This turreted building perched on the ramparts of Vervins is full of character, with pretty, individually decorated rooms. Recent reports include (for the first time) niggles about service and housekeeping. But no complaints about the food, except that the menus do not offer a very wide choice. More reports, please.

■ 45 Rue du Général Leclerc, 02140 Vervins (Aisne) **Tel** 23.98.00.11 **Fax** 23.98.00.72 **Meals** breakfast, lunch, dinner **Prices** rooms 350F-500F; breakfast 60F, menus 180F-400F **Rooms** 16, all with bath, central heating, phone, TV, radio, minibar; some have air-conditioning **Credit cards** AE, DC, MC, V **Closed** mid-Jan to mid-Feb

Western France

Our Western France region has three major components of interest to tourists. First there is the Loire valley and its immediate surroundings, including the atmospheric Sologne, south of Orleans. There are almost as many Charming Small Hotels here as there are Renaissance châteaux. Secondly, the hilly Limousin, fading into the northern fringes of Périgord, around Angoulême and Limoges. And finally the hinterland of the Atlantic coast, including the canals of Poitou-Charente. We have entries in all these areas, but also dotted around the *départements* in between, and on the western side of the region on the fringes of the Massif Central.

Contenders in Western France
Aubigny-sur-Nère, Château de la Verrerie 48.58.06.91 Splendid turreted château in gracious parkland, run by aristocratic owners.
Blois, Le Vieux Cognet 54.56.05.34 Simple but well furnished B&B in quiet spot on banks of the Loire.
Challans, Château de la Vérie 51.35.33.44 Richly furnished manor-house in extensive grounds; pool, tennis. Cheverny,
Château du Breuil 54.44.20.20 18thC château in large grounds, with an elegant salon and comfortable bedrooms with antiques.
Chouzé-sur-Loire, Château des Réaux 47.95.14.40 Fairytale château, stylishly decorated and handsomely furnished.
Dompierre-les-Églises, Le Moulin des Combes 55.68.62.09 Ancient watermill turned luxury B&B, with British owner.
Grez-Neuville, La Croix d'Etain 41.95.68.49 Handsome little manor-house B&B in pleasant village on the Mayenne.
Le Gua, Le Moulin de Châlons 46.22.82.72 Pale stone mill beside the Seudre with grassy grounds and charming rooms.
Loches, Hôtel George Sand 47.59.39.74 Riverside Logis with abundant beams and traditional decor.
Mondoubleau, Le Grand Monarque 54.80.92.10 Friendly Logis with neat (some cramped) rooms, in mature grassy garden.
Mont-près-Chambord, Manoir de Clénord 54.70.41.62 Secluded country house, tastefully furnished and family-run.
Montbazon-en-Touraine, Domaine de la Tortinière 47.26.00.19 Dinky fairytale château, smartly furnished, in wooded grounds with views and pool.
Onzain-en-Touraine, Domaine des Hauts de Loire 54.20.72.57 Elegantly furnished but characterful converted hunting lodge (Relais & Châteaux).
La-Roche-sur-Yon, Logis de la Couperie 51.37.21.19 Country house, just outside the town, run as an elegant but home-like guest-house.
St-Lambert-des-Levées, La Croix de la Voulte 41.38.46.66 Ancient country house B&B in lush gardens.
Tours, Jean Bardet 47.41.41.11 Smooth, elegant setting for some of the best food in France.
Velluire, Auberge de la Rivière 51.52.32.15 Unpretentious waterside Logis with some pleasant rooms.

Western France

Converted mill, Bannegon

Auberge du Moulin de Chaméron

The Moulin de Chameron is a curious animal, and difficult to categorise. At the heart of it is the original 18th-century water-mill – now a combination of country museum and charmingly traditional restaurant. But the bedrooms are housed across the garden in a pair of unremarkable modern buildings of rather towny appearance – comfortable and peaceful, but thin on charm. So should it be thought of as a restaurant with rooms rather than a hotel? We think to do so would be to underestimate its appeal as a place to stay for more than a one-night stopover – at least in summer, when the wooded garden and neat pool come into play, along with the restaurant's tented dining terrace beside the mill stream. Jean Merilleau's cooking is excellent, and not overpriced.

Nearby Meillant castle (25 km); Noirlac abbey (30 km).

Bannegon 18210 Charenton-du-Cher
Tel 48.61.83.80
Fax 48.61.84.92
Location in countryside between Bannegon and Neuilly, 40 km SE of Bourges; with garden and ample car parking
Meals breakfast, lunch, dinner
Prices rooms 350F-650F; menus 150F-220F, children's 60F **Rooms** 13 double, 8 with bath, 5 with shower (5 twin); one family room with bath; all rooms have central heating, phone, TV
Facilities 2 dining-rooms, bar, 2 sitting-rooms; swimming-pool, fishing
Credit cards AE, MC, V
Children welcome
Disabled no special facilities
Pets accepted in bedrooms; charge **Closed** mid-Nov to early Mar; Tue in low season
Proprietors M. Candoré and M. Merilleau

Western France

Château and manor house hotel, Briollay

Château de Noirieux

'A gem of a hotel, situated at the western end of the Loire château-belt; whereas most hotels on the Loire tourist trail are over-priced and under-enthusiastic, this one gets most things right and is thoroughly professional in the nicest way.' So says one of our most conscientious reporters. Since he's started so well, we'll let him finish.

'Dating from the seventeenth century, with Art Deco additions in 1927, it opened as a hotel in 1991. It is set in magnificent grounds, with views down to the Loir. It is outstandingly comfortable; a good test was that during three days of almost continuous rain we always felt cossetted. The salons are beautifully furnished and comfortable, the dining-room light and airy, with a terrace for fine weather. Bedrooms are split between the main building and two others – all well furnished, some quite opulently.

'The cuisine is inventive and of a high standard. The wine list is exemplary, with prices that don't take your breath away. We received a warm welcome, and all the staff were unfailingly helpful and courteous. The chateau is not cheap, but is excellent value in every respect.'

Nearby golf; Angers (12 km) – cathedral, château

26 Route du Moulin, 49125 Briollay
Tel 41.42.50.05
Fax 41.37.91.00
Location in countryside off D 52, (junction 14 off A11); with gardens and ample car parking
Meals breakfast, lunch, dinner
Prices rooms 600F-1,300F; breakfast 80F, menus 195F-450F
Rooms 19 double with bath; all rooms have central heating, phone, TV, minibar, hairdrier
Facilities dining-room, sitting-room/bar; jacuzzi, swimming-pool, tennis **Credit cards** AE, DC, MC, V **Children** accepted
Disabled 2 ground-floor bedrooms **Pets** accepted
Closed early Feb to mid-Mar; restaurant Sun, Mon mid-Oct to mid-Apr **Managers** Gérard and Anja Come

Western France

Le Fleuray

'I have no hesitation in recommending this small, well appointed hotel in the Loire valley,' says a reporter, 'where the loudest noise was the croaking of the little green bullfrogs in the pond.'

It was not always thus, as Peter Newington explains. 'My wife, children and I started work on this dilapidated house in April 1992; we opened, exhausted and poor, in November 1992. We have now built a good client base of locals for our restaurant, and get guests from all over France and worldwide. The hotel and restaurant are very much family-run, Hazel doing most of the cooking. In summer, we offer dining on the terrace, in winter in front of a log fire. Our bedrooms are named after local flowers. Breakfast includes hot home-made rolls, croissants, brioches, orange juice and fresh fruit.'

The old house has been modernized and decorated sympathetically, and has made a very agreeable place to stay while exploring chateau country. Our reporter confirms that Hazel's cooking is 'very good indeed', and found the Newingtons 'most welcoming hosts, without being intrusive.' And finally: prices of rooms and meals are very attractive.

Nearby Châteaux – Amboise, Chaumont, Chenonceaux, Tours.

Cangey 37530 Amboise
Tel 47.56.09.25
Fax 47.56.93.97
Location on D74, 7 km NE of Amboise; in gardens with ample car parking
Meals breakfast, dinner
Prices rooms 295F-375F; breakfast 45F, menus 98F-220F, children's 55F
Rooms 11 double, 4 with bath, 7 with shower; 9 rooms have central heating, 2 with electric heating, phone

Facilities dining-room
Credit cards MC, V
Children very welcome (special menus, games)
Disabled some ground floor rooms
Pets accepted
Closed late Oct to early Nov; Christmas and New Year
Proprietors Peter and Hazel Newington

Western France

Hôtel Diderot

Surprisingly few hotels have been in these pages since the first edition while generating a steady stream of entirely complimentary reports. But here is one – and one that is very modestly priced, to boot. 'Excellent' and 'superb' are the latest verdicts.

Creeper-covered and white-shuttered, it is a handsome townhouse set in a courtyard, which conveys the benefit (unusual for a modest hotel) of convenient private parking. The French-Cypriot proprietors are charming and unstintingly helpful, and breakfast (served on the shady terrace or in a rustic room with tiled floor and massive beams) is exceptionally tasty – thanks to Madame's home-made preserves. Bedrooms are simply furnished – as you might expect at these prices – but are spotlessly clean and some have fine views. Some now have smart new bathrooms.
Nearby Grand Carroi, ruined château, church of St-Maurice; châteaux – Azay-le-Rideau (20 km), Langeais (30 km).

4 Rue Buffon 37500 Chinon
Tel 47.93.18.87
Fax 47.93.37.10
Location in middle of town; with courtyard and private car parking
Meals breakfast
Prices rooms 250F-400F; breakfast 40F
Rooms 28 double, 17 with bath, 11 with shower (8 twin); 3 family rooms, all with bath; all rooms have central heating, phone

Facilities bar, breakfast room
Credit cards AE, DC, MC, V
Children welcome
Disabled some ground-floor bedrooms
Pets not accepted
Closed mid-Dec to mid-Jan
Proprietor Theo Kazamias

Western France

Hostellerie Ste-Catherine

The Tardoire valley is a pretty one, but the area around Montbron, east of Angoulême, is off the beaten tourist track and we presume this is why we hear so little from readers about this fine old house, once the residence of the Empress Joséphine.

The approach, along a winding drive through splendid wooded grounds, is appropriately imposing and the house – built in a pale, irregular stone – looks handsome but austere. But inside it is a different story: despite fine furnishings and immaculate housekeeping, there is none of the expected pretension, and a relaxed, informal atmosphere prevails.

Rooms are decorated and furnished with proper regard for both style and comfort: the dining-rooms (one leads in to the other) have tapestries on the walls, and a carved wooden mantlepiece stands over an old fireplace; the two sitting-rooms are inviting and relaxing. Most of the individually furnished and thoroughly comfortable bedrooms have views of the surrounding parkland; they do vary in size, and the prices reflect this. One menu and an 'interesting' *carte* are offered.

Nearby Angoulême (30 km) – cathedral, walk along ramparts; châteaux – de Brie (40 km); Rochechouart (40 km).

Route de Marthon 16220 Montbron
Tel 45.23.60.03
Fax 45.70.72.00
Location in park off D16, 4 km SW of Montbron, 28 km E of Angoulême; with ample car parking
Meals breakfast, lunch, dinner
Prices rooms 450F-800F; breakfast 49F, menu 170F
Rooms 14 double and 4 family rooms, most with bath or shower; all rooms have central heating, phone, TV
Facilities 2 dining-rooms, 2 sitting-rooms, bar; swimming-pool
Credit cards AE, DC, MC, V
Children accepted
Disabled no special facilities
Pets accepted
Closed never
Proprietor Marie-Michelle Rey

Western France

Château de Nieuil

'Our room was extremely comfortable, even though it was one of their smaller ones, and one of the best-value rooms of our holiday,' says a reporter on this fairy-tale Renaissance château, making the point that high prices can be worth paying if you get something special in return. Steep-roofed, turreted, and surrounded by parkland stretching away beyond its formal garden and ornamental 'moat', it is the picture of elegance. Inside, it is appropriately furnished throughout, with exquisite antiques, porcelain and tapestries. Some of the bedrooms are exceedingly grand.

It could be embarrassingly pretentious. But the delight of the place is that it is not at all pretentious or intimidating. The château has been in the Bodinaud family for over a hundred years, and the hotel is very much a family concern. Mme Bodinaud (an ex-design-lecturer) does all the interior decoration and oversees the cooking, earning a Michelin star for her imaginative food, while her husband administers a collection of 300 cognacs.

Since our last edition, the Bodinauds have opened a 'winter' restaurant, La Grange aux Oies, in converted stables. Their shared interest in art has also led to a gallery.

Nearby Angoulême (40km), Limoges (65 km).

Rte de Fontafie, 16270 Nieuil
Tel 45.71.36.38
Fax 45.71.46.45
Location in wooded park, 2 km E of Nieuil; with extensive grounds, car parking and garage for 8 cars
Meals breakfast, lunch, dinner
Prices rooms 630F-1,350F; suites 1,400F-2,100F; breakfast 75F; menus 240F-320F
Rooms 11 double, 3 suites, all with bath; all rooms have central heating, phone, TV, minibar; 5 have air conditioning
Facilities dining-room, sitting-room, bar; swimming-pool, tennis court
Credit cards AE, DC, MC, V
Children accepted
Disabled access possible to one bedroom and apartment
Pets welcome **Closed** Nov to Apr; restaurant 'La Grange aux Oies' mid-Apr to mid Dec
Proprietor Jean-Michel and Luce Bodinaud

Western France

33 Rue Thiers

This distinctive little guest-house continues to delight a steady stream of guests. 'The lovely Maybelle's welcome makes 33 Rue Thiers a particular favourite,' says one reporter. 'It proved to be the most memorable hotel I stayed in, and one I will certainly visit again,' says another.

33 Rue Thiers is a renovated 18thC townhouse in the heart of La Rochelle. Its owner and renovator is a half-American/half-French cook-book author, Maybelle Iribe. She opened for business in 1987, the word spread like wildfire and she now has a faithful band of enthusiastic guests who return year after year.

The public rooms are filled with antiques and (mainly) stylish modern furniture. The huge bedrooms are decorated in soothing pastel shades; to say they have been furnished individually is an understatement – they are a showcase for from Madame Iribe's eclectic collection of art and ornaments.

Sumptuous breakfasts and dinner can be eaten on the patio in the secluded little walled garden. Maybelle is happy to provide day-trippers with picnics.

Nearby old quarter, port, and lantern tower of La Rochelle; Ile de Rey.

33 Rue Thiers, 17000 La Rochelle
Tel 46.41.62.23
Location in street next to central market; with small walled garden and car parking
Meals breakfast, dinner, picnics
Prices rooms 380F-450F; breakfast 30F, dinner 120F
Rooms 5 double, one family room, all with bath; all rooms have central heating

Facilities dining-room, sitting-room, TV room
Credit cards not accepted
Children welcome; special meals, baby-sitting available
Disabled no special facilities
Pets well-behaved dogs accepted
Closed never
Proprietor Maybelle Iribe

Western France

Restaurant with rooms, Les Rosiers-sur-Loire

Auberge Jeanne de Laval

This is a quintessential restaurant with rooms – you go for Michel Augereau's Michelin-starred cooking, with the option of staying the night. You're unlikely to want to spend a holiday here, but the auberge makes an excellent stopover, whether you are touring the Loire château country or on your way south. The restaurant is a warmly welcoming room with light modern furniture beneath mellow exposed beams, and with an uncompromisingly modern glazed extension. In the same main building are four of the bedrooms – two overlooking the road, two the pretty garden. Most of the rooms are a fair walk away in the château-style Ducs d'Anjou annexe shown in our photo. They are quiet, spacious and tastefully decorated. Service in the annexe is limited to breakfast, which is served in the rooms or in the pretty garden.

Nearby Saumur (15 km); Angers (30 km) – cathedral, château.

54 Rue Nationale, Les Rosiers-sur-Loire 49350 Gennes
Tel 41.51.80.17
Fax 41.38.04.18
Location in middle of village, 15 km NW of Saumur; with flower gardens and car parking
Meals breakfast, lunch, dinner
Prices rooms 350F-600F; breakfast 50F, menus 170F-420F
Rooms 10 double, all but one with bath; all rooms have central heating, phone, TV, minibar
Facilities TV room, dining-room
Credit cards AE, MC, V
Children welcome
Disabled no special facilities
Pets dogs accepted in bedrooms
Closed mid-Nov to mid-Dec; mid to end Jan; Mon (except public holidays and high season)
Proprietors Augereau family

Western France

Château de la Vallée Bleue

The young Gasquets took over this handsome château in 1985, just in time to make an appearance in the first edition of this guide, and have been assiduously improving it ever since – a barn and stables have just recently been renovated to provide extra space. A report from a British resident in France with three young children sums up the Vallée Bleue precisely: 'Here is complete commitment. Service was friendly and discreet – the children treated like young adults. The restaurant was one of the best we've eaten in.'

Inside, the atmosphere of the house is, as always, warm and easy. Fresh flowers and a cosy log fire in the spacious entrance hall set the tone, and personal touches are in evidence in every room. The château overlooks gardens front and back, giving all the bedrooms – big, and comfortably furnished with antiques – a pleasant outlook; just visible, beyond cows grazing in the fields, are the terra-cotta roof-tops of the village. Public rooms are gracious and charming, furnished with solid antiques and looking on to the garden. Cooking is regionally based but *nouvelle*-oriented and way above average in execution.

Nearby Tour de la Prison (Museum of George Sand and Vallée Noire); Sarzay (10 km) – château; Nohant (5 km) – château.

Rte de Verneuil, St-Chartier
36400 La Châtre
Tel 54.31.01.91
Fax 54.31.04.48
Location just outside hamlet, on D69 9 km N of La Châtre; in 4 acre grounds with ample car parking
Meals breakfast, lunch, dinner
Prices rooms 390F-490F; breakfast 48F, menus 120F-250F, children 60F
Rooms 11 double (3 twin), 5 with bath 6 with shower; one single with shower; 2 family rooms with bath; all rooms have central heating, phone, TV, minibar, hairdrier
Facilities 2 dining-rooms, sitting-room, fitness room; swimming-pool, bowling area
Credit cards MC, V
Children welcome; special menus available
Disabled 3 ground-floor rooms
Pets accepted at extra charge
Closed Feb
Proprietor Gérard Gasquet

Western France

La Tonnellerie

The flow of readers' reports on this fine 19th-century wine merchant's house has dried to a trickle (perhaps because the cheapest rooms are no longer cheap) but its attractions seem to us to remain undiminished.

The hotel, in the small village of Tavers, close to the Loire and not far from Beaugency, is set around a central courtyard-garden which is at the heart of its appeal. There is a pretty little swimming-pool, shady chestnut trees; tables for summer meals stand on the lawn and further away from the house on terrace areas. The country atmosphere extends indoors to the dining-rooms, both looking on to the garden, one in 'winter garden' style, the other handsomely rustic, with tiled floor and mellow woodwork. Cooking is *nouvelle* in style but recognizes the traditions of the region, and is above average in execution.

In recent years Mme Pouey has steadily improved the hotel, adding four 'apartments/suites' (pastel walls, flowery drapes, polished antiques, smart tiled bathrooms) and refurbishing other bedrooms.

Nearby Beaugency – Hôtel de Ville, Tour St-Firmin, church of Notre-Dame; châteaux – Chambord (25 km), Blois (30 km).

12 Rue des Eaux-Bleues, Tavers 45190 Beaugency
Tel 38.44.68.15
Fax 38.44.10.01
Location in middle of village, 3 km W of Beaugency; with garden, and private and public car parking
Meals breakfast, lunch, dinner
Prices rooms 705F-880F, apartments 880F-1,435F; breakfast 55F, menus 125F-310F
Rooms 12 double (7 twin), 3 suites, 5 apartments, all with bath; all rooms have central heating, phone, TV, hairdrier
Facilities 2 dining-rooms, sitting-room; swimming-pool, tennis, bicycle hire
Credit cards AE, MC, V
Children welcome; cots and special meals **Disabled** ground-floor rooms; lift/elevator **Pets** accepted
Closed 2 Jan to end Feb
Proprietor Marie-Christine Pouey

Western France

Le Prieuré

A few years ago we came close to dropping this hotel from the guide through lack of support from readers, but our perseverance has been rewarded by a renewed burst of enthusiastic reports. 'I certainly endorse the inclusion of Le Prieuré,' says one. 'At just over 800F for two it must rank as our most expensive stopover, but well worth it.' Another reporter (who describes the prices as 'reasonable') sums up Le Prieuré as 'excellent in every respect,' with 'first-rate food'.

Tonnay-Boutonne is a small, quiet village lying between the old military town of Rochefort and St-Jean-d'Angély, a former wine port. Set slightly back from the (not very busy) main road in a large grassy garden, Le Prieuré is a typical Charentaise building: plain but handsomely symmetrical, with white-shuttered windows. It was the family home of the proprietors before they opened it as a hotel, and retains a friendly atmosphere. The bedrooms and bathrooms have been revamped, leading a reporter to call them 'lovely' and justifying a move from two-star to three-star status a couple of years ago.

Nearby Rochefort – 17thC Corderie Royale, Navy Museum; La Roche Courbon (25 km) – château; Saintes (30 km).

17380 Tonnay-Boutonne
Tel 46.33.20.18
Fax 46.33.25.55
Location in village 21 km E of Rochefort; with large garden and ample car parking
Meals breakfast, lunch, dinner
Prices rooms 250F-450F; breakfast 45F, menu 140F
Rooms 16 double (6 twin), 2 family rooms; 15 with bath, 3 with shower; all rooms have phone, TV

Facilities reception/sitting-area, TV/sitting-room, 2 dining-rooms
Credit cards MC, V
Children welcome
Disabled no special facilities
Pets accepted
Closed Christmas/New Year
Proprietors M. and Mme Paul Vernoux

The West

Village inn, Angles sur l'Anglin

Le Relais du Lyon D'or

Reports would be especially welcome on Le Relais du Lyon D'or (new to the guide this year) which is situated at the heart of a village that has been designated one of the most beautiful in France. The building, which was once a royal tythe depot and dates back to the 14thC, now provides comfortable accommodation with five individually designed bedrooms (with more planned) open log fires, rustic beams and terracotta tiled floors. Food is based on seasonal local produce.

■ 4 Rue d'Enfer, 86260 Angles sur l'Anglin (Vienne) **Tel** 49.48.32.53 **Fax** 49.84.02.28 **Meals** breakfast, lunch, dinner **Prices** rooms 350F; breakfast 35F; menus from 98F **Rooms** 5, all with bath or shower, central heating, phone **Credit cards** MC, V **Closed** 15 Jan to Mar

---

Château hotel, Amboise

Château de Pray

A 13thC château steeped in history and in a magnificent position high up above the Loire, with superb views from the windows and terraces. All the rooms have been smartly redecorated recently, and four swish suites have been added across the garden.

■ 37400 Amboise (Indre-et-Loire) **Tel** 47.57.23.67 **Fax** 47.57.32.50 **Meals** breakfast, lunch, dinner **Prices** rooms 520F-750F; breakfast 50F, menus from 195F **Rooms** 19, all with bath, phone, TV **Credit cards** AE, DC, MC, V **Closed** Jan

---

Village hotel, Bassac

L'Essille   11/9/98

It's years since we first heard of this modest hotel in a peaceful small village on the banks of the Charente, and a new report earns an entry: 'Comfortable hotel in delightful garden; very quiet; simple food; good parking.' 'Warm welcome, friendly but efficient service,' says an earlier report.

■ 16120 Bassac (Charente) **Tel** 45.81.94.13 **Fax** 45.81.97.26 **Meals** breakfast, lunch, dinner **Prices** rooms 250F-340F; breakfast 35F, menus 100F-220F **Rooms** 10, all with bath, central heating, phone, TV **Credit cards** MC, V **Closed** One week in Jan; restaurant only, Sun evening and Mon lunch

---

Converted abbey, Beaugency

L'Abbaye

The setting of this medieval abbey is its main feature – on the banks of the Loire, facing the old arched bridge of Beaugency. Lofty dining-hall and reception. Bedrooms are spacious and well equipped. A recent visitor's verdict: 'On the expensive side, but the ambience is worth it'.

■ 2 Quai de l'Abbaye, 45190 Beaugency (Loiret) **Tel** 38.44.67.35 **Fax** 38.44.87.92 **Meals** breakfast, lunch, dinner **Prices** rooms 420F-680F; menu 190F **Rooms** 18, all with bath, central heating, phone, TV **Credit cards** AE, DC, MC, V **Closed** never

The West

Village hotel, Bléré

Le Cheval Blanc

This smart-looking three-fireplace Logis on the main square of Bléré comes highly recommended, particularly for the 'outstanding' warmth of welcome and friendly service from the young staff. Food is 'imaginative and delicious,' value for money 'difficult to beat in the area.'

■ Place de l'Église, 37150 Bléré (Indre-et-Loire) **Tel** 47.30.30.14 **Fax** 47.23.52.80 **Meals** breakfast, lunch, dinner **Prices** rooms 290F-390F; breakfast 36F, menus 99F-265F **Rooms** 12, all with bath or shower, central heating, phone, TV, minibar, hairdrier **Credit cards** AE, DC, MC, V **Closed** Jan and Feb; restaurant only, Sun and Mon dinner except Jul and Aug

---

Village hotel, Brinon-sur-Sauldre

Auberge de la Solognote

The attractions of this rather dull-looking house are within – elegantly rustic furnishing and restrained, tasteful decoration, and excellent (Michelin-starred) food. The light, attractive bedrooms earn top marks for comfort – especially those in the converted outhouse.

■ 18410 Brinon-sur-Sauldre (Cher) **Tel** 48.58.50.29 **Fax** 48.58.56.00 **Meals** breakfast, lunch, dinner **Prices** rooms 310F-420F; menus 160F-330F **Rooms** 13, all with bath or shower, central heating, phone, TV **Credit cards** MC, V **Closed** mid-Feb to mid-Mar; restaurant only, Tue eve and Wed; Tue, Wed lunch in summer

---

Country hotel, Buzançais

L'Hermitage

An excellent Logis de France, occupying a mini manor house in leafy grounds beside the Indre. Breakfast can be had in the garden, which also provides flowers and vegetables. Reporters are enthusiastic – warm welcome, good housekeeping, excellent good-value food in an otherwise pricey area.

■ 36500 Buzançais (Indre) **Tel** 54.84.03.90 **Fax** 54.02.13.19 **Meals** brea kfast, lunch, dinner **Prices** rooms 290F-325F; breakfast 28F, menus 85F-225F **Rooms** 14, all with central he ating, phone, TV **Credit cards** MC, V **Closed** Sun evening and Mon, except July/Aug

---

Riverside hotel, Châteauneuf-sur-Sarthe

Hôtel de la Sarthe

Our most recent reporter was happy with this modest Logis on a beautiful stretch of the Sarthe, but light sleepers can be disturbed by noise from the nearby through-road. The flowery rooms are simple but satisfactory; food is well prepared and excellent value. Very welcoming proprietors.

■ 1 Rue du Port, 49330 Châteauneuf-sur-Sarthe (Maine-et-Loire) **Tel** 41.69.85.29 **Meals** breakfast, lunch, dinner **Prices** rooms 190F-265F; breakfast 30F, menus 90F-200F **Rooms** 7, all with bath or shower, central heating **Credit cards** MC, V **Closed** 3 weeks Oct; restaurant only, Sun dinner, Mon lunch and dinner out of season

The West

Village hotel, Chaumont-sur-Tharonne

La Croix Blanche

The 200-year-old tradition of women chefs continues at this cosy hotel, furnished with gleaming country antiques and floral-patterned fabrics. The 'superb' food is the attraction; the style of cooking is largely Périgordian (foie gras and so on). A recent visitor thought the hotel itself 'in need of a facelift'.

■ 41600 Chaumont-sur-Tharonne (Loir-et-Cher) **Tel** 54.88.55.12 **Fax** 54.88.60.40 **Meals** breakfast, lunch, dinner **Prices** rooms 290F-500F; DB&B 420F-500F; breakfast 45F, menus 145f-350F **Rooms** 16, all with bath, central heating, phone, TV, radio, minibar **Credit cards** AE, DC, MC, V **Closed** never

---

Village hotel, Chenonceaux

La Roseraie

A reader alerted us to this recently opened hotel, formerly the Ottoni, run by a 'delightful' Parisienne, Mme Fiorito. The bedrooms are tastefully decorated, the beamed dining-room is charming, but the highlight is the sunny dining terrace. There is now a heated swimming-pool, too. The splendid château is only a couple of minutes away.

■ 7 Rue du Dr Bretonneau, 37150 Chenonceaux (Indre-et-Loire) **Tel** 47.23.90.09 **Fax** 4 7.23.91.59 **Meals** breakfast, lunch, dinner **Prices** rooms 255F-465F; breakfast 38F, menus 98F-148F Rooms 18, all with central heating, phone, satellite TV **Credit cards** AE, DC, MC, V **Closed** mid-Nov to mid-Feb

---

Riverside hotel, Coulon

Au Marais

The Marais in question is a huge area of marshes west of Niort. This friendly little inn on the banks of the Sèvre-Niortaise river makes a pleasant and peaceful stop-over. The rooms are decorated in bright pastel tones and immaculately kept.

■ 46-48 Quai Louis-Tardy, 79510 Coulon (Deux-Sèvres) **Tel** 49.35.90.43 **Fax** 49.35.81. 98 **Meals** breakfast **Prices** rooms 250F-600F; breakfast 38F **Rooms** 18, all with bath, central heating, phone, TV **Credit cards** AE, MC, V **Closed** never

---

SERT'98

Country guest-house, Fondettes

19/9/

Manoir du Grand Martigny

Henri and Monique Desmarais are fluent in English, and actively seek to attract English-speaking guests to their 16thC manor house, in wooded grounds not far from the Loire. They renovated the house in the mid-1980s, and it makes a captivating place to stay, with splendid bedrooms and elegant public rooms. Excellent breakfasts.

■ Vallières, 37230 Fondettes (Indre-et-Loire) **Tel** 47.42.29.87 **Fax** 47.42.24.44 **Meals** breakfast **Prices** rooms 460F-700F with breakfast **Rooms** 7, all with bath, central heating **Credit cards** not accepted **Closed** mid-Nov to Mar

The West

Village inn, Fontgombault

Auberge de l'Abbaye

'An interesting overnight stop' sums up this unpretentious, tiny 16thC auberge – described as 'barely more than a cottage' by a recent reporter. Bedrooms are small and basic but the food is excellent and the service 'delightful' – as is the village setting, close to Fontgombault Abbey. Reservation in advance is recommended.

■ 36220 Fontgombault (Indre) **Tel** 54.37.10.82 **Meals** breakfast, lunch, dinner **Prices** rooms 130F-200F; breakfast 28F, menu 115F **Rooms** 5 **Credit cards** V **Closed** never

---

Riverside hotel, Gien

Hôtel du Rivage

Christian Gaillard's modern-classic (Michelin-starred) cooking is the main attraction of this unpretentious but quite chic modern hotel. Rooms are generally comfortable, with new mattresses promised for the beds, and good value. Lovely views of the Loire are shared by some bedrooms and the pretty dining-room.

■ 1 Quai de Nice, 45500 Gien (Loiret) **Tel** 38.37.79.00 **Fax** 38.38.10.21 **Meals** breakfast, lunch, dinner **Prices** rooms 300F-600F, suites 685F-785F; menus 155F-390F **Rooms** 19, all with bath or shower, central heating, phone, TV **Credit cards** AE, DC, MC, V **Closed** early Feb to Mar

---

Converted mill, Loches

Le Moulin

Andrew and Sue wrote to suggest that their 19thC watermill might make an entry here, and they were right. The house is on a small island in the Indre, with lawns down to the water. All the bedrooms are recently renovated, and furnished with stripped pine or antiques. French-trained Andrew Page cooks, and you can eat separately or communally.

■ St-Jean, St-Germain, 37600 Loches (Indre-et-Loire) **Tel** 47.94.70.12 **Fax** 47.94.77. 98 **Meals** breakfast, dinner **Prices** rooms 280F with breakfast; menus 110F **Rooms** 5, all with bath, central heating **Credit cards** not accepted **Closed** Jan, Nov, Dec

---

Town hotel, Lusignan

Le Chapeau Rouge

This 17thC coaching inn is now a friendly Logis run by the welcoming Nau family (father cooks, mother takes orders, son waits at table and runs the bar). 'Excellent' food is served in the beamed and rustic dining-room; bedrooms are simple but pleasantly furnished. 'Excellent value.'

■ 1 Rue Nationale, 86600 Lusignan (Vienne) **Tel** 49.43.31.10 **Meals** breakfast, lunch, dinner **Prices** 220F-300F; breakfast 30F **Rooms** 10, all with bath or shower, phone, TV **Credit cards** MC **Closed** Sun evening and Monday; 2 weeks Oct, 2 weeks Feb

The West

Restaurant with rooms, Marans

La Porte Verte

This neat, shuttered house sits quietly on the quayside with its own invitingly shady courtyard. A good, predominantly fishy menu (and wonderful puds) from Didier Montéran's kitchen. Bedrooms are tasteful, although there are idiosyncratic touches. Two are in the Montérans' own house along the quay. Reports on the new quayside *terrasse* please.

■ 20 Quai Foch, 17230 Marans (Charente-Maritime) **Tel** 46 01 09 45 **Meals** breakfast, lunch, dinner **Prices** rooms 150F-250F; menus 110F-165F **Rooms** 4, all with shower, central heating **Credit cards** MC,V **Closed** 17 Feb to 4 Mar; Wed; Sun dinner low season

---

Château hotel, Montrichard

Château de Chissay

A small-scale fairytale château in the heart of château country, renovated in the late 1980s, with rooms ranging from the affordable to the rather less so. Cooking is above average, including fish from the Loire. Swimming-pool.

■ Chissay-en-Touraine, 41400 Montrichard (Loir-et-Cher) **Tel** 54.32.32.01 **Fax** 54.32. 43.80 **Meals** breakfast, lunch, dinner **Prices** rooms 450F-1,500F; breakfast 60F; menus 185F-295F **Rooms** 31, all with bath, central heating, phone **Credit cards** AE, DC, MC, V **Closed** mid-Nov to mid-Mar

---

Château hotel, Montrichard

Château de la Menaudière

Despite its elegant furnishings, the atmosphere of this lovely little château is not intimidating. There are two intimate and rather hushed dining-rooms, and the food is good; breakfast can be had in the courtyard in summer, and there is a pubby bar in the stables. Bedrooms are well furnished, with smart bathrooms.

■ 41401 Montrichard (Loir-et-Cher) **Tel** 54.32.02.44 **Fax** 54.71.34.58 **Meals** breakfast, lunch, dinner **Prices** rooms 520F-670F; menus 190F-280F **Rooms** 25, all with bath, central heating, phone, TV, minibar **Credit cards** AE, DC, MC, V **Closed** Nov to Mar; restaurant only, Sun dinner, Mon lunch and dinner out of season

---

Restaurant with rooms, Mosnac

Moulin de Marcouze

The food (two Michelin stars) is the main draw of this smartly converted mill – Dominique Bouchet is a graduate of the Tour d'Argent in Paris. The modern bedrooms, like the dining-room, employ a light, simple style, with antique and reproduction furniture on plain quarry-tiled floors. Swimming-pool.

■ Mosnac, 17240 Saint-Genis-de-Saintonge (Charente-Maritime) **Tel** 46.70.46.16 **Fax** 4 6.70.48.14 **Meals** breakfast, lunch, dinner **Prices** rooms 525F-700F; breakfast 70F, menus 140F-420F **Rooms** 9, all with bath, central heating, air-conditioning, phone, TV, minibar **Credit cards** AE, MC, V **Closed** Nov to Feb; restaurant, Tue, and Wed lunch

The West

Riverside hotel, Olivet

Le Rivage

Position and food are the keys to this ordinary-looking hotel. It's in a peaceful spot on the banks of the Loiret, with a riverside terrace; the food is regionally-based and rated 'excellent' and 'beautifully presented'. Chatty, friendly owner. Tennis court.

■ 635 Rue de la Reine Blanche, 45160 Olivet (Loiret)
Tel 38.66.02.93 **Fax** 38.56.31. 11 **Meals** breakfast, lunch, dinner
Prices rooms 350F- 470F; breakfast 45F-50F, menus 155F-270F
Rooms 17, all with bath or shower, central heating, phone, TV, minibar
Credit cards AE, DC, MC, V **Closed** 3 weeks in Jan; restaurant only, Sun dinner Nov to Easter

---

Manor house hotel, Ouchamps

Relais des Landes

This 17thC mansion has a splendidly peaceful setting, in neat gardens leading off to the ponds and woods of the Sologne. Restful, spacious, well equipped bedrooms (most in low outbuildings); traditional food is served in a tiled, beamed dining-room. Reports welcome.

■ 41120 Ouchamps (Loir-et-Cher) **Tel** 54.44.03.33
Fax 54.44.03.89 **Meals** 20breakfast, dinner **Prices** rooms 495F-745F;
DB&B 565F-855F **Rooms** 28, all with bath, central heating, pho ne, TV,
minibar **Credit cards** AE, DC, MC, V **Closed** mid-Nov to end Mar

---

Town hotel, Pons

Auberge Pontoise

Ambitious and competent cooking (Michelin-starred) is the chief attraction of this simple, unpretentious hotel. The rooms (some facing the garden) are of a fair size, and there is a pleasant courtyard where meals are served in summer. Reports welcome.

■ 23 Ave Gambetta, 17800 Pons (Charente-Maritime)
Tel 46.94.00.99 **Fax** 46.91.33.40 **Meals** breakfast, lunch, dinner
Prices rooms 250F-420F; menus 160F-320F **Rooms** 22, all with bath or shower, central heating, phone, TV **Credit cards** AE, MC, V **Closed** 5 weeks Dec to Jan; Sun dinner and Mon out of season

---

Converted mill, La Roche-l'Abeille

Moulin de la Gorce

A tranquil setting and renowned cooking (two stars from Michelin) are the main attractions of this neat, low-lying 16thC mill building, beside a lake amid wooded grounds. Bedrooms – some richly furnished, some more bland – are split between the main building and an ancient nearby mill. Relais & Châteaux.

■ 87800 La Roche-l'Abeille (Haute-Vienne) **Tel** 55.00.70.66
Fax 55.00.76.57 **Meals** breakfast, lunch, dinner **Prices** rooms 350F-900F,
apartment 1,300F; breakfast 75F; menus 180F-480F **Rooms** 10, all with bath, phone, TV **Credit cards** AE, DC, MC, V **Closed** Oct to Apr

The West

Château hotel, St-Hilaire-de-Court

Château de la Beuvrière

A beautifully restored medieval château with 11thC origins – complete with conical slate roofs atop its round towers. Inside, the scale is more domestic than in many châteaux, the atmosphere welcoming. Outside, extensive grounds. New to the guide a couple of years ago; reports, please.

■ St-Hilaire-de-Court, 18100 Vierzon (Cher) **Tel** 48.75.14.63 **Fax** 48.75.47.62 **Meals** breakfast, lunch, dinner **Prices** rooms 350F-460F, suite 600F; menus 140F-198F **Rooms** 15, all with bath or shower, central heating, phone **Credit card** AE, DC, V **Closed** Sun night and Mon

---

Country hotel, St-Maixent-l'Ecole

Le Logis Saint-Martin

Here is a neatly restored old house, completely secluded in wooded grounds but conveniently close to the RN11 and the A10. The rooms are individually and tastefully furnished, and the food is taken increasingly seriously. Breakfast can be had on the terrace.

■ Chemin de Pissot, 79400 St-Maixent-l'Ecole (Deux-Sèvres) **Tel** 49.05.58.68 **Fax** 49.76.19.93 **Meals** breakfast, lunch, dinner **Prices** rooms 360F-460F; breakfast 55F; menus 140F-160F **Rooms** 11, all with bath or shower, central heating, phone, hairdrier, TV **Credit cards** AE, DC, MC, V **Closed** Jan; restaurant Mon, Oct to Feb

---

Country house hotel, St-Martin-du-Fault

La Chapelle-Saint-Martin

A neat, shuttered country house in lovely manicured grounds. The suave interior is designer-decorated and luxuriously furnished, mixing antiques, modern conveniences and rich fabrics in the best of taste; bedrooms are equally impressive. Michelin-starred food. Relais & Châteaux.

■ St-Martin-du-Fault, 87510 Nieul (Haute-Vienne) **Tel** 55.75.80.17 **Fax** 55.75.89.50 **Meals** breakfast, lunch, dinner **Prices** rooms 690F-980F, suites 1,300F-1,500F; DB&B 750F-850F **Rooms** 14, all with bath, central heating, phone, TV **Credit cards** AE, MC, V **Closed** Jan and Feb

---

Château hotel, St-Patrice

Château de Rochecotte

An affordable opportunity to sample life in a château of the grandest style, looked after by the charming Mme Pasquier and her equally charming staff. Bright fabrics, elegant modern furniture and light decoration complement the classical proportions of the rooms. The cuisine is appropriately gastronomique.

■ St-Patrice, 37130 Langeais (Indre-et-Loire) **Tel** 47.96.16.16 **Fax** 47.96.90.59 **Meals** breakfast, lunch, dinner **Prices** rooms 580F-930F, suites 1,250F; menus 195F-285F **Rooms** 30, all with bath, central heating, phone, TV **Credit cards** AE, DC, MC, V **Closed** Feb

The West

Village inn, Souvigny-en-Sologne

Auberge de la Croix Blanche

This family-run brick-and-timber auberge occupies a prime spot in the middle of a deliciously pretty village in the Sologne (the annexe is some 150 metres from the hotel itself). Bedrooms are small and simple with smartly tiled bathrooms. The *cuisine traditionelle et copieuse* is highly regarded.

■ Rue Eugenie Labiche, Souvigny-en-Sologne, 41600 Lamotte-Beuvron (Loir-et-Cher) **Tel** 54.88.40.08 **Meals** breakfast, lunch, dinner **Prices** rooms 120F-280F; breakfast 30F, menus 75F-230F **Rooms** 9, all with central heating, phone **Credit cards** V **Closed** mid-Jan to Feb; Tue dinner, Wed lunch and dinner

---

Restaurant with rooms, Thouars

Le Clos Saint-Médard

This stylishly simple restaurant with four neatly furnished rooms occupies a fine half-timbered 13thC building with a spiral staircase and huge stone fireplaces. Cooking is ambitious, 'gastronomic and imaginative'. Panoramic views over the Thouet valley.

■ 14 Place Saint-Médard, 79100 Thouars (Deux-Sèvres) **Tel** 49.66.66.00 **Fax** 49.96.15. 01 **Meals** breakfast, lunch, dinner **Prices** rooms 240F-320F; DB&B 300F **Rooms** 4, all with bath, central heating, phone, TV **Credit cards** AE, MC, V **Closed** one week in Feb

Eastern France

Area introduction

Our Eastern France region takes in Burgundy, the Jura and most of the Alps – an exceptionally rewarding area for lovers of food, wine and the great outdoors. We have a great many potential entries for this area, listed below.

Contenders in Eastern France

Beaune, Le Cep 80.22.35.48 Fairly pricey B&B in centre, now much enlarged.

Bourg-St-Maurice, Hôtel l'Autantic 79.07.01.70 Modern stone-faced chalet on edge of town, with comfy rooms.

Le-Bourget-du-Lac, Ombremont 79.25.00.23 Tastefully decorated R&C villa overlooking lake; pool.

Bresson, Chavant 76.25.25.38 Upmarket, elegantly furnished auberge with flower-filled dining terrace; excellent food.

Buxy, Château de Sassangy 85.96.12.40 Tall 18thC château in lovely grounds, with freshly decorated rooms.

Chamonix-Mont-Blanc, Hôtel Albert 1er
50.53.05.09 Solid old town hotel with the best food in town.

Chorey-les-Beaune, Château de Chorey-les-Beaune 80.22.06.05 Tastefully decorated, family-run B&B in solid 17thC château.

Cordon, Le Cordonant 50.58.34.56 Good-value modern chalet hotel in a country setting with excellent views.

Courchevel 1850, La Sivolière 79.08.08.33 Warmly welcoming hotel, run with dedication; quiet position, but close to centre.

Lods, La Truite d'Or 81.60.95.48 Old riverside mill in a narrow Jura valley, now a modest, rustic Logis.

Loué, Laurent 43.88.40.03 Smart Relais & Châteaux place with extravagant decor, attractive gardens with pool.

Lyon, La Tour Rose 78.37.25.90 Ambitious restaurant with spectacularly individual rooms decorated by Lyon silk makers.

Megève, Le Fer à Cheval 50.21.30.39 Tastefully rustic furnishings in a wood-built chalet on edge of town.

Mionnay, Alain Chapel 78.91.82.02 Luxury restaurant (one of best in France) with very expensive rooms.

Monêtier-les-Bains, l'Auberge du Choucas 92.24.42.73 Former farmhouse, still charming, with simple quiet rooms.

Le-Moulin-du-Milieu, Le Moulin 81.44.35.18 Eccentric house with large garden in a remote setting, recently opened.

Onlay, Château de Lesvault 86.84.32.91 Home-like little 19thC manor in grounds, with special appeal for writers and artists.

Replonges, La Huchette 85.31.03.55 Boldly decorated, shuttered house in grassy grounds with a large pool; good food.

St-Martin-en-Bresse, Au Puits Enchanté 85.47.71.96 Neat little Logis with exceptionally stylish decor and good-value food.

St-Sauveur-en-Rue, L'Auberge du Château de Bobigneux
77.39.24.33 Dinky rustic 16thC château offering simple rooms and country cooking at very low prices.

Saulieu, Bernard Loiseau 80.64.07.66 A temple of gastronomy, in an old inn, beautifully renovated, plus rustic-style extensions.

Veyrier-du-Lac, Auberge de l'Eridan 50.60.24.00 Swanky villa on lake shore; super-chef Marc Veyrat cooks.

Vienne, La Pyramide 74.53.01.96 Famous restaurant, revived under a new chef; tasteful, comfortable rooms.

Eastern France

Manor house hotel, Aloxe-Corton

Hôtel Clarion

'Highly recommended,' enthuses a recent German visitor, 'especially for its modern style in a traditional building, the superb garden views and the excellent breakfasts.'

The tiny village of Aloxe-Corton is a place of pilgrimage for lovers of great white wine. Its symbol is the château of Corton-André, a picturesque building of gleaming coloured tiles and tidy tunnels full of *premiers crus*. Next to it lies the Hôtel Clarion, a 17th-century mansion which has been cleverly converted into a small and unconventional hotel. The style is a mix of modern and old, art deco furnishings set against old timberwork and beamed ceilings. Bedrooms are well co-ordinated, mainly in matching fabrics of pastel shades. Although varied in size and price, all are thoroughly comfortable and well-equipped. Bathrooms, in marble, are large and luxurious.

Other merits of the hotel are the comfortable salon (beams, open fireplace) opening out on to the park and vineyards, and the large garden. Those breakfasts include eggs, cheese and fresh fruit in addition to the usual coffee and croissants.

Nearby Vineyards; Beaune – infirmary, wine museum; Le Rochepot (25 km) – château; Dijon (35 km).

21420 Aloxe-Corton
Tel 80.26.46.70
Fax 80.26.47.16
Location on edge of village, 3.5 km N of Beaune on N74; in large garden with ample car parking
Meals breakfast
Prices rooms 485F-790F
Rooms 10 double (7 twin), all with bath; one family room with bath ; all rooms have central heating, phone, TV, minibar

Facilities sitting-room; bicycles
Credit cards MC, V
Children welcome; cots, special meals, baby-sitting available
Disabled one ground-floor bedroom specially equipped
Pets accepted
Closed never
Proprietor Christian Voarick

Eastern France

Converted abbey, Annecy-le-Vieux

L'Abbaye

Annecy-le-Vieux is not the lovely medieval heart of Annecy, but a sprawling residential area north of the lake, and to be honest both the inspectors we've recently sent here have fretted about this weak spot in an otherwise captivating (although idiosyncratic) hotel. In promoting it to a full entry, we're influenced by a reader who summarises it as 'a very attractive hotel with delightful bedrooms,' with no niggles about the location.

L'Abbaye was indeed an ancient abbey. A stone archway leads into a quaint cobbled courtyard surrounded by a wooden balcony. The dining-room is a splendid, vaulted room sporting a motley array of decoration: gold mythological masks, chandeliers, Renaissance fresco, Indian print napkins. In summer, tables are set up in the shade of huge trees. The bedrooms have been beautifully furnished – again in a variety of styles – and with every modern convenience. (We're not surprised to hear that the hotel has recently stepped up to four-star status.)

It's rather surprising to find a disco in a hotel like this, but it is separate and does not disturb the peace. The food is good, and well priced; service is casual in terms of dress, but effective.

Nearby lake; Annecy (old town, churches, château)

15, Chemin de l'Abbaye,
74940 Annecy-le-Vieux
Tel 50.23.61.08
Fax 50.27.77.65
Location in rural setting,
2 km NE of Annecy; with
garden and car parking
Meals breakfast, dinner
Prices rooms 400F-650F;
breakfast 50F, menu 120F
Rooms 15 double, 2 suites,
one apartment, all with bath;
all have central heating,
phone, TV, minibar

Facilities dining-room, bar,
piano bar, terrace
Credit cards AE, DC, MC, V
Children welcome
Disabled no special facilities
Pets accepted
Closed restaurant only, Mon
Proprietors M. Menges and
M. Burnet

Eastern France

Town mansion, Auxerre

Parc des Maréchaux

This substantial 1850s house, restored from near-dereliction by Espérance Hervé and her doctor husband, enjoys clear support from readers, not least because it offers excellent value.

The Hervés have cut no corners: the welcoming ambience, confident style and solid comfort of the house would do credit to any professional hotelier. For a bed-and-breakfast establishment, the public rooms are exceptionally comfortable; as well as the sitting-room, the smart little bar looking over the garden is appreciated.

The large bedrooms are beautifully done out in restrained colours, and handsomely furnished using warm wooden beds and chests in traditional styles. One reader warned against those on the noisy road side and advises booking one that overlooks the garden – the secluded, leafy 'park' from which the hotel takes its name. But Madame advises that the road-side rooms have now been soundproofed. Breakfast, which can be had outside in summer, as an alternative to the pretty breakfast room, is 'outstanding,' says one reporter, 'adequate, with more copious options,' says another.

Nearby cathedral, abbey church of St-Germain; Chablis (20 km)

6 Ave Foch 89000 Auxerre
Tel 86.51.43.77
Fax 86.51.31.72
Location close to middle of town; with gardens and car parking
Meals breakfast
Prices rooms 300F-460F (under 7s free); breakfast 45F
Rooms 19 double (7 twin), 2 single, 3 family rooms; all with bath; all rooms have central heating, phone, TV
Facilities sitting-room, bar, breakfast room
Credit cards AE, V
Children welcome
Disabled 3 ground-floor bedrooms; lift/elevator
Pets accepted
Closed never
Proprietor Espérance Hervé

Eastern France

Château de Vault-de-Lugny

Recent visitors report enthusiastically on this impressive and expensive château, new to the guide a few years ago – only a couple of miles from the dear little Moulin des Templiers (page 114), but as sharp a contrast in style as you will find. 'Superb and welcoming hotel,' runs one report. 'We enjoyed both the food and the ambience, and will go again.'

The house, of plain medieval rather than fancy Renaissance origin, was restored and opened as a hotel in the mid-1980s. Some of the very grand bedrooms retain their aristocratic style, with period decoration and sparse antique furnishings that contribute more to atmosphere than comfort; others have something of a modern designer feel, with subtly coloured fabrics, and comfortable furniture that looks suspiciously like reproduction rather than the real thing. Bathrooms are ritzy, as they should be at these prices.

The extensive, well-wooded grounds include a well-used kitchen garden, contributing to the proprietors' *cuisine traditionelle*, and a fair stretch of trout fishing, as well as a tennis-court. Hot-air balloon flights can be arranged.

Nearby Avallon – ramparts; Vézelay (10 km)

89200 Avallon
Tel 86.34.07.86
Fax 86.34.16.36
Location 4 km W of Avallon, 1 km N of Pontaubert, on D427 outside village of Vault-de-Lugny, in large grounds with ample car parking
Meals breakfast, lunch, dinner, snacks
Prices rooms 700F-2,200F with breakfast; dinner 265F; reductions for 5 nights plus
Rooms 12 double (4 twin), all with bath; all rooms have central heating, phone, TV, minibar; most have hairdrier
Facilities sitting-room/bar, sitting-room, restaurant; tennis, fishing
Credit cards AE, MC, V
Children welcome; babysitting available
Disabled easy access, room on ground floor
Pets welcome (50F charge)
Closed mid-Nov to early Apr
Proprietor Elisabeth Audan

Eastern France

Converted mill, Chaublanc

Moulin d'Hauterive

We've no reason to doubt that this ancient watermill is as attractive as ever, but reports are few and far between; if you pay a visit, do drop us a line about it.

The wheels of the mill were still turning less than 30 years ago; only for the last decade or so has it been enjoying a new lease of life as a country hotel – offering an unusual blend of rural seclusion, good living and sporting activities. It is a handsome creeper-clad building, three storeys high, surrounded by a collection of lower outbuildings. Beyond them are the little pool (with a lift-up cover/roof which is doubtless a great aid to child safety and energy conservation when the pool is not in use, but diminishes the pleasure of swimming) and tennis court.

The interior is the epitome of rustic chic. The building contributes a network of beams, smooth stone-flagged floors, white-washed or rough pale stone walls. Against this are placed bright fabrics, delicate mellow antiques, gleaming ornaments, and vivid bowls of flowers. Bedrooms are romantically done out in pastel shades – beds are often draped or canopied with lacy fabrics. The young Moilles were new to hotel keeping when they set up the Moulin. Madame has gained a formidable reputation for her inventive dishes (two red *toques* from Gault-Millau).

Nearby Archéodrome (10 km) – archeological centre; Beaune (15 km) – medieval infirmary, wine museum.

Chaublanc 71350 St-Gervais-en-Vallière
Tel 85.91.55.56
Fax 85.91.89.65
Location 16 km SE of Beaune, off D970; in grounds with ample car parking
Meals breakfast, lunch, dinner
Prices rooms 530F-650F, suites 850F; DB&B 580F-730F; menus 160F-400F
Rooms 11 double, 11 family rooms, all with bath or shower; all rooms have central heating, phone, TV, minibar
Facilities 2 dining-rooms, bar, 3 seminar rooms; swimming-pool, tennis, spa, billiards, heliport, sauna, solarium, fitness room
Credit cards AE, DC, V
Children accepted
Disabled one room
Pets dogs accepted in bedrooms at extra charge
Closed Christmas, Jan
Proprietors Christiane and Michel Moille

Eastern France

Les Grands Crus

The walls are vertical and plastered, the exposed beams are straight and smooth, the windows are easily opened casements: this is a modern hotel, built as recently as 1977, and so not as immediately charming as many older places in these pages. But the Grands Crus has been done out in traditional Burgundian style, with quarry-tiled floors, lime-washed walls, tapestry fabrics and a carved-stone fireplace, and it drips with geraniums in summer – so to a degree it combines the charm of the old with the comfort of the new. More importantly, perhaps, it offers a warm welcome and friendly service – factors which repeatedly impress themselves on our reporters.

The bedrooms are not the last word in stylish decoration, but they are peaceful, spacious and thoughtfully furnished, and look out over the famous Gevrey-Chambertin vineyards. A better-than-average breakfast is served in the small flowery garden in fine weather; if you're confined indoors, there may be delays because of a shortage of space in the breakfast room, off reception. There are plenty of restaurants nearby for other meals, including some notably good ones.

Nearby Dijon – Grand Duke's palace, Place de la Libération.

Rte des Grands Crus 21220 Gevrey-Chambertin
Tel 80.34.34.15
Fax 80.51.89.07
Location in middle of village, 10 km SW of Dijon; with garden and ample car parking
Meals breakfast
Prices rooms 350F-430F; breakfast 45F; children under 4 free
Rooms 24 double (8 twin) all with bath; all rooms have phone
Facilities sitting-room
Credit cards MC, V
Children welcome
Disabled no special facilities
Pets accepted but not to be left in rooms
Closed Dec to Feb
Proprietor Mme Marie-Paule Farnier

Eastern France

Chalet hotel, Chamonix

Auberge du Bois Prin

Despite increasing competition (notably from the newish Jeu de Paume, see page 116) the Bois Prin remains our favourite spot in (or at least near) Chamonix. This is partly because of its stunning views across the valley to the spires and glaciers of Mont Blanc, Europe's highest peak. But an inspection visit also confirms its merits as a cossetting place to stay.

The Bois Prin is a traditional-style dark-wood chalet, in a pretty, flowery garden close to the foot of the Brévent cable-car, on the north side of the deep, steep-sided Chamonix valley. The Carriers have run the hotel since it was built (by Monsieur's parents) in 1976. The first impression may be of a surprising degree of formality, with crisply dressed staff. But in fact the informal and friendly approach of the young Carriers sets the tone. Bedrooms face Mont Blanc, and are luxuriously furnished, with rich fabrics and carved woodwork (much of it Denis's own work) and a sprinkling of antiques; the best have a private terrace. Food is excellent, with a good choice of menus and a 'wonderful' cheeseboard.

Nearby Mt Blanc and Le Brévent – cable-car rides, walking, rock climbing, skiing; Mont Blanc tunnel for easy access to Italy.

69 Chemin de l'Hermine, Les Moussoux 74400 Chamonix
Tel 50.53.33.51
Fax 50.53.48.75
Location on hillside, NW of town; with garden and ample car parking and garages
Meals breakfast, lunch, dinner
Prices rooms 870F-1,120F with breakfast; menus 170F-420F
Rooms 9 double (5 twin), all with bath; 2 family rooms, with bath; all rooms have phone, TV, minibar
Facilities dining-room, seminar room
Credit cards AE, DC, MC, V
Children welcome; special meals, high-chair available
Disabled no special facilities
Pets accepted
Closed mid-Apr to early May, late Oct, Nov
Proprietors Monique and Denis Carrier

Eastern France

Village mansion, Mailly-le-Château

Le Castel

We have had mixed reports, over the years, on this pleasant old *maison bourgeoise*. We're coming to the view that it's a matter of expectations. It is a modest hotel – a two-fireplace Logis, with rooms and meals at very attractive prices. But because the house and its name are rather grand, some visitors perhaps expect too much. Our latest reporter, who stayed two nights, takes a balanced view: 'Pleasant welcome (in English), good rooms, good food; restricted menus understandable in view of reasonable prices.'

Built at the end of the last century, Le Castel is a large shuttered house lying in the shadow of the village church, with a well-kept garden and a flowery terrace shaded by lime trees, where you can have breakfast. There are two dining-rooms, separated by a small salon with Empire-style furnishings and a handsome fireplace. Bedrooms vary widely – from spacious ones with touches of grandeur, such as chandeliers and drapes over bedheads, to much smaller and simpler rooms. Some much-needed refurbishment has been undertaken recently, and continues. Madame is 'the perfect hostess'.

Nearby Vézelay (30 km) – Romanesque buildings; Avallon (30 km) – ramparts; Chablis (45 km) – vineyards.

Place de l'Église 89660 Mailly-le-Château
Tel 86.81.43.06
Fax 86.81.49.26
Location in church square of village, 30 km S of Auxerre; with garden, terrace and car parking
Meals breakfast, lunch, dinner
Prices rooms 155F-400F, suite 420F; menus 75F-170F
Rooms 10 double (5 twin), 7 with bath, 2 with shower; 2 family rooms with bath ; all rooms have central heating, phone
Facilities 2 dining-rooms, sitting-room
Credit cards MC, V
Children accepted
Disabled one ground-floor bedroom
Pets accepted
Closed Wed
Proprietors M. and Mme Breerette

Eastern France

Chalet hotel, Manigod

Chalet Hôtel de la Croix-Fry

The inspector who was lucky enough to find herself spending a night in this cosy wooden chalet could scarcely contain her enthusiasm, summing it up in the end as her favourite in a week-long tour which included several delectable places.

Mountain chalets come in many styles, but the pretty-as-a-cuckoo-clock variety, two a penny in Switzerland, is all too rare in France. But this is one – built in dark wood, its terrace overflowing with bright flowers. Inside, the immediate impression is of rustic simplicity, with wood the warm, dominant material; an open fire burns on cool evenings, with benches and sofas covered by animal skins in front of it. The bedrooms, too, are charmingly rustic in style – even in the modern annexe-chalets, which offer flexible and comfortable accommodation (with kitchenettes) for all sizes of family.

Style apart, the peaceful setting is the attraction, with superb views across the valley from the terrace and the picture windows of the dining-area. The welcoming owners and staff strike the perfect balance of attentive service without intrusion. Good, nourishing mountain food completes a happy picture.

Nearby skiing; Vallée de Manigod, Thônes (10 km); Annecy.

Rte du Col de la Croix-Fry, Manigod 74230 Thônes
Tel 50.44.90.16
Location at the col, 5 km NE of Manigod, on D16 6 km S of La Clusaz; in countryside, with garden and ample car parking
Meals breakfast, lunch, dinner
Prices rooms 500F-1,500F; breakfast 80F; menus 140F-360F
Rooms 12 double with bath; all rooms have central heating, phone, satellite TV
Facilities dining-room, sitting-room, bar; heated swimming-pool, tennis, ski bus
Credit cards AE, MC, V
Children accepted
Disabled no special facilities
Pets not accepted in dining-room
Closed mid-Sep to mid-Dec, mid-Apr to mid-Jun
Proprietor Mme Marie-Ange Guelpa-Veyrat

Eastern France

Les Récollets

The Brionnais is a rural region, with gently rolling hills and lush meadows where Charollais cattle graze. It is a part of Burgundy that few foreigners bother with, which we hope explains why we get so few reports on this near-ideal combination of French chic and home comforts. More reports would be very welcome.

The small market town of Marcigny provides an excellent base for touring the region – it is close to the Loire, and not far from the famous cattle market of St-Christophe-en-Brionnais. It is also the location of this, one of the most delightful hotels in the region. We use the word 'hotel' loosely: this is really a private home open to guests.

Josette Badin, who runs the place with Burgundian *bonhomie*, has furnished the rooms superbly, from the dining-room with its hand-painted cupboards to the antique-laden bedrooms. There are log fires, home-made *brioches* for breakfast, hand-made chocolates by the bedside (along with sleeping tablets, indigestion pills and painkillers). Indeed, every need is catered for, and the only house-rule is 'do as you please'.

Officially, only breakfast is served, but ask in advance and Josette will be happy to prepare a simple meal: soup or omelette – even *foie gras*, followed by Charollais beef.

Nearby Mill Tower Museum; La Clayette (25 km); Charlieu Abbey (30 km); Château Drée (30 km).

Place du Champ de Foire
71110 Marcigny
Tel 85.25.05.16
Fax 85.25.06.91
Location on edge of small town 22 km S of Paray; in grounds with ample car parking
Meals breakfast; lunch and dinner on request
Prices rooms 330F-600F with breakfast; menus 170F-200F
Rooms 6 double (2 twin), all with bath; 3 family rooms, all with bath; all rooms have central heating, phone
Facilities TV room, library, breakfast/dining-room
Credit cards AE, V
Children accepted
Disabled one ground-floor bedroom
Pets accepted
Closed never
Proprietor Mme Josette Badin

Eastern France

Village inn, Mercurey

Hôtellerie du Val d'Or

Jean-Claude Cogny and his family keep standards as high as ever in this early 19th-century coaching inn, on the main street of the prestigious but rather dull wine village of Mercurey. It is easy to see what brings the customers back: in a region of culinary excellence and exorbitant prices, many are daunted by the formal (or even pretentious) style of most hotels, and long to find some village-inn simplicity. The friendly Val d'Or obliges, and combines this with excellent cooking (Michelin-starred) and comfortable, neatly decorated bedrooms – though some are rather small. There is an attractive gravelled garden.

Nearby Château de Germolles (10 km); Buxy (20 km).

Grande-Rue 71640 Mercurey
Tel 85.45.13.70
Fax 85.45.18.45
Location in middle of village, 9 km S of Chagny; with garden
Meals breakfast, lunch, dinner
Prices rooms 320F-550F; meals 160F-410F, children's meals 85F
Rooms 10 double (3 twin), one single, 2 family rooms; all with bath or shower; all rooms have central heating, phone, TV
Facilities 2 dining-rooms, lounge/bar
Credit cards MC, V
Children accepted
Disabled no special facilities
Pets not accepted
Closed Mon and Tue lunch
Proprietor Jean-Claude Cogny

Eastern France

Auberge du Rostaing

We don't get many reports on this completely peaceful and relaxed *auberge* in an unspoiled area west of the Jura hills, but they are all positive. 'We are sure to return,' says the latest.

This is an area that is great for getting away from it all, with lovely walks (or bicycle rides) for the active. And this simple place, well run by a charming Franco-Swiss couple, seems entirely in harmony. It also has more to offer than most similarly simple competitors: an inviting sitting-room with music, games and books (and emphatically no TV), a shady courtyard garden where meals and drinks are served in summer, a large airy dining-room with an open fireplace and rustic furniture, and nine fresh, spacious and simple bedrooms – some of them in an adjacent building, reached by an outside staircase and a balcony decked with climbing vines and geraniums.

Madame Eckert does the cooking – good and wholesome, with lots of Swiss influences; *fondue* and *raclette* sometimes crop up, and there is a 'marvellous' daily cheese platter. Many of the guests come back year after year and it is easy to see why.

Nearby forest walks, bicycle rides, vineyards; Château-Chalon (5 km); Cirque de Ladoye (10 km); Poligny (10 km)

39230 Passenans
Tel 84.85.23.70
Fax 84.44.66.87
Location on outskirts of village, 11 km SW of Poligny on D57, follow Route des Vins; with garden
Meals breakfast, lunch, dinner
Prices rooms 125F-235F; breakfast 24F, menus 59F-165F
Rooms 7 double (2 twin), 5 with shower; 2 family rooms with bath; all rooms have central heating
Facilities dining-room, sitting-room; bicycles for hire
Credit cards DC, MC, V
Children accepted; reductions by arrangement
Disabled no special facilities
Pets accepted
Closed Mon evenings except high season; Dec, Jan
Proprietor Félix Eckert

Eastern France

Le Pontot

Most visitors to this rambling fortified house – the only hotel inside the walls of the old town of Vézelay, just a short walk from the famous basilica – are captivated by its combination of character and luxury.

Rebuilt after the Hundred Years War, and added to in the 18th century, it has only recently become a hotel. Since 1984 the American owner, architect Charles Thum, and manager Christian Abadie have skilfully converted the building into a rather special bed-and-breakfast. (Who needs a restaurant when the famous Espérance lies just down the road?) The bedrooms include a large Louis XVI apartment, with canopied beds, fireplace and private dressing room; and another with stone paving, 16thC beamed ceiling and antique, country-style, furnishings.

Breakfast is quite a sumptuous affair, served as it is on gold-encrusted, royal blue Limoges porcelain. On cool days, it is eaten in front of a blazing fire in the handsome, panelled, Louis XVI salon; but in summer you sit outside in the delightful walled garden. A reader warns that bedrooms can be chilly in October.

Nearby St-Père-sous-Vézelay (2 km); Avallon (15 km); Auxerre (50 km); Chablis and Sancerre (50 km) – vineyards.

Place du Pontot 89450 Vézelay
Tel 86.33.24.40
Fax 86.33.30.05
Location in middle of town; with walled flower garden and car parking
Meals breakfast
Prices rooms 350F-1050F (child sharing room 100F); breakfast 60F
Rooms 9 double, one single, all with bath and shower (4 twin); all rooms have phone, radio
Facilities sitting-room, bar, breakfast room
Credit cards DC, MC, V
Children accepted
Disabled not suitable for wheelchairs
Pets accepted; 50F charge
Closed Nov to Easter
Manager Christian Abadie

The East

Town hotel, Arnay-le-Duc

Chez Camille

Armand Poinsot's excellent cooking (traditional but light) is only one attraction of this captivating little hotel. The mostly compact bedrooms are tastefully decorated and cluttered with antiques – and effectively double-glazed against noise from the RN 6. Much cheaper rooms in the modern Clair de Lune annexe.

■ 1 Place Edouard-Herriot, 21230 Arnay-le-Duc (Côte-d'Or)
Tel 80.90.01.38 **Fax** 80.9 0.04.64 **Meals** breakfast, lunch, dinner
Prices rooms 400F-600F; menus 130F-250F **Rooms** 14, all with bath,
central heating, phone, TV **Credit cards** AE, DC, V **Closed** never

---

Converted mill, Avallon

Moulin des Ruats

Up to now, we have not been quite convinced by this old flour mill, despite its idyllic setting. But it has been taken over by the Rossis, of Auberge de la Benvengudo in Provence. The place has the potential to be completely captivating, and they have the energy and taste to make it happen.

■ Vallée du Cousin, 89200 Avallon (Yonne) **Tel** 86.34.07.14
Fax 86.31.65.47 **Meals** breakfast, lunch, dinner **Prices** 300F-650F;
breakfast 50F; menus 150F-230F **Rooms** 24, all with bath or shower,
central heating, phone **Credit cards** V **Closed** mid-Nov to mid-Feb;
restaurant only, Mon eve out of season

Converted mill, Avallon

Moulin des Templiers

A recent report confirms our affection for this modest, captivating stop-over on the way through Burgundy. Breakfast is served on the riverside terrace on fine days, otherwise in a tiny room – there may be a queue. The pretty bedrooms are mostly small, and the smallest is minute. No alcohol is served.

■ Vallée du Cousin, Pontaubert, 89200 Avallon (Yonne) **Tel** 86.34.10.80
Meals 20breakfast **Prices** rooms 250F-350F; breakfast 36F **Rooms** 14, all
with shower, phone **Credit cards** not accepted **Closed** Nov to mid-Mar

---

Château hotel, Bagnols

Château de Bagnols

Some expensive château hotels are simply smart, or luxurious, or full of character, or in exceptionally privileged settings. Bagnols is entirely extraordinary – a medieval fortress restored and furnished to be perfect in every detail. Send for the brochure before you dismiss the idea of paying the prices. 'Loved it; would certainly go back,' says our ecstatic nominating reader.

■ 69620 Bagnols (Rhône) **Tel** 74.71.40.00 **Fax** 74.71.40.49
Meals breakfast, lunch, dinner **Prices** rooms 2,200F-3,000F with
breakfast, suites 4,000F-5,000F **Rooms** 20, all with bath, central
heating, phone, TV, hairdrier **Credit cards** AE, DC, MC, V **Closed** end-Oct
to mid-Apr

The East

Converted mill, Bonnevaux-le-Prieuré

Le Moulin du Prieuré

Eight neat bedrooms are located in little modern chalets in the garden of this converted watermill which offers complete peace, wonderful scenery and competent cooking. You prepare your own breakfast (an arrangement that suits trout-fishing guests).

■ 25560 Bonnevaux-le-Prieuré (Doubs) **Tel** 81.59.28.79 **Fax** 81.59.21.47 **Meals** breakfast, lunch, dinner **Prices** rooms 350F; breakfast 30F, menus 280F-350F (at least one meal obligatory) **Rooms** 8, all with bath or shower, phone, TV, minibar **Credit cards** AE, DC, MC, V **Closed** mid-Nov to early Mar, Sun evening, Mon

---

Country inn, La Celle-Saint-Cyr

La Fontaine aux Muses

'We absolutely loved it,' says a weary traveller refreshed by the 'delightful' pool of this creeper-covered rural auberge, which also offers golf, tennis and a music room where the family often play. Simple rooms opening on to the garden. Good simple cooking with an emphasis on fish; slow service.

■ Route de la Fontaine, 89116 La Celle-Saint-Cyr (Yonne) **Tel** 86.73.40.22 **Fax** 86.73 .48.66 **Meals** breakfast, lunch, dinner **Prices** rooms 340F-650F; breakfast 36F, menu 175F **Rooms** 17, all with bath or shower, central heating, phone **Credit cards** MC, V **Closed** Mon; restaurant only, Tue lunch

---

Restaurant with rooms, Chablis

Hostellerie des Clos

You go here for the food; the modern, tasteful but unremarkable rooms are a bonus. The designer-decorated dining-room is light and stylish; the light, innovative cooking (one Michelin star, two toques from Gault-Millau) makes full use of the local white wines.

■ Rue Jules Rathier, 89800 Chablis (Yonne) **Tel** 86.42.10.63 **Fax** 86.42.17.11 **Meals** breakfast, lunch, dinner **Prices** rooms 250F-570F; breakfast 50F, menus 168F-420F **Rooms** 26, all with bath, central heating, phone, TV, radio, minibar **Credit cards** MC, V **Closed** 2 weeks Christmas and New Year; Wed and Thu lunch from Oct to Apr

---

Château hotel, Chagny

Hostellerie du Château de Bellecroix

An approving report from a discriminating reader restores this creeper-covered château to the guide. It combines 12thC and 18thC architecture to magical effect. Comfortable bedrooms, some in the turrets, with plenty of antiques and views over the parkland. Large pool. 'Excellent' food.

■ Route Nationale 6, 71150 Chagny (Saône-et-Loire) **Tel** 85.87.13.86 **Fax** 85.91.28.62 **Meals** breakfast, lunch, dinner **Prices** rooms 590F-950F; breakfast 62F, menus 250F-350F **Rooms** 21, all with bath or shower, central heating, phone, TV, minibar **Credit cards** AE, DC, MC, V **Closed** 20 Dec to 15 Feb; restaurant only, Wed; Jul, Aug

The East

Town hotel, Chagny

Hôtel Lameloise

Jacques Lameloise maintains the reputation of this calm shuttered house, established by his father Jean, as one of the best restaurants in France. It is a comfortable hotel, too, with tastefully furnished bedrooms and solidly traditional public areas. Relais & Châteaux, but not at all snooty.

■ 36 Place d'Armes, 71150 Chagny (Saône-et-Loire) **Tel** 85.87.08.85 **Fax** 85.87.03.57 **Meals** breakfast, lunch, dinner **Prices** rooms 650F-1,500F; menus 360F-590F **Rooms** 19, all with bath, phone, TV; some have air-conditioning **Credit cards** AE, MC, V **Closed** Wed, Thu until 5 pm; mid-Dec to mid-Jan

---

Chalet hotel, Chamonix

Hôtel du Jeu de Paume

Parisian chic comes to the mountains: this offshoot of the Jeu de Paume in Paris, newly built in traditional chalet style, has immediately become one of the most desirable places to stay in the Chamonix valley. Pine-panelled bedrooms. Small indoor pool.

■ 705, Route du Chapeau, Le Lavancher, 74400 Chamonix (Haute-Savoie) **Tel** 50.54.03.76 **Fax** 50.54.10.75 **Meals** breakfast, lunch, dinner **Prices** rooms 680F-1,250F; breakfast 55F, menus 160F **Rooms** 22, all with bath, central heating, phone, TV, radio, minibar, hairdrier **Credit cards** AE, DC, MC, V **Closed** mid-May to mid-Jun, mid-Oct to mid-Dec

---

Town hotel, Charolles

Hôtel de la Poste

A prime example of an unassuming provincial hotel doing a sound job. The white-painted building is immaculately maintained, as is the smart bar-salon; and the dining-room has been made positively ritzy by small-town standards. It is also possible to dine outside in the newly created garden.

■ 2 Ave de la Libération, 71120 Charolles (Saône-et-Loire) **Tel** 85.24.11.32 **Fax** 85. 24.05.74 **Meals** breakfast, lunch, dinner **Prices** rooms 270F-360F, 2 suites 340F-600F; breakfast 45F, menus 180F-360F **Rooms** 13, all with bath or shower, central heating, phone, TV **Credit cards** AE, MC, V **Closed** Sun evening, Mon; Nov

---

Village hotel, Chassignelles

Hôtel de l'Ecluse No. 79

The *écluse* is the nearby lock on the canal in front of this infant enterprise – a peaceful row of houses boldly but sympathetically converted to provide (at present) five tastefully furnished bedrooms with smart bathrooms, as well as pleasantly rustic dining-rooms and a bar. Charming *patronne*, modest prices.

■ 89000 Chassignelles (Yonne) **Tel** 86.75.18.51 **Fax** 86.75.02.04 **Meals** breakfast, lunch, dinner **Prices** rooms 175F-300F; breakfast 25F, menus 75F-140F, children's 45F **Rooms** 5, all with bath or shower, central heating, phone, TV, hairdrier **Credit cards** DC, MC, V **Closed** 3 weeks in Jan

The East

Village hotel, Châteauneuf

Hostellerie du Château

The picturesque hostellerie, cleverly converted from a 15thC presbytery close to the château, is in keeping with the medieval village around it: old stone walls, quiet rustic rooms and terraced gardens. In the beamed restaurant where wholesome Burgundian dishes are the order of the day. 'Very good value,' says a recent report.

■ Châteauneuf, 21320 Pouilly-en-Auxois (Côte-d'Or) **Tel** 80.49.22.00 **Fax** 80.49.21.27 **Meals** 20breakfast, lunch, dinner **Prices** rooms 270F-430F; menu 120F-220F **Rooms** 17, all with bath or shower, central heating, phone **Credit cards** AE, MC, V **Closed** Dec to mid-Feb

---

Town inn, Châtillon-sur-Seine

Hôtel de la Côte d'Or

This creeper-covered family-run auberge in a leafy garden offers prettily decorated rooms at modest prices, friendly but proper service and food that is interesting and competently cooked (and served on the terrace when the weather permits).

■ Rue Charles-Ronot, 21400 Châtillon-sur-Seine (Côte-d'Or) **Tel** 80.91.13.29 **Fax** 80. 91.29.15 **Meals** breakfast, lunch, dinner **Prices** rooms 320F-600F; breakfast 35F; menus 95F-180F **Rooms** 10, all with central heating, phone, TV **Credit cards** AE, DC, MC, V **Closed** Jan

---

Country house hotel, Chonas-l'Amballan

Domaine de Clairefontaine

Of the Girardons' two operations (see also the Marais St Jean) this has the higher reputation for food, with one Michelin star. The handsome old house in splendid, peaceful park-like grounds, is family-run without pretension, and offers entirely comfortable rooms at modest prices.

■ Chonas-l'Amballan, 38121 Reventin-Vaugris (Isère) **Tel** 74.58.81.52 **Fax** 74.58.80.93 **Meals** breakfast, lunch, dinner **Prices** rooms 180F-380F; breakfast 45F, menus 150F-350F **Rooms** 16, all with bath or shower, central heating, phone **Credit cards** AE, DC, MC, V **Closed** Dec, Jan; Sun evening and Monday lunch out of season

---

Farmhouse hotel, Chonas-l'Amballan

Le Marais Saint-Jean

For some years now in the same ownership as the Clairefontaine, this neat farmhouse conversion has a private-home atmosphere, much of which has recently undergone redecoration. Modern comforts blend with the original timbered ceilings, beams and quarry tiles. Good food served in a beamed dining-room or on a sunny terrace.

■ Chonas-l'Amballan, 38121 Reventin-Vaugris (Isère) **Tel** 74.58.83.28 **Fax** 74.58.81.9 6 **Meals** breakfast, lunch, dinner **Prices** rooms 650F-700F; breakfast 60F, menus 165F-320F **Rooms** 10, all with bath, phone, satellite TV, minibar **Credit cards** AE, DC, MC, V **Closed** Feb to mid Mar, Nov; restaurant only, Wed and Thurs lunch.

The East

Town hotel, Cluny

Hôtel de Bourgogne

The most comfortable and central hotel in Cluny, this attractive stone mansion, dating from 1817, is built around a garden and courtyard. The elegant setting and Burgundian specialities of the restaurant draw many non-residents despite the loss of its Michelin star a couple of years ago.

■ Place de l'Abbaye, 71250 Cluny (Saône-et-Loire) **Tel** 85.59.00.58 **Fax** 85.59.03.73 **Meals** breakfast, lunch, dinner **Prices** rooms 455F-1150F; breakfast 55F, menus 200F-420F **Rooms** 15, all with bath, central heating, phone, TV **Credit cards** AE, DC, MC, V **Closed** mid-Nov to Feb, Tue; restaurant Tue, and Wed lunch

---

Riverside hotel, Condrieu

Hôtellerie Beau Rivage

The 'beau rivage' is that of the Rhône – not an entirely appropriate description, given the nearby chemical works. But the immediate surroundings of this elegantly furnished Relais & Châteaux place are 'most agreeable', the staff welcoming and the Michelin-starred food 'excellent'.

■ 69420 Condrieu (Rhône) **Tel** 74.59.52.24 **Fax** 74.59.59.36 **Meals** 20break fast, lunch, dinner **Prices** rooms 500F-820F; breakfast 60F, menus 165F-600F **Rooms** 24, all with bath or shower, central heating, phone **Credit cards** AE, DC, MC, V **Closed** never

---

Village hotel, Curtil-Vergy

Hôtel Le Manassès

What better way to spend an overnight stop in Burgundy than in the heart of a working vineyard in the Hautes Côtes de Nuits? The 'beautifully furnished' and well equipped rooms in a converted outbuilding offer remarkable value, and in the next-door wine museum Yves Chaley will treat you to a taste of his wines. Recommended restaurants nearby.

■ 21220 Curtil-Vergy (Côte-d'Or) **Tel** 80.61.43.81 **Fax** 80.61.42.79 **Meals** breakfast **Prices** rooms 380F; breakfast 50F **Rooms** 7, all with bath, central heating, phone, TV, minibar **Credit cards** MC, V **Closed** Dec to Feb

---

Country hotel, Doussard

Marceau Hôtel

Recommended 'without reservation,' says a visitor of this plain-looking but welcoming family-run hotel, near lake Annecy. The beautiful mountain views are not the only attraction: bedrooms are spacious and dotted with antiques, there is a cosy sitting-room, a rambling garden and a panoramic dining terrace.

■ Bout du Lac, 74210 Doussard (Haute-Savoie) **Tel** 50.44.30.11 **Fax** 50.44.39.44 **Meals** breakfast, lunch, dinner **Prices** rooms 440F-660F; breakfast 50F, menus 130F-330F **Rooms** 16, all with bath or shower, central heating, phone, TV, radio **Credit cards** AE, DC, MC, V **Closed** Oct to Jan

The East

Château hotel, Fleurville

Château de Fleurville

Unlike so many château hotels, this is not a formal, luxury establishment – the atmosphere is pleasantly relaxed and it is reasonably priced. Many original 16thC features have been retained and, despite various modernizations, there is still a medieval atmosphere. Bedrooms are simply furnished. Tennis and swimming-pool.

■ 71260 Fleurville (Saône-et-Loire) **Tel** 85.33.12.17 **Fax** 85.33.95.34 **Meals** breakfast, lunch, dinner **Prices** rooms 440F, apartment 800F; breakfast 45F, menus 170F-260F **Rooms** 15, all with bath, central heating, phone **Credit cards** DC, MC, V **Closed** mid-Nov to 26 Dec; restaurant only, Mon lunch

---

Village inn, Givry

Hôtel de la Halle

The façade of this town-centre Logis is undistinguished and furniture and decoration are not at all special. What captivates British visitors and local regulars alike is the scrupulous house-keeping, excellent traditional Burgundian cuisine and exceptionally low prices.

■ Place de la Halle, 71640 Givry (Saône-et-Loire) **Tel** 85.44.32.45 **Fax** 85.44.49.45 **Meals** breakfast, lunch, dinner **Prices** rooms 210F-280F; breakfast 25F, menus 55F-260F **Rooms** 10, all with bath or shower, central heating, phone **Credit cards** AE, DC, MC, V **Closed** mid-Nov to early Dec

---

Chalet hotel, Goumois

Hôtel Taillard

A steady flow of readers approve of this pretty chalet in a wooded valley on the Swiss border. They like the wonderful views from the breakfast terrace, the delightful garden, the comfortable rooms, the friendly atmosphere and (not least) the food – 'delicious, if slightly repetitive'.

■ 25470 Goumois (Doubs) **Tel** 81.44.20.75 **Fax** 81.44.26.15 **Meals** breakfast, lunch, dinner **Prices** rooms 275F-435F; breakfast 50F; menus 135F-370F **Rooms** 17, all with bath or shower, central heating, phone, TV **Credit cards** AE, DC, MC, V **Closed** mid-Nov to mid-Mar

---

Château hotel, Igé

Château d'Igé

This turreted, creeper-covered castle retains its medieval atmosphere despite its conversion into a luxurious Relais & Châteaux hotel. Above-average food is served in front of a huge open hearth in the massively beamed dining-room – a marked contrast to the pleasant new conservatory.

■ 71960 Igé (Saône-et-Loire) **Tel** 85.33.33.99 **Fax** 85.33.41.41 **Meals** breakfast, lunch, dinner **Prices** rooms 480F-710F, suites 875F-1,100F; breakfast 65F, menus 190F-360F **Rooms** 13, all with bath, central heating, phone, TV, hairdrier **Credit cards** AE, DC, V **Closed** Dec to Mar

The East

Bed and breakfast farmhouse, Levernois

Le Parc

Beaune has a dearth of reasonably priced accommodation but the Parc, 5 km away, offers excellent value and a pleasant rural setting. It is a simple hotel, converted from an old farmhouse, and run rather like a private home. Breakfast is served in a pretty courtyard.

■ Levernois, 21200 Beaune (Côte-d'Or) **Tel** 80.24.63.00 **Fax** 80.24.21.19 **Meals** breakfast **Prices** rooms 180F-450F **Rooms** 25, all with bath or shower, central heating, phone, TV **Credit cards** MC, V **Closed** 10 days in early Dec

---

Village hotel, Meursault

Hôtel les Charmes

This 18thC maison bourgeoise sits peacefully in a park-like garden with mature trees. A refined private-house atmosphere prevails: in the bedrooms the furniture is antique and elegant, the decorative schemes individual and harmonious. Secure parking. Fairly new to the guide – reports welcome.

■ 10 Place du Murger, 21190 Meursault (Côte-d'Or) **Tel** 80.21.63.53 **Fax** 80.21.62.89 **Meals** breakfast **Prices** rooms 390F-550F; breakfast 45F **Rooms** 14, all with bath, central heating, phone, TV, minibar **Credit cards** MC, V **Closed** Dec to Mar

---

Village bed-and-breakfast, Meursault

Les Magnolias

In a pleasantly quiet location, Les Magnolias is a polished and unusually stylish place – a group of old houses around a small courtyard, with spacious bedrooms that have been individually decorated with some panache. Expect to drive to a restaurant. New to the guide a couple of years ago; more reports, please.

■ 8 Rue Pierre Joigneaux, 21190 Meursault (Côte-d'Or) **Tel** 80.21.23.23 **Fax** 80.21.29.10 **Meals** breakfast **Prices** rooms 380F-750F; breakfast 45F **Rooms** 12, all with bath or shower, central heating, phone; TV on request **Credit cards** AE, MC, V **Closed** Dec to Feb

---

Medieval inn, Pérouges

Ostellerie du Vieux Pérouges

The Ostellerie is at the heart of the perfectly preserved little medieval town of Pérouges. Excellent meals are served in the charming old dining rooms, while slices of *galette Pérougienne* (a sort of sugary pizza) are dispensed from the kitchen window. Bedrooms are in four other houses, the best splendidly old (and pricey).

■ Place du Tilleul, Pérouges, 01800 Meximieux (Ain) **Tel** 74.61.00.88 **Fax** 74.34.77.9 0 **Meals** breakfast, lunch, dinner **Prices** rooms 390F-900F; menus 170F-390F **Rooms** 29, all with bath, phone **Credit cards** V **Closed** never

The East

Town hotel, St-Florentin

La Grande Chaumière

This attractive pink, turn-of-the-century building with a leafy garden makes a pleasant gastronomic stop-over on the route south. It's not strong on character: bedrooms are in an essentially modern style, the Michelin-starred restaurant light and smartly furnished.

■ 3 Rue des Capucins, 89600 St-Florentin (Yonne) **Tel** 86.35.15.12 **Fax** 86.35.33.14 **Meals** breakfast, lunch, dinner **Prices** rooms 350F-550F, suites 650F-850F; breakfast 54F; menus 135F-275F **Rooms** 10, all with bath or shower, central heating, phone, TV **Credit cards** AE, DC, MC, V **Closed** first week Sep, mid-Dec to mid-Jan; Wed out of season

Country inn, St-Lattier

Le Lièvre Amoureux

One reporter reckons the food at this old hunting lodge is of star quality. Michelin disagrees, but there are other attractions – not least the leafy garden and the pool, which is directly accessible from the pine-panelled rooms in the modern 'outbuildings'; in the main building there are more traditional alternatives.

■ La Gare, 38840 St-Lattier (Isère) **Tel** 76.64.50.67 **Fax** 76.64.31.21 **Meals** breakfast, lunch, dinner **Prices** rooms 320F-450F; breakfast 55F, menus 175F-285F **Rooms** 14, all with bath, central heating, phone, TV, hairdrier **Credit cards** DC, MC, V **Closed** Nov to mid-Feb

Converted abbey, Tonnerre

L'Abbaye Saint-Michel

Not everyone likes the way this ancient abbey has been elevated to Relais & Châteaux status – using plate glass or stainless steel as readily as stone and wood. But the innovative cooking deserves its toques and stars from gastronomic guides. One dining-room is a stone vault, the other gives views of the countryside.

■ Montée de Saint-Michel, 89700 Tonnerre (Yonne) **Tel** 86.55.05.99 **Fax** 86.55.00.10 **Meals** breakfast, lunch, dinner **Prices** rooms 700F-1,750F, suites 1,850F-2,050F; breakfast 85F, menus 300F- 630F **Rooms** 14, all with bath, central heating, phone, TV, minibar **Credit cards** AE, DC, MC, V **Closed** Jan

Converted mill, Val-Suzon

Hostellerie du Val-Suzon

This 18thC mill is now a country inn, with beams and flowery prints in the bedrooms and cuisine praised as 'nouvelle-oriented, with excellent fish dishes – a memorable experience'. Breakfast breads are notably good. The modern annexe is a short walk up the hillside.

■ RN 71, Val-Suzon, 21121 Fontaine-lès-Dijon (Côte-d'Or) **Tel** 80.35.60.15 **Fax** 80.35 .61.36 **Meals** breakfast, lunch, dinner **Prices** rooms 350F-500F, suites 600F-800F;menus 190F-400F **Rooms**17, all with bath or shower, central heating, phone, alarm; 9 have TV, radio **Credit cards** AE, DC, MC, V **Closed** restaurant only, Wed and Thu lunch, except May to Oct

The East

Ski resort hotel, Val-Thorens

Fitz Roy

The ski resort of Val-Thorens as a whole virtually closes down in summer (although there is some glacier skiing), and this exceptionally civilized and welcoming hotel is no exception. Light, pine-furnished bedrooms. Serious food – about the best in the resort. Special outings to high-altitude chalets for dinner, and a music festival in January.

■ 73440 Val-Thorens (Savoie) **Tel** 79.00.04.78 **Fax** 79.00.06.11 **Meals** breakfast, lunch, dinner **Prices** DB&B 900F-1,650F **Rooms** 36, all with spa bath, central heating, air conditioning, phone, TV, radio, minibar, hairdrier **Credit cards** AE, DC, MC, V **Closed** early May to 2 Dec

---

Lakeside hotel, Veyrier-du-Lac

La Demeure de Chavoire

A splendid combination of traditional elegance and modern comfort, set in a pretty garden on the shores of lovely lake Annecy. Every room has been thoughtfully and richly furnished; the bedrooms are all individually decorated in romantic style, and named after local beauty spots and Annecy's famous writers.

■ Route d'Annecy-Chavoire, 74290 Veyrier-du-Lac (Haute-Savoie) **Tel** 50.60.04.38 **Fax** 50.60.05.36 **Meals** breakfast, snacks **Prices** rooms 650F-1,000F, suites 1,100F-1,550F; breakfast 68F **Rooms** 13, all with bath, central heating, phone, TV, radio, minibar, hairdrier **Credit cards** AE, DC, MC, V **Closed** never

The South-west

The Limousin hills represent the watershed between the basins of the Charente and the Loire, to the north, and that of the Garonne and its tributaries, to the south; and the start of our South-west region. For many British visitors, the valleys of the Dordogne and the Lot represent an ideal, not only of France but of life itself – life in a kind climate and a fertile landscape. And the concentration of our kind of hotel here is second only to that in Provence. To the west lie the peerless vineyards of Bordeaux, a nd the forests and limitless beaches of the Landes. To the south, Gascony and the Basque country of the Pyrenees.

Contenders in the South-west

Barcus, Chez Chilo 59.28.90.79 Idiosyncratic village hotel, smartly furnished; good food.

Cadéac-les-Bains, Hostellerie du Val d'Aure 62.98.60.63 Secluded Logis in wooded grounds with pool and tennis, near the ski resort of St-Lary.

Les Courrières, Les Murailles 53.05.58.09 English-run farmhouse B&B (option to dine with owners) tastefully restored; in large garden with pool.

Gramat, Château de Roumegouse 65.33.63.81 Prettily furnished mini-château surrounded by woods; pool.

Grenade-sur-l'Adour, Pain Adour et Fantaisie 58.45.18.80 Handsome riverside house with stylishly modern furnishings and knockout food – 2 stars, 4 *toques*.

Lascabanes, La Petite Auberge 65.31.82.51 A captivating group of stone farm buildings in a quiet country setting; charmingly simple stone-walled rooms.

Loubressac, Château de Gamot 65.38.58.50 Little 17thC château furnished in period, run as a B&B in summer by its Parisian owners; pool, but not available July and August.

Mussidan, Le Bastit 53.81.32.33 Carefully furnished country house in flowery garden (with pool) run by friendly Anglo-French couple.

Paulhiac, L'Ormeraie 53.36.45.96 Carefully converted farmhouse in lovely country setting, run in house-party style by retired publisher.

Port-de-Lanne, La Vieille Auberge 58.89.16.29 Warmly furnished village Logis with pleasant garden and pool.

St-Jean-de-Luz, Parc Victoria 59.26.78.78 Immaculate, elegantly furnished villa in leafy gardens with excellent pool.

St-Pierre-de-Côle, Domaine de Doumarias 53.62.34.37 Simply but tastefully furnished country B&B with pool in lush garden.

St-Robert, La Maison Anglaise 55.25.19.58 Freshly decorated 19thC villa in peaceful setting with long views; carefully run by English proprietors.

Segos, Domaine de Bassibé 62.09.46.71 Small, intimate, comfortable hotel with lovely views and good chef.

Toulouse, Hôtel des Beaux Arts 61.23.40.50 Designer style in central Toulouse.

Valence-sur-Baïse, La Ferme de Flaran 62.28.58.22 Freshly decorated farmhouse with dining terrace and pleasant pool, in countryside; decent food.

The South-west

Village hotel, Aïnhoa

Hôtel Ohantzea

This is by some margin the cheapest of our main recommendations in the Pyrénées-Atlantiques, and accordingly simple – but no less charming for that. Set on the road through an attractive mountain village, the timbered Ohantzea has been in the Ithurria family for three centuries, and old family furniture is dotted around the house, which is satisfyingly rustic and tasteful throughout – uneven wooden floors, beamed ceilings. The bedrooms are notably spacious, and some have balconies. The menus offer fair value and the dining-room is pleasant enough. M. and Mme Ithurria are a charming, outgoing couple who make everyone feel at home.

Nearby St-Pée-sur-Nivelle (10 km); Sare (10 km) – cog railway.

Aïnhoa 64250 Cambo-les-Bains
Tel 59.29.90.50
Location in middle of village, 10 km SW of Cambo-les-Bains; with garden and car parking behind
Meals breakfast, lunch, dinner
Prices rooms 240F-300F; menus 120F-220F
Rooms 10 double, 9 with bath and shower (3 twin); all rooms have central heating, phone
Facilities sitting-room, 2 dining-rooms
Credit cards AE, DC, MC, V
Children welcome
Disabled no special facilities
Pets accepted
Closed Dec and Jan
Proprietor M. Ithurria

The South-west

Le Chatenet

This lovely 17thC manor house has prompted a steady flow of approving reports from readers over the years of its inclusion in the guide, and the latest gives the clearest possible view: 'We left wanting to stay longer, and we will certainly go back.'

The appeal of the place stems not only from its rural surroundings – down a country track off the busy riverside road, blissfully far removed from the tourist bustle of Brantôme – but also from its informal atmosphere: despite evidently heavy investment in rich furnishings, the Laxtons attach importance to maintaining the family-home feel, and it shows. There are vases of fresh flowers on low tables, deep armchairs, and country antiques in both the sitting-room and breakfast room, which form part of the Laxtons' home. Bedrooms are spacious, with elegant decoration. In the cosy clubhouse there's an 'honesty' bar and room for wet-weather activities. Outside, deckchairs are scattered invitingly around the garden beneath shady trees, and there is plenty of space for children.

Breakfasts (Magdeleine has a repertoire of 10 sorts of home-made *confiture*) are served on a covered terrace in fine weather, and guests may have the use of an outdoor barbecue. If do-it-yourself doesn't appeal, there are several excellent restaurants nearby. The 'very cordial' welcome is 'enhanced by the dog'.

Nearby Brantôme – monks' garden, belfry, troglodyte caves; Bourdeilles (10 km) – château; Chancelade (30 km) – abbey.

24310 Brantôme
Tel 53.05.81.08
Fax 53.05.85.52
Location 1.5 km SW of town, off D78; in large grounds with ample car parking
Meals breakfast
Prices rooms 550F-590F, suites 800F
Rooms 8 double, all with bath (6 twin); 2 suites; one cottage with 2 double rooms; all rooms have central heating, phone; TV on request

Facilities sitting-room, breakfast room, clubhouse with billiards; heated swimming-pool, tennis
Credit cards MC, V
Children welcome if well behaved **Disabled** access easy; 2 ground-floor bedrooms, one specially equipped
Pets welcome if well behaved
Closed at times Nov to Apr – phone to check
Proprietors Philippe and Magdeleine Laxton

The South-west

Converted mill, Brantôme

Moulin de l'Abbaye

Our visits to this exquisite little mill have always left us wishing to stay longer; why, we wonder, do we not hear from more readers about it? Could the Relais & Châteaux prices be to blame?

The setting is the thing. The shady riverside terrace, illuminated in the evening, is an idyllic place for a drink or a meal while admiring Brantôme's unusual angled bridge, the tower of the abbey or the swans gliding by. Wonderful views over the river and the old houses of one of the prettiest villages in France are also to be had from many of the bedrooms – all beautifully decorated and comfortably furnished (some have four-poster beds and antiques, others are more modern).

Traditional Périgord dishes with a *nouvelle* touch earn the restaurant 3 *toques* from Gault-Millau and a star from Michelin. The dining-room is as pleasant a place to enjoy this excellent cuisine as the terrace it leads to, though we can raise no enthusiasm for the 'Monet-style' colour scheme. There are fresh flowers, sparkling glass and silverware, and soft lighting in the evening. Staff are correct and courteous; service is efficient.

Nearby Monk's garden, belfry; Antonne-et-Trigonant (3 km) – 15thC Périgord manor; Bourdeilles (10 km) – château.

1 Rte de Bourdeilles 24310 Brantôme
Tel 53.05.80.22
Location on edge of town, 20 km N of Périgueux; with garden, and ample car parking across road
Meals breakfast, lunch, dinner
Prices rooms 550F-950F, apartments 1,000F-1,350F; breakfast 75F, menus 220F-450F
Rooms 17 double,
3 apartments, all with bath; all rooms have central heating, TV, minibar
Facilities dining-room, sitting-room
Credit cards AE, DC, MC, V
Children welcome
Disabled no special facilities
Pets dogs accepted
Closed Nov to May; restaurant only, Mon lunch
Manager M. Dessum

The South-west

Manor house hotel, Le Buisson-de-Cadouin

Manoir de Bellerive

Our most recent report on this fine Napoléon III manor house sums up its attractions comprehensively: 'Magnificent rooms, spectacular grounds, very friendly staff'. Sadly our correpondent didn't sample dinner, which is the latest development in the Manoir's gradual progress towards full hotelhood.

The Manoir is set in lovely peaceful grounds which stretch down to the banks of the Dordogne. Sun beds and tables are liberally scattered over the lawns, and there is a swimming-pool and tennis court tucked away between the pine trees and flower borders. If you prefer to watch the world – and the slow-moving river – go by from a more elevated position, you can sit out on the balustraded first-floor terrace. Once you step inside the lofty entrance hall, you are transported back in time. The elegant staircase sweeps up to spacious and very comfortable designer-decorated bedrooms. Breakfast can be taken on the terrace or in a room with murals on the pale walls.

For six months of the year (mid-March to mid-June and mid-September to mid-November), the hotel is also used as a conference centre. At other times, peace reigns.

Nearby walking, golf; Lascaux – caves; Les Eyzies; Sarlat (35 km).

Route de Siorac 24480 Le Buisson-de-Cadouin
Tel 53.27.16.19
Fax 53.22.09.05
Location in countryside, 800 m SE of Le Buisson-de-Cadouin on D25; with grounds and ample car parking
Meals breakfast, dinner; lunch at weekends
Prices rooms 420F-750F; breakfast 55F-65F; menu 115F-185F

Rooms 16 double, 8 with bath, 8 with shower (6 twin); all rooms have central heating, phone, satellite TV, minibar **Facilities** sitting-room, breakfast room, sauna, jacuzzi, conference facilities; swimming-pool, tennis court
Credit cards MC, V
Children accepted
Disabled access difficult
Pets accepted
Closed Nov to mid-Apr
Proprietor Mme Huin

The South-west

Le Moulin du Roc

A steady flow of approving reports from readers confirm the attractions of this delectable old walnut-oil mill, one of that rare breed of hotels that give you the sensation of pampering without charging £100 a night for a room. 'Absolutely stellar,' says the most recent – although the Moulin is less stellar than it used to be (these days it rates 'only' one Michelin star).

The setting on the banks of the Dronne (a few miles upstream of Brantôme) is wonderfully romantic; the waterside gardens are lush, secluded, shady and bursting with colour. Inside the rough-stone 17thC building, old beams, fireplaces, mill machinery, fine old carved furniture, rich fabrics and massive oil paintings – together with plenty of ornaments and flower arrangements – create a style that is highly individual, or even eccentric. Some may find it rather heavy. The same cannot be said of the food: in the land of *foie gras*, Solange Gardillou manages to build on culinary traditions to produce remarkably light and inventive dishes. Breakfasts are a treat, with home-made rolls and jams, beautifully served. Bedrooms vary in size, but do not disappoint – pretty, cosy, with their full share of antiques.

Nearby Brantôme; Bourdeilles (15 km) – château.

24530 Champagnac-de-Belair
Tel 53.54.80.36
Fax 53.54.21.31
Location in hamlet, on D82 and D83, 6 km NE of Brantôme; with large garden and ample car-parking
Meals breakfast, lunch, dinner
Prices rooms 380F-680F; breakfast 55F, menus 150F-280F, children's 100F
Rooms 10 double (2 twin), 4 suites; all with bath; all rooms have central heating,
phone, TV, minibar
Facilities sitting-room, dining-room; heated swimming-pool, tennis court, terrace
Credit cards AE, DC, MC, V
Children welcome
Disabled two ground-floor rooms **Pets** accepted
Closed mid-Nov to mid-Dec, mid-Jan to mid-Feb; restaurant only, Tue, Wed lunch
Proprietors M. and Mme Gardillou

The South-west

Manor house, Coly

Manoir d'Hautegente

A reader describes this creeper-clad manor house as 'so good that I wouldn't tell you about it if it were not already in the guide'. We'll just have to hope that he doesn't mind our promotion of the Manoir – new to the guide a few years ago – to a full entry.

The house, set in beautiful wooded grounds, has been in the Hamelin family for about 300 years, and is now run by Edith Hamelin and her son Patrick. It was built as a forge in the 13th century, later became a mill (using the stream that runs beside it), was then embellished and turned into a family residence and was finally converted into a hotel – but with the private-home feel entirely intact. Public rooms and the spacious, comfortable bedrooms are imaginatively decorated with family antiques and paintings. Dinner in the pretty vaulted dining-room is a five-course affair – 'first-class cuisine' which inevitably includes home-produced *foie gras*, another of the Hamelins' commercial successes. Wines are reasonably priced.

In the pleasant grassy grounds there is a smart pool that gets plenty of sun. A warm welcome from the family awaits.

Nearby châteaux; Lascaux (15 km); Sarlat (25 km).

Coly 24120 Terrasson
Tel 53.51.68.03
Fax 53.50.38.52
Location in countryside, 6 km SE of Le Lardin on the D62; with grounds and car parking
Meals breakfast, dinner
Prices rooms 500F-950F; breakfast 55F, menus 190F-250F
Rooms 12 double, all with bath (2 twin); all rooms have central heating, phone; hairdrier, TV

Facilities dining-room, sitting-room; heated swimming-pool
Credit cards MC, V
Children welcome
Disabled one ground-floor room
Pets accepted if well behaved
Closed Nov to Easter
Proprietors Edith Hamelin and Patrick Hamelin

The South-west

Les Glycines

'I reckon it's the best in town now,' says a trusted reporter of this handsome 19th-century house – the 'town' being the touristy capital of the prehistory business. Les Glycines stands close to the station on the edge of Les Eyzies, in the lush and beautiful gardens that are one of the hotel's chief attractions; the name means wisteria, and that lovely flower is to be found here in abundance. There is also a swimming-pool and a terrace for drinks, so it's an excellent place for good weather.

Indoors there are also plenty of sitting-areas, well supplied with reading material, meaning this is also an hotel where it's not unpleasant to while away time in poor weather. The dining-room and covered terrace are very attractive, too. The bedrooms are comfortable but unremarkable – few are notably spacious; those at the back are superior. There are more rooms than we generally allow in a country hotel, but the hotel does not feel large, partly because some of the rooms are in a connected annexe.

The food is 'very good,' and Madame, although rather chic and cool at first, softens when she gets to know you.

Nearby Château de Fages (15 km); Sarlat (21 km); Lascaux caves (25 km); Beynac (30 km) – village and castle.

24620 Les Eyzies-de-Tayac
Tel 53.06.97.07
Fax 53.06.92.19
Location on edge of town, on main road; with large gardens and ample car parking
Meals breakfast, lunch, dinner
Prices rooms 355F-410F; breakfast 52F; DB&B 402F-450F; menus 140F-190F
Rooms 25 double, all with bath or shower (12 twin); all rooms have central heating, phone
Facilities 2 sitting-rooms, dining-room, bar; swimming-pool
Credit cards AE, MC, V
Children accepted
Disabled access possible
Pets accepted
Closed Nov to Easter; restaurant Sat lunch out of season
Proprietors M. and Mme Henri Mercat

The South-west

La Daille

Another Dorgogne establishment that combines the best of France and Britain. The mellow stone, red-roofed buildings are surrounded by gardens with glorious herbaceous borders that could only be the work of British green fingers. Rich local produce is transformed into wonderful light dishes that stand in sharp contrast to the typical Périgord menu.

British *emigrés* Barbara and Derek Brown have been running this unusual establishment, in wonderful unspoilt and hilly countryside just south of the Dordogne, for nearly 20 years now – and have built up a regular local clientele for their afternoon teas and ambitious set dinners. La Daille is a small-scale *pension* catering for no more than 7 residents and 14 non-resident diners (half board obligatory, minimum stay three days unless you can sneak in a night or two between bookings). The double bedrooms are in a modern single-storey building – thoroughly comfortable, with big bathrooms and terraces – across the garden from the original farmhouse, which contains the cool, rustic dining-room. The one (equally comfortable) single is in an old outbuilding.

Nearby golf, canoeing; Domme (15 km) – *bastide*, Sarlat (25 km)

Florimont-Gaumiers 24250 Domme
Tel 53.28.40.71
Location in countryside, 2 km S of Gaumiers (signposted from village); in large grounds with ample car parking
Meals breakfast, afternoon tea, dinner
Prices DB&B (with wine) 455F
Rooms 3 double (2 twin), one single, all with bath or shower; all rooms have central heating
Facilities dining-room, terrace
Credit cards not accepted
Children accepted over 7
Disabled access difficult
Pets not accepted
Closed Nov to 1 May
Proprietors Mr and Mrs Derek Vaughan Brown

The South-west

Château de la Treyne

We've had our eye on this little château beside the Dorgogne since an inspector came back a <u>few</u> years ago with a report littered with emphatically underscored adjectives – 'gorgeous ... impeccable ... exceptionally comfortable'. Of course, it is not cheap; perhaps we should be grateful that elevation to Relais & Châteaux status has not pushed prices up further.

Michèle Gombert-Devals' house has made a splendid small hotel. It starts with the advantage of a beautiful position, in woods on a low cliff cut by the meandering river Dordogne. But the compelling attraction of the château is the near-ideal balance struck between the impressiveness of a fortified manor-house and the intimacy of a genuine home. The building dates from the early 14th century, but was substantially rebuilt in the 1600s; it is now tastefully equipped with a happy mix of furnishings – comfy sofas in front of an open fire, as well as grand antiques.

There are long walks to enjoy in the grounds, and a very beautiful formal garden before which you can take breakfast. Excellent regional food is served – on the delightful terrace perched above the river in good weather.

Nearby Souillac – abbey church; Rocamadour, Sarlat.

Lacave 46200 Souillac
Tel 65.32.66.66
Fax 65.37.06.57
Location 3 km W of village on D43, 6 km SE of Souillac; in large grounds beside river, with ample private car parking
Meals breakfast, lunch, dinner
Prices rooms 900F-1,800F; DB&B 350F; breakfast 70F, menus 180F-280F
Rooms 14 double, all with bath; all rooms have central heating, air conditioning, phone, TV
Facilities 3 sitting-rooms, dining-room, bar, billiard room, meeting-room; sauna, swimming-pool, tennis
Credit cards AE, DC, MC, V
Children welcome
Disabled access difficult
Pets accepted if well behaved
Closed 15 Nov to Easter
Proprietor Mme Michèle Gombert-Devals

The South-west

Farmhouse hotel, Mauroux

Hostellerie Le Vert

Le Vert goes from strength to strength. The attractions of this secluded 17th-century farmhouse have been greatly increased by the construction of a swimming-pool. It will doubtless remain the kind of hotel you look forward to returning to at the end of the day; it also looks set to become the kind you're disinclined to leave at all.

There is just a small side door to lead you inside. Within, all is original stone walls and beams. The dining-room opens out on to a terrace with wide views; through an arch at one end is a small sitting-room – ideal for an aperitif. The bedrooms are all comfortably and tastefully modernized, and have lovely views. The largest are quite grand and furnished with antiques. But the most attractive are in the little annexe a couple of yards from the entrance – the lower one stone-vaulted, the upper one beamed, with a marble floor. The garden has chairs and tables, and is improving in colour despite dry summers. The Philippes are a friendly and hard-working couple – he cooks (interestingly and competently), she serves (and speaks excellent English).

Nearby Bonaguil (15 km) – château; Biron castle (35 km); Monpazier (50 km) – *bastide*; Cahors (50 km) – medieval bridge.

Mauroux 46700 Puy-l'Evêque
Tel 65.36.51.36
Location in countryside, off D5 10 km SW of Puy-l'Evêque; 10 km SE of Fumel; in garden, with ample private car parking
Meals breakfast, lunch, dinner
Prices rooms 230F-360F; breakfast 38F, menus 100F-150F
Rooms 7 double, all with bath or shower; all have central heating, phone, TV
Facilities dining-room, sitting-room, terrace, swimming-pool
Credit cards AE, MC, V
Children welcome – children's menu 50F
Disabled no special facilities
Pets welcome at extra charge
Closed Dec to mid-Feb
Proprietors Eva and Bernard Philippe

The South-west

Au Bon Coin du Lac

We see no sign of slippage in the high standards of Jean-Pierre Caule, the third generation of his family to run Au Bon Coin, or indeed the exacting standards of Mme Caule, who oversees things front of house.

The two-storey, stone and painted-wood house has a superb lakeside setting, with neat little footpaths inviting you to walk around the grounds. But the hotel's *raison d'être* is its Michelin-starred restaurant, and M. Caule's culinary skill as head chef (seafood is his speciality). The generally expensive feel of the place is reflected in the menu – and the prices. The dining-room has an uncluttered view of the lake and is charmingly furnished: round tables, white table-cloths, floral china and floral-covered chairs. The service is formal, as you would expect in a restaurant in this price range, but nevertheless friendly.

The bedrooms are large and luxurious; not impersonal, but rather uniform. Despite the many activities on the lake – sailing, fishing – the swings nearby and the special children's menu, this is not really a place for a family holiday. But it is ideal for those who want four-star treatment, a relaxed and friendly atmosphere and excellent food.

Nearby Lakes; beaches (5 km); Landes forest (30 km); Sabres (40 km) – railway to Marquèze Ecomuseum.

34 Ave du Lac, Mimizan
40200 Landes
Tel 58.09.01.55
Fax 58.09.40.84
Location amid forests, 2 km N of Mimizan; on edge of lake, with garden and car parking
Meals breakfast, lunch, dinner
Prices rooms 360F-650F; menus 160F-350F; reduced rates for children
Rooms 5 double, all with bath and shower; 4 suites, all with bath and shower; all rooms have central heating, phone, TV, radio, minibar
Facilities sitting-room, dining-room
Credit cards AE, V
Children welcome; special meals, baby-listening available
Disabled ground-floor bedrooms
Pets accepted
Closed Feb; restaurant only, Sun dinner, and Mon out of season
Proprietor Jean-Pierre Caule

The South-west

Château Cordeillan-Bages

This is a château in the Bordeaux manner – not a Loire-style extravagance, but a harmoniously proportioned, single-storey stone mansion dating from the 17thC, with an associated five-acre expanse of vineyard (formerly an important one, and now-gradually gaining in stature again). The house was completely restored in 1989 and the decoration is stylish and restful. There is something of the feel of an English country house about the intimate sitting-rooms and elegant dining-room, – until you walk out on to the terrace to be confronted by vines. The bedrooms are very comfortable, with the sure hand of the interior designer given full rein.

Chef Thierry Marx, who has taken over the kitchen at Château Cordeillan-Bages since our last edition, uses his skills to create new dishes based on seasonal produce, as well as traditional regional food, and of course, the wine-list is long.

The *Ecole du Bordeaux*, based within Château Cordeillan-Bages, organizes a wide choice of courses for both professional and amateur wine lovers, with visits to other châteaux in this famous wine-growing region.

Nearby Château Mouton-Rothschild (museum) (5 km).

Route des Châteaux, 33250 Pauillac
Tel 56.59.24.24
Fax 56.59.01.89
Location in wine village on D2, 40 km N of Bordeaux; in own grounds, with ample car parking
Meals breakfast, lunch, dinner
Prices rooms 830F-900F; junior suite 960F-1100F; breakfast 65F-95F, menus 180F-290F
Rooms 25 double, all with bath; all rooms have central heating, phone, TV, radio, minibar, hairdrier, safe
Facilities sitting-rooms, bar, dining-room, breakfast room
Credit cards AE, DC, V
Children welcome; babysitting available **Disabled** lift/elevator, access ramp, ground-floor rooms, toilets **Pets** small ones accepted **Closed** 10 Dec to end Jan; restaurant only, Mon and Sat lunch
Manager Alain Rabier

The South-west

Domaine de la Rhue

Curiously, we have no reports from readers recently on this lovely little hotel, peacefully set amid rolling countryside out of sight of any other building, yet only a few kilometres away from touristy Rocamadour. But we have great confidence in the charming young proprietors, Eric and Christine Jooris.

You might be somewhat disappointed to discover that the hotel does not occupy the magnificent family-owned château, but is set in the adjoining stable block. But your disappointment would be short-lived; this superb 19th-century stone building has been carefully and imaginatively converted into a dozen pretty, spacious bedrooms. Several are suitable for families, and some now have discreet kitchenettes. Breakfast is served in a pleasant salon (stone-flagged, with an open fireplace), and the Joorises are happy to make snack lunches, which can be eaten beside the glorious swimming-pool in front of the hotel.

You might also want to take advantage of Eric's other passion; he is a qualified hot-air balloon pilot and offers his guests the chance to see Rocamadour from the air – 'an experience not to be missed'.

Nearby hot-air ballooning; walks; Rocamadour (7 km); Padirac (10 km), Loubressac (20 km); Carennac (20 km).

La Rhue 46500 Rocamadour
Tel 65.33.71.50
Fax 65.33.72.48
Location in countryside, 55 km S of Brive La Gaillarde on N20 towards Cressenssac, then N140. Turn right 1 km before crossing with D673 (Racamadour-Padirac); with grounds and ample car parking
Meals breakfast
Prices rooms 370F-570F; breakfast 42F-65F

Rooms 11 double, one suite, several suitable for families, all with bath; all rooms have phone
Facilities sitting-room; swimming-pool
Credit cards MC, V
Children accepted
Disabled access easy
Pets accepted
Closed Nov to Easter
Proprietors Eric and Christine Jooris

The South-west

Les Vieilles Tours

This mellow country house does not have a blot-free record with readers – M. Zozzoli, an artist, does not always radiate bonhomie – but there is no doubt that the 'ayes' have it, for the moment. 'Delightful and extremely accommodating,' reports one visitor.

It is a beautifully restored stone building, dating from the 13th and 17th centuries, with its medieval atmosphere largely preserved. The dining-room is in the oldest part of the building, with rich pink and floral fabrics contrasting with the original stone walls, tiled floors and old timbers. The cosy sitting-room occupies the first floor of an interesting circular turret-wing. The views across open countryside are completely uninterrupted, giving a feeling of privacy and isolation to the spacious, attractively furnished rooms (most of them in a new but traditional-style building). Roger Zozzoli's paintings (for sale) are hung throughout the hotel. Madame cooks, making full use of local produce in her three dinner menus (one changing daily) – 'very good, excellently presented and good value,' says one report, but bear in mind that choice may be limited.

Nearby château; Moulin de Cougnaguet (10 km); Autoire (20 km) – village, mouth of Autoire Gorges; Carennac (20 km).

Lafage 46500 Rocamadour
Tel 65.33.68.01
Location in countryside 2.5km outside Rocamadour, on D673 to Payrac; with grounds and ample car parking
Meals breakfast, dinner; lunch by arrangement
Prices rooms 210F-450F; DB&B 250F-365F; breakfast 40F-60F, menus 110F-320F, children's 56F
Rooms 9 double, 9 family, 17 with bath, one with shower; all have phone; 10 rooms with TV
Facilities 2 sitting-rooms (one with TV), dining-room; swimming-pool
Credit cards MC, V
Children welcome
Disabled access easy
Pets accepted, but not in restaurant
Closed Nov to Easter
Proprietor M. and Mme Zozzoli

The South-west

La Pélissaria

Recent reports leave us in no doubt that the Matuchets' distinctive little hotel is as compelling as ever. And the chances of finding a room vacant have increased since they bought an old house next door to the main one, providing three additional large bedrooms (two double beds in each).

The 13th-century house clings to the steep hillside on the edge of the lovely medieval hilltop village of St-Cirq-Lapopie. It was lovingly restored by the Matuchets themselves, and its quirky character is such that you descend the stairs to the bedrooms, which look out on to the tiny garden and enjoy stunning views over the Lot valley. The bedrooms – two of them detached from the house, down the garden – are light, airy and comfortable, with close attention to detail in the furnishings.

Dinner, served in the elegant and intimate beamed dining-room (with roaring log fire on cold nights) is adventurous and delicious; Madame does all the cooking, so the choice of dishes is naturally limited. M. Matuchet is a musician, and tapes of his music provide a background to dinner. Breakfast is served al fresco or in your room if you prefer.

Nearby Pech-Merle caves and museum; Cahors (35 km).

St-Cirq-Lapopie 46330
Cabrerets
Tel 65.31.25.14
Fax 65.30.25.52
Location in village, 30 km E of Cahors; with garden; parking difficult
Meals breakfast, dinner
Prices rooms 400F-600F, suite 640F; breakfast 49F, dinner from 150F
Rooms 8 double, 6 with bath, 2 with shower (4 twin); 2 suites with bath; all rooms have phone, TV
Facilities dining-room, sitting-room; swimming-pool
Credit cards MC, V
Children welcome
Disabled one adapted bedroom
Pets accepted
Closed mid-Nov to Apr; restaurant only, Thu and Fri
Proprietor Marie-Françoise Matuchet

The South-west

Arcé

Oh dear. 'The car-park was full of GB plates,' commented one reporter, 'so we beat a hasty retreat.' Bad news for those who like to escape while on their travels, but not entirely surprising: we're not the only British guide to list this delightful hotel – now run by the fifth generation of the Arcé family – and it does not face a lot of competition, here in the Basque foothills of the Pyrenees.

The setting – by a river in a typical Basque village – is a magical one, best appreciated from the dining terrace, which juts out over the water and is sheltered by a canopy of chestnut trees. The food is almost as good as the view, featuring plenty of local specialities (game, fish) – though Michelin withdrew its star a year or two ago. Inside the shuttered building are spacious public rooms – a beamed sitting-room with assorted furniture and a brick fireplace, a library with books in all languages, and a smart dining-room with picture windows. Some of the bedrooms are impressively large, with an apartment-sized sitting area; others open on to small terraces with mountain views. There is a smart swimming-pool across the river.

Nearby walking, fishing, bicycling; Pyrenees; Spanish border; Atlantic coast – beaches.

64430 St-Etienne-de-Baïgorry
Tel 59.37.40.14
Fax 59.37.40.27
Location in village 10 km W of St-Jean Pied-de-Port; with garden and car parking
Meals breakfast, lunch, dinner, snacks
Prices rooms 380F-680F; suite 870F-1,030F; breakfast 47F, menus 110F-260F
Rooms 22 double, 1 single, 20 with bath, 3 with shower; 6 family rooms with bath; 1 suite; all rooms have central heating, phone, TV, hairdrier
Facilities dining- room, sitting-rooms, games room; terraces, swimming- pool, tennis court
Credit cards MC, V
Children welcome
Disabled no special facilities
Pets accepted
Closed mid-Nov to mid-Mar
Proprietor M. Arcé

The South-west

Hostellerie St-Jacques

The more we learn about the Babayous' enterprise, the more thoroughly impressed we are by their sure understanding of holiday-makers' needs and priorities.

The front of the creeper-clad 18thC building gives little clue to what lies within – or, more to the point, what lies behind: the Babayou's 'summer sitting-room', which consists of lovely sloping gardens, with masses of colourful flowers, a fair-sized pool, tennis court and plenty of shade and space for children. Inside there is an unusually large dining-room/bar decorated in fresh summery colours, with big windows which open on to the terrace above the garden. All the bedrooms are comfortable, spacious and attractively decorated; several can accommodate families.

The food is rich and varied; even the basic menu is probably enough to satisfy most appetites. A buffet breakfast/brunch is served in the garden or by the pool. Occasionally there are lively evenings with dancing and games, or communal dinners devoted to exploration of regional cuisine. Not your cup of tea? Just give it a try; you might be surprised.

Nearby Montbrun (15 km) – fortress; Brantôme (30 km) – monks' garden, château de Richemont; Rochechouart (45 km).

24470 Saint-Saud-en-Périgord
Tel 53.56.97.21
Fax 53.56.91.33
Location in quiet village, 30_km N of Brantôme; with garden and car parking
Meals breakfast/brunch, lunch, dinner
Prices rooms 300F-450F, suites 750F; DB&B 255F-285F; breakfast 45F, menus 115F-290F
Rooms 22 double (7 twin), 2 suites, all with bath or shower; all rooms have central heating, phone; 10 have TV and minibar
Facilities 2 dining-rooms, bar, TV room; swimming-pool, tennis **Credit cards** MC, V
Children very welcome
Disabled no special facilities
Pets accepted
Closed mid-Oct to Mar; restaurant closed to non-residents Sun dinner and Mon
Proprietor Jean-Pierre Babayou

The South-west

Hôtel Arraya

Do any of our readers ever visit this polished country house? We've had it in the guide since the first edition, but we have to rely on our own inspections to keep up to date with Paul Fagoaga's stewardship. Happily, our impressions are entirely favourable, but reports would be welcome.

With its timbered, white-painted houses, Sare can claim to be the prettiest of all the extremely pretty Basque villages. In the heart of the village, this 16thC house was once a hostel for pilgrims on their way across the Pyrenees to Santiago.

Behind the slightly severe frontage on the main square lies a country-style hotel of great character. The sitting-room, bar and dining-room – not to mention every nook and cranny on stairways or landings – are filled with glorious old Basque furniture; sofas and chairs are comfortable and inviting, and flowers are everywhere. There are more antiques in the individually decorated bedrooms (not especially spacious, but bright and beautiful); some look out over the fine garden. As if all this is not enough, the cooking is good and there is a particularly well-chosen wine list; and there is even a splendid Gâteau Basque.

Nearby Cog railway up La Rhune; Aïnhoa (10 km) – Basque village; Ascain (5 km) – Basque church; St-Jean-de-Luz (14 km).

64310 Sare
Tel 59.54.20.46
Fax 59.54.27.04
Location in middle of village, 14 km SE of St-Jean-de-Luz; with garden and ample public car parking (private parking nearby)
Meals breakfast, lunch, dinner
Prices rooms 385F-530F; breakfast 50F; menus 130F-195F
Rooms 20 double, 17 with bath, 3 with shower (14 twin); one single with shower; all rooms have central heating, phone; TV on request
Facilities sitting-room, bar, dining-room
Credit cards AE, MC, V
Children welcome; special menu available
Disabled no special facilities
Pets accepted in restaurant only
Closed Nov to Apr
Proprietor Paul Fagoaga

The South-west

Le Vieux Logis

We continue to list this glorious old hotel, for our money one of the most civilized in a region with many attractive hotels, despite the fact that (to judge by our postbag) precious few readers are inclined to pay its prices. (If you decide to treat yourself to a stay here, do let us have a report.)

The Giraudel-Destords have lived in this complex of farm and village houses for nearly 400 years. The part which is now the dining-room once held pigs and wine barrels. Now, all has been designer-decorated to produce comfort of a high degree. The bedrooms are particularly delightful: individually furnished and very cosy in a sophisticated rustic style, with fine materials and furniture; some have four-poster beds. Public rooms are elegant and comfortable, and there are plenty of quiet nooks; the small salon has an open fire, and there are fine antiques throughout. The galleried dining-room is very attractive, and looks out on to the green and flowery garden, where you can have breakfast. The classic and modern cooking of Pierre-Jean Duribreux is excellent (two *toques* from Gault-Millau).

Nearby Les Eyzies-de-Tayac (25 km) – National Prehistoric Museum; Monpazier (30 km) *bastide*; Beynac (30 km).

24510 Trémolat
Tel 53.22.80.06
Fax 53.22.84.89
Location in village 15 km SW of Le Bugue; with garden and private car parking
Meals breakfast, lunch, dinner
Prices rooms 720F-1,500F; breakfast 72F, menus 180F-370F, children's 85F
Rooms 24 double (13 twin), all with bath; all rooms have central heating, phone, TV, minibar
Facilities 2 dining-rooms, 3 sitting-rooms, bar, conference room, swimming-pool
Credit cards AE, DC, MC, V
Children welcome
Disabled one adapted room; easy access to dining-room
Pets welcome
Closed never
Proprietor M. Bernard Giraudel

The South-west

Riverside hotel, Beynac

Hôtel Bonnet

There is a new manager at the helm of this old roadside favourite, beside the Dordogne at the foot of a showpiece village, so we include it despite criticisms of worn-out beds and indifferent food. Look (and bounce) before you book, and let us know your conclusions.

■ 24220 Beynac (Dordogne) **Tel** 53.29.50.01 **Fax** 53.29.83.74
Meals brea kfast, lunch, dinner **Prices** rooms 210F-330F; breakfast 35F; menus 160F-198F **Rooms** 22, all with bath or shower, **Credit cards** AE, DC, MC, V **Closed** end-Oct to 5 Apr

---

Village hotel, Carennac

Hostellerie Fénelon

This jolly-looking Logis – all red roofs and window boxes – in a lovely old village comes strongly recommended for Mme Raynal's warm welcome, the friendly and unobtrusive service of her staff, the 'very good home-style' cooking and the excellent value for money. There is a small pool with tables around it, and another terrace for dining.

■ 46110 Carennac (Lot) **Tel** 65.10.96.46 **Fax** 65.10.94.86
Meals breakfa st, lunch, dinner **Prices** rooms 280F-300F; breakfast 40F; DB&B 290F-310F; menus 88F-300F **Rooms** 16, all with bath or shower, central heating, phone, TV **Credit cards** MC, V **Closed** early Jan to mid-Mar

---

Town hotel, Condom

Hôtel des Trois Lys

Jeannette Manet will welcome you warmly to her lovely 17thC house, with its sandy stone walls and white shutters, and restrained elegant decoration within. The bedrooms are spacious and smart, with tasteful antique or reproduction furniture and fresh flowers. Swimming-pool.

■ 38 Rue Gambetta, 32100 Condom (Gers) **Tel** 62.28.33.33
Fax 62.28.41.85 **Meals** breakfast **Prices** rooms 260F-550F; breakfast 40F
Rooms 10, all with bath or shower, central heating, phone, TV, hairdrier
Credit cards AE, MC, V **Closed** Feb

Village inn, Dégagnac

Auberge sans Frontière

The recent proprietors of this simple auberge offer a 'professional but sincere' welcome, says our latest reporter. It is an integral part of sleepy Dégagnac, and not at all touristy – the dining-rooms also serve as a bar and sitting-room. Bedrooms are small-ish but comfortable and inviting. The food offers 'superb' value.

■ Dégagnac, 46340 Salviac (Lot) **Tel** 65.41.52.88 **Meals** breakfast, lunch, dinner **Prices** DB&B 220F-240F; menus 55F-135F **Rooms** 8, all with central heating **Credit cards** MC, V **Closed** never

The South-west

Village hotel, Domme

Hôtel de l'Esplanade

In a busy tourist village with splendid views over the Dordogne, this three-fireplace Logis is well furnished with taste and flair. Housekeeping is immaculate, service efficient – and particularly praised by a visitor who needed medical attention. Some bedrooms in annexes. Michelin-starred cuisine. Difficult car parking.

■ 24250 Domme (Dordogne) **Tel** 53.28.31.41 **Fax** 53.28.49.92
Meals breakfast, lunch, dinner **Prices** rooms 300F-590F; breakfast 50F, menus 160F-350F **Rooms** 25, all with bath or shower, central heating, phone, TV, hairdrier **Credit cards** AE, MC, V **Closed** Nov to mid-Feb; restaurant only, Mon and Sun dinner out of season

---

Village hotel, Escos

Relais des Voyageurs

This former presbytery – its pretty flower-filled garden used to be the cemetery of the next-door church – has been sy mpathetically converted. Some of the bedrooms are cramped – but the best are spacious and the dining-room is light and warm. 'We liked the informal atmosphere,' enthuse recent visitors.

■ Place de l'Église, 64270 Escos (Pyrénées-Atlantiques) **Tel** 59.38.42.39
Meals breakfast, lunch, dinner **Prices** rooms 110F-230F; menus 60F-150F **Rooms** 8, all with bath or shower, central heating, phone **Credit cards** MC, V **Closed** never

---

Converted mill, Les Eyzies-de-Tayac

Moulin de la Beune

This little mill on the bank of the river Beune is a peaceful place to stay, despite the bustle of the town. Bedrooms are excellent, with bright colour schemes. There's a simple breakfast room and an inviting restaurant ('very good value') in another mill building in the garden.

■ 24620 Les Eyzies-de-Tayac (Dordogne) **Tel** 53.06.94.33
Fax 53.06.98.06 **Meals** breakfast, lunch, dinner **Prices** rooms 260F, DB&B 320F; breakfast 40F, menus 85F-315F **Rooms** 20, all with bath or shower, central heating, phone **Credit cards** AE, MC, V **Closed** Nov to Mar; Tue lunch

---

Village hotel, Gluges

Hôtel les Falaises

This good-value family-run Logis enjoys an enviable position – huddled below a fine cliff, on the edge of a tiny medieval village beside the Dordogne – with a restful garden. Bedrooms are simple, light and well decorated.

■ Gluges, 46600 Martel (Lot) **Tel** 65.37.33.59 **Fax** 65.37.34.19
Meals breakfast, lunch, dinner **Prices** rooms 215F-305F **Rooms** 15, all with bath or shower, central heating, phone **Credit cards** MC, V **Closed** Dec to Feb

The South-west

Restaurant with rooms, Hossegor

Les Huitrières du Lac

Primarily a restaurant, specializing (as you might expect) in fish and seafood – though there are alternatives. The large dining-room and the best bedrooms share a view over the adjacent lake. Bedrooms are plain but spacious; some have balconies. Pleasant setting, good value.

■ 1187 Ave du Touring Club, 40150 Hossegor (Landes) **Tel** 58.43.51.48 **Fax** 58.41.73.11 **Meals** breakfast, lunch, dinner **Prices** rooms 300F-400F, DB&B 390F-490F; menus 95F-135F **Rooms** 9, all with bath, central heating, phone **Credit cards** AE, MC, V **Closed** Jan to early Feb

Riverside hotel, Lacave

Hôtel du Pont de l'Ouysse

The *raison d'etre* of this peaceful, small auberge is its stunning dining terrace overlooking the river, shaded by trees . The cooking makes use of local produce, including eel from the Ouysse. Prettily decorated rooms, smart new swimming-pool.

■ Lacave, 46200 Souillac (Lot) **Tel** 65.37.87.04 **Fax** 65.32.77.41 **Meals** breakfast, lunch, dinner **Prices** rooms 400F-700F; breakfast 60F, menus from 150F **Rooms** 12, all with bath, phone, TV **Credit cards** V **Closed** mid-Nov to end Feb

Riverside hotel, Lalinde

Le Château

His reputation for cooking established, Guy Gensou has turned to the building – an extraordinary little turreted affair, perched above the Dordogne; bedrooms and bathrooms have been refurbished and a cosy new sitting area designed. 'Service personal, friendly and welcoming' enthuses a recent visitor.

■ Rue de Verdun, 24150 Lalinde (Dordogne) **Tel** 53.61.01.82 **Fax** 53.24.74.60 **Meals** breakfast, lunch, dinner **Prices** rooms 350F-850F, demi-pension obligatory in high season 450F-700F; breakfast 60F, menus 160F-320F **Rooms** 7, all with bath or shower, phone, TV **Credit cards** MC, V **Closed** Jan; Mon out of season, Mon lunch Jul and Aug

Country inn, Lestelle-Bétharram

Le Vieux Logis

Smart modern additions have taken this thriving hotel in the foothills of the Pyrenees out of our normal size range. But the garden and pool are still very attractive, the cooking is well above average and the rooms are a bargain, even if they do lack character. Accommodation is in the main hotel or in wooden chalets dotted about the garden.

■ Rte des Grottes, 64800 Lestelle-Bétharram (Pyrénées-Atlantiques) **Tel** 59.71.94.87 **Meals** breakfast, lunch, dinner **Prices** rooms 210F-270F; menus 90F-200F **Rooms** 40, all with bath or shower, central heating, phone, TV **Credit cards** AE, MC, V **Closed** mid-Jan to Feb

The South-west

Country hotel, Montfort-en-Chalosse

Aux Tauzins

A reader's firm recommendation brings this three-fireplace Logis into the guide. With white walls, green shutters and low-pitched tiled roof, the building is typical of the area. The large dining-room has excellent country views, and many of the bedrooms have balconies. 'Friendly, efficient service, excellent food.' Pool and mini-golf.

■ 40380 Montfort-en-Chalosse (Landes) **Tel** 58.98.60.22 **Fax** 58.98.45.79 **Meals** breakfast, lunch, dinner **Prices** rooms 210F-260F; breakfast 30F, menus 95F-140F **Rooms** 16, all with bath or shower, central heating, phone, TV **Credit cards** MC, V **Closed** first 2 weeks Oct, last 3 weeks Jan

---

Village hotel, Plaisance

Le Ripa Alta

'Booked for one night, stayed for three,' says a report on this simple hotel. It revolves around the restaurant and the superb cooking of the 'hugely entertaining' Maurice Coscuella. Excellent breakfasts.

■ 3 Place de l'Eglise, 32160 Plaisance (Gers) **Tel** 62.69.30.43 **Fax** 62.69.36.99 **Meals** breakfast, lunch, dinner **Prices** rooms 170F-460F; breakfast 32F, menus 75F-275F, children's 50F **Rooms** 13, all with bath or shower, central heating, phone; most have TV **Credit cards** AE, DC, MC, V **Closed** Nov

---

Converted mill, Poudenas

Auberge à la Belle Gasconne

A detour to this pretty village to sample Marie-Claude Garcia's splendid cooking is highly recommended. The cosy bedrooms are in the lovingly converted 14thC watermill next door to her miller's house, jutting out into the Gélise river and there is a romantic terrace and a large garden. Swimming pool.

■ 47170 Poudenas (Lot-et-Garonne) **Tel** 53.65.71.58 **Fax** 53.65.87.39 **Meals** breakfast, lunch, dinner **Prices** rooms 500F-630F; breakfast 55F, menus 140F-280F **Rooms** 7, all with bath or shower, central heating, phone **Credit cards** AE, DC, MC, V **Closed** Jan and Feb; Sun evening and Mon except Jul to Sep

---

Village hotel, Puymirol

Les Loges de l'Aubergade

The Agenais is not noted for its gastronomic highlights; but Michel Trama's cooking – and especially his patisserie – is among the best in France. The 10 spacious bedrooms are highly individual, in a restrained modern Italian style.

■ 52 Rue Royale, 47270 Puymirol (Lot-et-Garonne) **Tel** 53.95.31.46 **Meals** breakfast, lunch, dinner **Prices** rooms 750F-1,450F; menus from 280F **Rooms** 10, all with bath or shower, central heating, air-conditioning, phone, TV **Credit cards** AE, DC, V **Closed** 2 weeks in Feb; restaurant only, Mon out of season.

The South-west

La Petite Auberge

Opened by its English owners in 1990, but run in a thoroughly French style, this converted farm – set in tranquil open countryside south of Bergerac – retains an informal 'family' atmosphere and is popular with foreign visitors and locals alike. Comfortable bedrooms. Outdoor giant chess set, swimming-pool.

■ 24500 Razac d'Eymet (Dordogne) **Tel** 53.24.69.27 **Fax** 53.27.33.55 **Meals** breakfast, lunch, dinner **Prices** rooms 180F-450F; breakfast 32F, menus 70F-200F **Rooms** 7, all with heating, phone; 2 two-bedroomed apartments **Credit cards** MC, V **Closed** restaurant only Sun and Mon

---

Hôtel de France

A classic two-fireplace Logis de France – an old flower-decked inn at the heart of a bustling market town, with a pretty and warmly inviting restaurant and modest but spacious bedrooms which can accommodate families, offering excellent value.

■ 3 Rue Marc Dufraisse, 24600 Ribérac (Dordogne) **Tel** 53.90.00.61 **Fax** 53.91.06.05 **Meals** breakfast, lunch, dinner **Prices** rooms 170F-265F; breakfast 28F, menus 68F-160F **Rooms** 20, all with bath or shower, phone **Credit cards** MC, V **Closed** never

---

Auberge des Pins

An excellent example of unpretentious French hotelkeeping – a three-fireplace Logis in a chalet-style building offering satisfactory accommodation and food in well-cared-for surroundings at moderate prices. The restaurant caters as much to locals as to travellers.

■ Route de la Piscine, 40630 Sabres (Landes) **Tel** 58.07.50.47 **Fax** 58.07.56.74 **Meals** breakfast, lunch, dinner **Prices** rooms 180F-650F; menus 100F-350F **Rooms** 24, all with bath or shower, central heating, phone, cable TV **Credit cards** AE, V **Closed** Jan

---

Auberge du Sombral

Despite Madame's cool reception, there is a lot to like about this beautifully restored house in the heart of a lovely medieval village. Excellent food is served in the elegantly rustic dining-room, and housekeeping is excellent – bedrooms are freshly decorated, though some are on the small side.

St-Cirq-Lapopie, 46330 Cabrerets (Lot) **Tel** 65.31.26.08 **Fax** 65.30.26.37 **Meals** breakfast, lunch, dinner **Prices** rooms 300F-350F; breakfast 45F; menus 80F-230F **Rooms** 8 all with bath or shower, phone **Credit cards** MC, V **Closed** mid-Nov to Mar; restaurant only, Tues eve and Wed, except in school holidays

The South-west

L'Abbaye

There is a captivating atmosphere about this friendly, constantly improving hotel. In the rustic, stone-flagged sitting-room you can see the old pastry oven and potager. The best bedrooms (first floor of newer annexe) are spacious and very attractive.

■ 24220 St-Cyprien (Dordogne) **Tel** 53.29.20.48 **Fax** 53.29.15.85 **Meals** breakfast, lunch, dinner **Prices** rooms 360F-680F; menus 140F-320F **Rooms** 24, all with bath or shower, phone **Credit cards** AE, MC, V **Closed** mid-Oct to Apr

---

Hostellerie de Plaisance

'Delighted to confirm your recommendation,' says a reader of this converted monastery, superbly positioned in the middle of St-Émilion – on top of a small cliff with captivating views, not least from the plush dining-room. Bedrooms are smart and comfortable. Good food, with a 'particularly good-value' three-course menu.

■ Place du Clocher, 33330 St-Émilion (Gironde) **Tel** 57.24.72.32 **Fax** 57.74.41.11 **Meals** breakfast, lunch, dinner **Prices** rooms 500F-790F, suites 1,350F; breakfast 56F, menus 140F-270F **Rooms** 12, all with bath, central heating, phone; most have air-conditioning **Credit cards** AE, DC, MC, V **Closed** Jan

---

Auberge du Poids Public

This thoroughly well run inn offers impressive views in all directions over the rolling uplands of the Lauragais. The dining-room is rustic and jolly; the bedrooms are rather grander in style. 'Food delicious, staff most helpful,' enthuses a visitor.

■ 31540 St-Félix-Lauragais (Haute-Garonne) **Tel** 61.83.00.20 **Fax** 61.83.86.21 **Meals** breakfast, lunch, dinner **Prices** rooms 250F-300F; menus 130F-305F **Rooms** 13, all with bath or shower, central heating, phone, TV, minibar **Credit cards** AE, V **Closed** Jan; Sun evening out of season

---

La Fayette

This little family-run hotel occupies a prime spot in the pedestrianised heart of the animated port and resort of St-Jean. The building is in Dutch style, all arches and red brick, and it has a street terrace for outside meals. Small, simple but cheerful bedrooms.

■ 18-20 Rue de la République, 64500 St-Jean-de-Luz (Pyrénées-Atlantiques) **Tel** 59.26.17.74 **Fax** 59.51.11.78 **Meals** breakfast, lunch, dinner **Prices** rooms 200F-350F; DB&B 450F **Rooms** 18, all with central heating, phone, TV **Credit cards** AE, DC, MC, V **Closed** never

The South-west

Hostellerie de Meysset

'Splendid room, very good food, pleasant owners, good views,' ran the reader's report that introduced this creeper-covered, typically Perigordian country house last year. Its style is traditional and unpretentious, though without floral excesses. The food leans towards traditional regional elements, too.

■ Rte des Eyzies, 24200 Sarlat (Dordogne) **Tel** 53.59.08.29 **Fax** 53.28.47.61 **Meals** breakfast, lunch, dinner **Prices** rooms 320F-450F; suites 580F-700F breakfast 45F, menus 145F-250F **Rooms** 26, all with bath or shower, phone **Credit cards** AE, DC, MC, V **Closed** Wed lunch; end Sep to end Apr

---

Château de Commarque

We get increasingly enthusiastic reports on this solid house, run by an English couple, with simple but comfortable self-contained apartments in the stables, grouped around a 'delightful' courtyard. Food is consistently rated 'excellent', and reasonably priced.

■ Sauternes, 33210 Langon (Gironde) **Tel** 56.76.65.94 **Fax** 56.76.64.30 **Meals** breakfast, lunch, dinner **Prices** rooms 180F-370F; menus 75F-175F **Rooms** 10, all with shower, central heating **Credit cards** MC, V **Closed** Feb; restaurant only, Wed out of season

---

La Bergerie

Mme Clavier has made her immaculate whitewashed house – built in southern single-storey style – a calm and civilized haven where the slow pace of life is infectious. The (obligatory) set dinner is based on whatever is fresh and good at the time. The bedrooms look on to the neat gardens.

■ Ave du Lac, 40140 Soustons (Landes) **Tel** 58.41.11.43 **Meals** breakfast, dinner **Prices** rooms 260F-380F; DB&B 360F-400F **Rooms** 12, all with bath, central heating, phone **Credit cards** DC, MC, V **Closed** Nov to Mar

---

La Source Bleue

An enthusiastic reader persuades us to restore this old paper-mill, to the guide. The beautiful and peaceful position beside the Lot remains a key attraction, and the rustic dining-room and the best of the bedrooms are charming. Pool. More reports, please.

■ Moulin de Leygues, Touzac, 46700 Puy-l'Evêque (Lot) **Tel** 65.36.52.01 **Fax** 65.24.65 .69 **Meals** breakfast, lunch, dinner **Prices** rooms 285F-450; breakfast 35F, menus 105F-220F **Rooms** 16, all with bath, central heating, phone; some have TV **Credit cards** AE, MC, V **Closed** Jan to Mar; resta urant only, Wed lunch

The South-west

Medieval manor, Vézac

Manoir de Rochecourbe

Every year we half-expect to hear that the elderly M. and Mme Roger have closed the doors of their rustic manor-house, which has been in the family for generations. Now we learn the good news that their son has taken over. A round tower housing the staircase gives the house a touch of grandeur, and the great beams and massive fireplaces inside do not disappoint.

■ Vézac, 24220 St-Cyprien (Dordogne) **Tel** 53.31.09.84 **Fax** 53.28.59.07 **Meals** breakfast **Prices** rooms 240F-550F; breakfast 45F **Rooms** 6, all with bath or shower, central heating, phone **Credit cards** AE, DC, MC, V **Closed** Dec to Apr

Château hotel, Vieux-Mareuil

Château de Vieux Mareuil

Behind the thick, ivy-clad stone walls of this 15thC fortified house lies a stylish little hotel, prettily decorated with plenty of attention to detail. Spacious bedrooms, home-like sitting-room, acres of parkland to explore. Well above-average food and outside dining. Pool. Reports welcome.

■ Route Angoulème-Périgueux, 24340 Vieux-Mareuil (Dordogne) **Tel** 53.60.77.15 **Fax** 53.56.49.33 **Meals** breakfast, lunch, dinner **Prices** rooms 600F-1,000F; breakfast 60F, menus 130F-300F **Rooms** 14, all with bath, central heating, phone, TV, hairdrier **Credit cards** AE, MC, V **Closed** end Oct to Apr; Mon, Sun dinner out of season

Massif Central

Area introduction

For many British visitors, the Massif is 'unknown France' – the high, remote area between Périgord on the west and the Rhône valley on the east. For guidebook purposes, it is a rather problematic region, particularly if (like all our regions) it is defined in terms of *départements*. The points where you might consider the physical Massif to begin and end don't always coincide happily with governmental boundaries (the *département* of Ardèche, for example, falls in our South of France region, but includes territory that is physically very much part of the Massif).

There is also a good case for considering this as 'unspoilt France'. Of course, tourism has had an impact, but it is slight compared with the impact on the much better-known areas to the west, east, north and south. There are bargains to be found as a result.

Boisset, Auberge de Concasty 71.62.21.16 Jolly little converted farmhouse with pool in grassy garden; country cooking.
Champagnac, Château de Lavendès 71.69.62.79 Simple but satisfactory Logis in countryside; basic pool.
Conques, Hostellerie de l'Abbaye 65.72.80.30 Comfortably furnished ancient house with beautiful country views.
Meyrueis, Château d'Ayres 66.45.60.10 Shuttered medieval house in leafy grounds with pool.

Reporting to the guide

We're very keen to hear from readers about their hotel-going experiences. We can't visit every hotel in the guide every year; even if we could, we wouldn't be staying in them all. And it's only when you stay in a place that you find out how the plumbing deals with the demand for hot water, what that much-vaunted 70F breakfast is really like, and what happens when you request something extraordinary like an extra pillow. So please do let us know how you get on next time you're travelling in France.

In particular, please do write when you like a small hotel, whether or not you've chosen it with our help. People are pretty good at letting us know when we've got a place wrong (usually, we hope, because the place has gone downhill). Places that come up to expectations don't always trigger a reaction.

It doesn't have to be a detailed, feature by feature description of the hotel (though highly detailed reports are always very welcome). The key thing is to let us know what you felt about the place, as a customer. We've suggested a structure for readers' reports on page 11, but you certainly don't have to stick to that; if you'd find it easier to dash off a few lines in whatever order they come to mind, please do just that.

Massif Central

Manor house hotel, Castelpers

Château de Castelpers

If our calculations are correct, Yolande Tapié de Celeyran has now been at the helm (and the stove) of this family-home-turned-hotel for more than 30 years – and she shows no sign of weakening. Her house makes a relaxing retreat. It dates from the 17th century and ranges from the purely rustic to the Gothic in style, with a tower, arched windows and rooms of character furnished comfortably with antiques. But it is not a château hotel in the grand manner; families can feel at ease, with swings and spacious lawns (dotted with ancient trees) for children to play on and trout streams to explore, and prices that reflect the modest size of some of the bedrooms. Good food, served in front of an open fire in winter. More reports would be very welcome.

Nearby Château du Bosc (10 km); Sauveterre-de-Rouergue (20 km).

Castelpers 12170 Requista
Tel 65.69.22.61
Fax 65.69.25.31
Location in countryside 9 km SE of RN88, 10 km S of Naucelle; in wooded park with private car parking
Meals breakfast, lunch, dinner
Prices rooms 285F-485F; menu 135F
Rooms 6 double (4 twin), 2 family rooms; 3 with bath, 5 with shower; all rooms have phone, 5 have TV
Facilities sitting-room, 2 dining-rooms; fishing
Credit cards AE, MC, V
Children welcome if well behaved **Disabled** one specially equipped ground-floor bedroom **Pets** accepted, but not in dining-room
Closed Oct to Mar; restaurant occasional evening or days only
Proprietor Mme de Saint Palais

Massif Central

Hôtel Sainte-Foy

Promotion to a full entry was long overdue for this delectable hotel in a lovely old village; as it is, we are somewhat behind the French tourist authorities, who in 1993 promoted the Sainte-Foy to four-star status – the first hotel in Aveyron to achieve the rating. Marie-France and Alain Garcenot, proprietors since they took over from an aunt in 1987, are justifiably proud of their achievement, but the facilities that are required for star-ratings are not the basis of the hotel's appeal.

Hôtel Sainte-Foy is a lovingly restored, partly timbered old house which takes its name from the great abbey church directly opposite. The house has been beautifully furnished with close attention to detail and to the character of the building. The warm glow of wood is everywhere. The large two-part sitting-room is particularly well furnished with antiques. Bedrooms are highly individual, tasteful and large, with views either over the church or the flowery courtyard garden. You can dine here or in the intimate but pleasantly spacious rooms inside. The increasingly inventive cooking (daily changing menus) gets good reviews.

Nearby Church of Ste-Foy (remarkable tympanum and treasury).

Conques 12320 St-Cyprien-sur-Dourdou
Tel 65.69.84.03
Fax 65.72.81.04
Location in heart of village, 40 km N of Rodez; with private car parking
Meals breakfast, lunch, dinner
Prices rooms 450F-1,100F; breakfast 58F; menus 160F-330F; lunch 100F
Rooms 15 double (10 twins), 2 single, all with bath; all rooms have central heating, phone
Facilities 3 dining-rooms, sitting-room, bar, interior patio, conference room; 2 terraces; exercise room
Credit cards AE, MC, V
Children accepted
Disabled no special facilities
Pets accepted
Closed end Oct to Easter
Proprietors Marie-France and Alain Garcenot

Massif Central

Le Grand Écuyer

One reporter reckons that the cooking of Yves Thuriès is less impressive than it was a few years ago. But he still gets a star from Michelin and two *toques* from Gault-Millau, and the other attractions of this ancient hunting lodge in the glorious medieval village of Cordes are undiminished.

Le Grand Écuyer is a classified historic monument, transformed into a comfortable, elegant and atmospheric hotel. The dining-room is medieval in style, with old stone walls and tiled floors, dark beamed ceiling, old prints and so on, blending well with the lacy white table-cloths, shining silver, painted plates and tapestry chairs. The sitting-room and 'rather gloomy' bar are more domestic, with deeply upholstered armchairs, low tables and potted plants. Bedrooms (varying in size) are inviting – beamed ceilings, monumental stone fireplaces, rugs on expanses of polished floor – and are beautifully furnished with antiques. Bathrooms are modern. M. Thuriès and his friendly staff ensure that a graciously informal atmosphere prevails.

Nearby Rue Droite (14thC houses); Fôret Grésigne (15 km) – marked trails; Albi – *la ville rouge.*

Rue Voltaire 81170 Cordes
Tel 63.56.01.03
Fax 63.56.18.83
Location in middle of village, 25 km NW of Albi; with public car parking nearby
Meals breakfast, lunch, dinner
Prices rooms 600F-850F, suite 1,400F; menus 170F-360F
Rooms 12 double, one suite, all with bath; all rooms have central heating, phone, radio
Facilities 2 dining-rooms, breakfast room, sitting-room, bar
Credit cards DC, MC, V
Children accepted
Disabled no special facilities
Pets accepted
Closed Nov to Easter
Proprietor Yves Thuriès

Massif Central

Country hotel, Coulandon

Le Chalet

Reviewing the entry of this Logis deep in the Bourbonnais countryside always raises an editorial smile, and not only because of the proprietor's name. We first visited it on a summer evening when its secluded, wooded garden (park-like in style) seemed idyllic; the big fish pond was perfect for strolling around, drink in hand, before pausing a while on the little raised terrace and then proceeding in to dinner.

It's a modest, traditional place. Rooms (in the chalet-style building itself, and in converted outbuildings) vary in style and size; none is notably stylish, but the best are cheerfully comfortable (with exposed beams and bright wallpaper). There are regional specialities in the traditional-style dining-room, and the service is amiable.

Nearby Moulins – timbered houses, cathedral.

03000 Coulandon
Tel 70.44.50.08
Fax 70.44.07.09
Location in countryside 6 km W of Moulins, off D945; with large grounds and ample car parking
Meals breakfast, lunch, dinner
Prices rooms 290F-460F; breakfast 45F, menus 110F-230F
Rooms 19 double, 5 with bath, 14 with shower (5 twin);
9 family rooms, 6 with bath, 3 with shower; all rooms have central heating, phone, TV
Facilities dining-room, sitting-room; fishing, swimming-pool
Credit cards AE, DC, MC, V
Children accepted
Disabled 6 ground-floor bedrooms
Pets accepted
Closed mid-Dec to end Jan
Proprietor M. H. Hulot

Massif Central

Demeure de Flore

A new shop, *L'Insolite*, selling antiques, has been added to this exceptionally charming hotel, in the foothills of the mountains of Haut-Languedoc. It was opened by Monike and Jean-Marie Tronc in 1992, and they have created something close to our ideal hotel. Their 19th-century *maison de maitre* may be an undistinguished building, but it sits prettily in a mature, wooded *jardin anglais*, far enough from the passing RN112 to feel quite secluded. And within, there is a delightful ambience. None of your traditional French clashes of patterns here: stylish floral prints are set against warm, plain backgrounds. The house has lots of floor-to-ceiling windows, and the general effect is light and fresh. Carefully chosen antiques and ornaments give the feel of a lived-in but cared-for family home. The eight bedrooms are individually furnished in the same careful way.

In good weather meals are served out on the terrace, and 'a bite of lunch' can be had by the smart little pool. We haven't tried the food – *cuisine 'maison bourgeoise'*, says Monike – so reports on this entry would be particularly welcome. **Nearby** Castres (35 km), Albi (60 km), Toulouse (100 km); Mediterranean beaches within reach.

106 Route Nationale, 81240 Lacabarede
Tel 63.98.32.32
Fax 63.98.47.56
Location opposite service station on outskirts of village on RN 112 between St-Pons and Mazamet; in gardens with ample car parking
Meals breakfast, lunch, dinner
Prices rooms 400F-500F; breakfast 54F, menus 100F-150F

Rooms 10 double, one suite, all with bath; all rooms have central heating, phone, TV, hairdrier
Facilities sitting-room, dining-room; swimming-pool
Credit cards MC, V
Children accepted
Disabled one adapted room
Pets not accepted except by special arrangement
Closed Feb
Proprietor Monike Flore Tronc

Massif Central

Farmhouse hotel, Moudeyres

Le Pré Bossu

This remote little place prompts more reports from readers than just about anywhere else in the guide – and they tell different stories. 'Absolutely delightful', says one; 'over-rated', another. A common reservation is an occasional lack of warmth, physical and metaphorical. But the latest is wholehearted: 'Excellent; comfortable; food outstanding and beautifully served; worth every franc – we will go again.'

Moudeyres is a remote village high (1,200 metres) in the volcanic Mézenc massif, surrounded by fields of wild flowers (in the spring) and mushrooms (in the autumn). The village consists of thatched rough-stone houses, many beautifully restored. The Pré Bossu is no exception, although it was built as recently as 1969, with old materials. The Flemish owners have worked hard to create an attractive and comfortable house. Starting with beams, wood floors and ingle-nook fireplace, they have added fine antique dressers, lace curtains, wild flowers, plants and books. It is all fresh and well-kept. Bedrooms are rustic, too – clean and simple, with good shower rooms; tranquillity is assured. Food is ambitious and reliable, earning a Michelin star.

Nearby Restored 18thC farm; Le Puy – volcanic rock formations.

43150 Moudeyres
Tel 71.05.10.70
Fax 71.05.10.21
Location on edge of village, 25 km SE of Le Puy, beyond Laussonne; in garden, with ample car parking
Meals breakfast, lunch, dinner
Prices rooms 350F-480F; breakfast 55F, menus 165F-360F
Rooms 10 double, 5 with bath, 5 with shower (4 twin); one family room; all rooms have central heating, phone
Facilities bar, TV room, dining-room
Credit cards AE, MC, V
Children accepted
Disabled no special facilities
Pets accepted in bedrooms, but not in dining-room
Closed mid-Nov to Easter
Proprietor Carlos Grootaert

Massif Central

Longcol

This splendid turreted medieval farmhouse is immersed in woods a few miles from Najac. 'Farming hamlet' might be a more accurate description, since the hotel consists of multiple stone buildings, mostly grouped around the central swimming-pool and all equipped with distinctive bell-shaped slate roofs and neat small-paned windows.

The *long col* is a loop in the river Aveyron, which meanders through gorges below this secluded spot. The Luyckx family bought the original farm in 1982, and spent six years restoring it before opening for business. Since then they have gone from strength to strength, doubling the number of rooms without altering the atmosphere of a polished but welcoming home. They are keen antique collectors, and it shows; the low-beamed rooms are full of beautiful pieces of furniture, tapestries and Asian artefacts. Bedrooms are equally original and comfortable, but vary in size. Meals are served in the light, airy dining-room, or on the little walled terrace in summer – or by the angular swimming-pool, which shares the woody views. Food is taken seriously, and there is an excellent wine list.

Nearby Najac – medieval houses and castle.

La Fouillade 12270 Najac
Tel 65.29.63.36
Fax 65.29.64.28
Location in large wooded grounds NW of village, NE of Najac; with garden and car parking
Meals breakfast, lunch, dinner
Prices rooms 550F-800F; meals 125F-290F
Rooms 17 double, 15 with bath, 2 with shower; all rooms have central heating, phone, TV, radio, minibar
Facilities dining-room, sitting-room, billiard room, terrace; swimming-pool, tennis court
Credit cards AE, V
Children welcome; baby-sitting available
Disabled no special facilities
Pets welcome
Closed mid-Nov to Easter; restaurant only, Tue out of season
Proprietors Luyckx family

Massif Central

Hôtel du Midi-Papillon

Every year we receive a long hand-written bulletin from Jean-Michel Papillon, the fourth generation of Papillons to run this lovable old post inn, spelling out the latest improvements. And practically every year we receive enthusiastic reports, underlining the fact that the essential appeal of the place is unchanged. Readers say 'wonderful' food, 'faultless' welcome, 'outstanding' value.

The Midi is the rural Logis at its best: a village inn amid grand countryside, offering welcoming rooms (of varying sizes) and excellent food at irresistible prices. It is very much a family-run place, with Mme overseeing the dining-room while Jean-Michel cooks. Vegetables come from the garden, poultry is home-raised, jams and croissants home-made.

The dining-room is divided into three sections, so that although the Papillon family try to accommodate their diners as fairly as possible, some will have the pleasure of dining on the terrace with a splendid river view, while others may find themselves in the intimate *salon* with leather furniture. Perhaps worth expressing a preference.

Nearby Gorges de la Dourbie (10 km); Montpellier-le-Vieux.

12230 St-Jean-du-Bruel
Tel 65.62.26.04
Fax 65.62.12.97
Location by river, in village on D991, 40 km SE of Millau; with garden and garages
Meals breakfast, lunch, dinner
Prices rooms 79F-195F; menus 72F-197F
Rooms 12 double, 8 with bath (3 twin); 2 single; 5 family rooms, 3 with bath, 2 with shower; all rooms have central heating, phone
Facilities 3 dining-rooms, bar, sitting-room, TV room; swimming-pool, jacuzzi
Credit cards MC, V
Children welcome; special menus available
Disabled access to dining-room only
Pets accepted
Closed mid-Nov to Easter
Proprietors Papillon familly

Massif Central

Manor house hotel, St-Martin-Valmeroux

Hostellerie de la Maronne

This 19th-century country house, set in a beautiful peaceful valley in the Auvergne, has had its critics in the past but these days earns nothing but praise from readers. Or nearly so: our latest reporter notes that the place has quite a formal air, but this is more to do with the elegant style of furnishing than the style of operation – she also commends the owners and staff as 'very welcoming and friendly.'

With its small modern swimming-pool and tennis court surrounded by lovely gardens and sweeping countryside, the *hostellerie* makes a fine retreat whether you are in search of peace or of outdoor exercise. Much has changed during Alain de Cock's tenure: a smart dining-room has been built into the hillside, other public areas have been attractively refurbished, newly built bedrooms have replaced the least attractive of the old ones, and others have been remodelled.

Food is taken seriously, with 'excellent' results. There is now a range of menus (reaching up to *gastronomique* levels), each offering no choice, as well as a reasonable *carte*. The wine list is quite wide-ranging. Gault-Millau awards a *toque*.

Nearby Salers (10 km); Anjony (20 km) – château.

Le Theil 15140 St-Martin-Valmeroux
Tel 71.69.20.33
Fax 71.69.28.22
Location in countryside 3 km E of St-Martin, on D37; with gardens, ample car parking
Meals breakfast, lunch, dinner
Prices rooms 350F-550F; DB&B 355F-455F; breakfast 40F-50F; menu 140F-300F
Rooms 21 double, all with bath; all rooms have central heating, phone, minibar; 10 have balcony or terrace
Facilities dining-room, sitting-room, breakfast room, seminar room; swimming-pool, tennis, *pétanque*, sauna, garden
Credit cards MC, V
Children welcome; baby-sitting by arrangement
Disabled lift/elevator
Pets accepted but not in dining-room
Closed Nov to Mar
Proprietor Alain de Cock

Massif Central

Riverside hotel, St-Sernin-sur-Rance

Hôtel Carayon

'Excellent,' is all our latest reporter says of this thriving three-fire-place Logis in a handsome medieval village in hilly countryside not far from the Tarn (of which the Rance is a tributary). Nothing much has changed chez Carayon, evidently.

The hotel (once called the France but, after a century in the same hands, now known by the family name) is a white-painted, shuttered building with café tables in front; most of the rooms are in a smart modern extension. The hotel enjoys a lovely view over the valley of the Rance (shared by the restaurant and its terrace, and many of the rooms), the welcome is warm and – not least – Pierre Carayon's cooking is excellent. What is more, the menu prices are modest, earning a prized red *repas* rating from Michelin. The reputation of the Carayon is for good honest regional fare, fresh ingredients and large portions – nothing *nouvelle* about it. The Carayons are an attractive and friendly couple (Pierre speaks good English, having worked in London). **Nearby** Vallée du Tarn (20 km); Monts de Lacaune (30 km).

Place du Fort 12380 St-Sernin-sur-Rance
Tel 65.99.60.26
Fax 65.99.69.26
Location in village, 50 km E of Albi, 63 km SW of Millau; with garden, car parking and garages
Meals breakfast, lunch, dinner
Prices rooms 189F-369F, 2 suites 600F-700F; menus 72F-300F
Rooms 26 double, 14 with bath, 10 with shower (8 twin); 10 family rooms/suites, 5 with bath, 3 with shower; all rooms have central heating, phone, minibar; 10 rooms have TV
Facilities 2 dining-rooms, TV room, games room; tennis, 2 swimming-pools, mini-golf
Credit cards AE, DC, MC, V
Children welcome
Disabled 3 bedrooms specially equipped **Pets** accepted
Closed Sun dinner and Mon out of season
Proprietor Pierre Carayon

Massif Central

Château de Boussac

Increased public exposure – now in other British hotel guides as well as this one – does not seem to have affected the delicate balancing act conducted by the Marquis and Marquise de Longueil, who continue to welcome guests into their home with captivating charm.

The Château de Boussac lies between Vichy and Moulin, tucked away in the Bourbonnais – quite difficult to find. Solid, turreted and moated, the château could be a tourist sight in its own right; it is built around a courtyard, and the main reception rooms, furnished with Louis XV antiques and chandeliers, open on to a vast terrace with an ornamental lake and formal gardens.

But the château is very much lived-in. By day the Marquis dons his overalls and works on the estate, but comes in to cook at least one course of the evening meal and chat to his guests. His wife looks after the rooms with care – there are fresh flowers everywhere, and the antiques are highly polished. Dinner *en famille* can be a rather formal affair, but the food is hard to fault and the Marquis, who speaks English, will make you feel at home.

Nearby Souvigny (35 km) – Gothic/Romanesque church; Vichy (40 km) – spa town; Moulins (50 km) – half-timbered houses.

Target 03140 Chantelle
Tel 70.40.63.20
Fax 70.40.60.03
Location in countryside, off D42, 12 km NW of Chantelle, 50 km W of Vichy; in large park, with ample car parking
Meals breakfast, dinner
Prices rooms 600F-1,100F; breakfast 55F, menus 220F-320F with wine
Rooms 4 double (3 twin), one suite, all with bath; all rooms have central heating
Facilities dining-room, sitting-room
Credit cards MC, V
Children accepted if well behaved
Disabled no special facilities
Pets accepted if well behaved
Closed Nov to Feb (except by reservation in advance)
Proprietors Marquis and Marquise de Longueil

Massif Central

Château de Trancis

We should welcome reports from readers who leave the beaten tourist track to find this impressive place – a classic little Loire-style château on the 500-metre-high fringes of the Auvergne regional park. This unlikely thing is more easily understood when you know that the Italianate architectural flourishes are of 20th-century origin. And its opening as an elegant hotel is perhaps more easily understood when you discover that it is run by an English couple, travel writers Innes and Fiona Fennell.

They have refurbished it to create the kind of harmonious and stylish ambience that is distinctly rare in and around the Massif Central. Bedrooms are well equipped and individually decorated, with antique furniture and rugs on polished floors. Public rooms embrace an ornate Louis XIV salon, a 'German' dining-room and an 'English' library. The view from the terrace across the smart little pool, where candlelit dinners are served in summer, is pleasant and soothing.

A house-party atmosphere prevails, with the Fennels' five-course dinners served only to residents. Note that they do not normally accept children.

Nearby Dordogne gorges, Parc Régional des Volcans d'Auvergne.

15210 Ydes
Tel 71.40.60.40
Fax 71.40.62.13
Location on D15, off D22, 2 km N of village of Saignes, 3 km E of Ydes; in countryside, with car parking in grounds
Meals breakfast, dinner
Prices rooms 560F-950F, suite 1,300F, including breakfast; DB&B 580F-900F; menu 280F
Rooms 6 double (one twin), one suite, all with bath or shower; all rooms have central heating, phone, TV, minibar, tea/coffee kit, hairdrier, electric fan
Facilities 3 sitting-rooms, 2 dining-rooms; 2 terraces, park, swimming-pool
Credit cards MC, V
Children not accepted
Disabled difficult access
Pets no dogs **Closed** mid-Oct to end Mar
Proprietors Innes and Fiona Fennell

Massif Central

Medieval inn, Cordes

Hostellerie du Vieux Cordes

A simpler base than the Grand Ecuyer, this stone-built 13thC building is set at the top of the old hill town giving long views, notably from the grassy terrace. Inside, furniture is generally simple and rustic, except in the plush little sitting-room. 'Friendly service, excellent food, good value,' says a recent report.

■ Rue St-Michel, 81170 Cordes (Tarn) **Tel** 63.56.00.12 **Fax** 63.56.02.47 **Meals** breakfast, lunch, dinner **Prices** rooms 265F-420F; breakfast 40F, menus 80F-160F **Rooms** 21, all with bath or shower, central heating, phone, TV **Credit cards** AE, DC, MC, V **Closed** Jan

---

Country hotel, Cuq-Toulza

Cuq en Terrasses

A full entry in the making, if ever there was one: opened in 1993 after three years of restoration by its British designer owners, Tim and Zara Whitmore, this old presbytery is beautifully and sympathetically done out, with lots of hand-made tiles and natural materials. Great views, flowery garden, pool.

■ Cuq-le-Château, 81470 Cuq-Toulza (Tarn) **Tel** 63.82.54.00 **Fax** 63.82.54.11 **Meals** breakfast, lunch, dinner **Prices** rooms 400F-900F; breakfast 50F, menus 130F-150F **Rooms** 8, 6 with bath, 2 with shower; all with central heating, phone, TV; **Credit cards** MC, V **Closed** never

---

Manor house hotel, La Malène

Manoir de Montesquiou

'Good-sized room, good food, very good views,' says a contented reader of this attractive castle-like 15thC manor house. Your bedroom may be in one of the turrets; it may have a grand four-poster; it is sure to be comfortable and well looked after. Family run with care and good humour.

■ 48210 La Malène (Lozère) **Tel** 66.48.51.12 **Fax** 66.48.50.47 **Meals** breakfast, lunch, dinner **Prices** rooms 430F-760F; breakfast 60F, menus 165F-250F **Rooms** 12, all with bath or shower, central heating, air-conditioning, phone; some have TV **Credit cards** DC, MC, V **Closed** mid-Oct to early Apr

---

Village inn, Montsalvy

Auberge Fleurie

The two attractive dining-rooms – polished wood dressers, gleaming copper, red-check tablecloths – are the focal point of this delightful creeper-covered auberge. We last visited after it changed hands a few years ago; reports on the now well-established new regime are welcome.

■ Place du Barry, 15120 Montsalvy (Cantal) **Tel** 71.49.20.02 **Meals** breakfast, lunch, dinner **Prices** rooms 120F-160F; breakfast 25F, menus 50F-180F **Rooms** 13, all with central heating **Credit cards** AE, DC, MC, V **Closed** restaurant only, mid-Jan to mid-Feb

Massif Central

Village hotel, Najac

L'Oustal del Barry

This spick-and-span little Logis, in the same family for five generations, will not be the same after Jean-Marie Miquel's tragic death in 1994, but the charming Catherine will doubtless continue to offer the genuine welcome, excellent food and notably good value for which it is known. Rooms are spacious but ordinary.

■ Place du Bourg, 12270 Najac (Aveyron) **Tel** 65.29.74.32
Fax 65.29.75.32 **Meals** breakfast, lunch, dinner **Prices** rooms
350F-550F with breakfast; menus 98F-320F **Rooms** 22, all with
central heating, phone, TV **Credit cards** AE, MC, V **Closed** Nov to Mar

---

Farmhouse hotel, Pont-de-L'Arn

La Métairie Neuve

The Metairie is a tastefully renovated old farm with its heritage properly respected – exposed beams, stone walls, polished tiled floors – and with a relaxed atmosphere. Mme Tournier is a charming hostess who keeps the antique-furnished public areas looking immaculate.

■ Pont-de-L'Arn, 81660 Mazamet (Tarn) **Tel** 63.61.23.31
Fax 63.61.94.75 **Meals** breakfast, lunch, dinner **Prices** rooms
340F-450F; menus 100F-250F **Rooms** 11, all with bath, central
heating, phone, TV **Credit cards** DC, MC, V **Closed** 15 Dec to
20 Jan; restaurant only, Sat (Oct to Mar) , Sat lunch (Apr to Sep)

Village inn, Vitrac

La Tomette

'This hotel has all the qualities of peace, welcome, attractive setting and very good food that characterise your selections,' a reader says of the Tomette – a jolly inn, much expanded and improved over the last 15 years, evidently without the loss of its essential appeal. Pleasant garden, pool.

■ 15220 Vitrac (Cantal) **Tel** 71.64.70.94 **Fax** 71.64.77.11
Meals breakfast, lunch, dinner **Prices** rooms 220F-440F; breakfast 40F,
menus 60F-180F **Rooms** 18, all with bath or show er, central heating,
phone, TV **Credit cards** AE, MC, V **Closed** Jan to Mar

The South

Area introduction

Mediterranean France: sea, sun, wine, flowers, fruit, mountains, Roman remains. Heaven on earth – and with more guide entries and potential entries (listed below) than any other region.

Contenders in the South

Aigues-Mortes, Les Arcades 66.53.81.13 Characterful restaurant with individually decorated rooms in ancient building.

Aix-en-Provence, Hôtel des Augustins 42.27.28.59 Converted monastery in centre of Aix; garden for breakfast.

Aix-en-Provence, Hôtel des Quatre-Dauphins 42.38.16.39 Prettily designer-decorated little place in Mazarin quarter.

Avignon, Hôtel de la Mirande 90.85.93.93 Extravagantly elegant town hotel, opened in 1990.

Montfavet, Les Frênes 90.31.17.93 Elegant mansion, beautiful garden, and superb pool. Good food.

Les-Baux-de-Provence, Mas de l'Oulivie 90.54.35.78 Newly built, in traditional *mas* style, with attractive pool among olives.

Les-Baux-de-Provence, La Cabro d'Or 90.54.33.21 Starred restaurant, with lovely pool/gardens and comfortable rooms.

Bonnieux, Hostellerie Le Prieuré 90.75.80.78 Delightful 17thC abbey in small hillside village.

Castillon-du-Gard, Le Vieux Castillon 66.37.00.77 Luxurious and stylish conversion of old houses in ancient hilltop village.

Collias, Hostellerie Le Castellas 66.22.88.88 Stylish, slightly slick little place in centre of old village; small garden, pool.

Coursegoules, Auberge de l'Escaou 93.59.11.28 Simple, tastefully modernized inn, in quiet, isolated hill village.

Gordes, Les Romarins 90.72.12.13 Tastefully furnished house overlooking the village; pool.

Gordes, Les Bories 90.72.00.51 Expensive picturesque restaurant with rooms overlooking valley in medieval village.

Joucas, Mas des Herbes Blanches 90.05.79.79 Very attractive old *mas* with fine views; well-equipped rooms; pool; good food.

Joucas, Le Phebus 90.05.78.83 Stylishly decorated, welcoming farmhouse-style place, good food, attractive pool.

Malemort-du-Comtat, Château Unang 90.69.91.37 18thC house in formal gardens surrounded by vineyards, elegantly furnished but informally run as a B&B.

Montpellier, Hôtel le Guilhem 67.52.90.90 Tastefully done out old house in old town, with lovely terrace; B&B only.

Pernes-les-Fontaines, Hôtel l'Hermitage 90.66.51.41 Elegant, patchily furnished Logis in pleasant gardens with pool.

Le-Puy-Ste-Reparade, Domaine de la Cride 42.61.96.96 Home-like restored farmhouse in a leafy garden with pool.

Roquebrune-sur-Argens, La Maurette 94.45.46.81 Hilltop farmhouse with views; rooms open on to the garden.

Russamp-Est, Mas des Aigras 90.34.81.01 Simple but stylish farmhouse B&B in leafy gardens with pool, tennis.

St-Remy, Mas de la Tour 90.92.61.00 Traditional-style house with rooms opening on to flowery garden and pool.

Ste-Maxime-sur-Mer, La Croisette 94.96.17.75 Pastel-coloured villa with secluded garden and good views; seafood specialities.

Vence, Château du Domaine St Martin 93.58.02.02 Elegantly furnished Relais & Châteaux place, in splendid high setting; terrace, lovely pool, tennis.

The South

Mas d'Entremont

This farmhouse-style hotel just outside Aix, has a blemish-free record of reports from readers (including one who has been going there for over a decade) and impressed a recent inspector mightily.

The hotel consists of low red-roofed buildings clustered around a courtyard – modern constructions, but using lots of old materials. Within are wooden beams and pillars, rustic furniture, tiled floors and open fireplaces. Bedrooms are also rustic, comfortable and quite stylish. Five (relatively small, but all with terrace or balcony) are in the main building, the rest (bigger) spread around the gardens in bungalows. The setting is peaceful, and the gardens are a delight – with a big swimming-pool shielded by cypresses, plenty of secluded corners, and a pond with fountain, lilies and lazy carp. Overlooking this is a beautiful summer dining-room, with windows that slide away, effectively creating a roofed terrace.

Cuisine is classic in style, with a strong Provençal influence, and excellent in quality, attracting a full house for Sunday lunch. The Marignanes create a relaxed family atmosphere.

Nearby Aix-en-Provence; Abbaye de Silvacane (25 km).

Montée d'Avignon 13090 Aix-en-Provence
Tel 42.23.45.32
Fax 42.21.15.83
Location in countryside just off N7, 2 km NW of Aix; with large grounds and car parking
Meals breakfast, lunch, dinner
Prices rooms 640F-840F, suite 960F; breakfast 70F; DB&B 1,200F-1,400F (for two); menus 200F-230F
Rooms 17 double (7 twin) all with bath; all rooms have air-conditioning, phone, satellite TV, minibar, safe, private terrace
Facilities dining-room, sitting-areas; swimming-pool, tennis
Credit cards MC, V
Children accepted; some rooms have side-rooms
Disabled lift/elevator
Pets accepted
Closed Nov to mid-Mar; restaurant only, Sun dinner and Mon lunch
Proprietors Marignane family

The South

Town villa, Aix-en-Provence

Villa Gallici

This is certainly one of the most expensive and one of the smallest hotels in Aix; from where we stand it is absolutely the best. We've called it a town villa; suburban villa might be more accurate, while country villa might convey more of the feel of the place, set in a beautiful garden just north of the centre.

It is a deliciously peaceful, relaxing place, where distinctions between indoors and out seem to blur. A shady terrace is converted to an outdoor sitting-room by deep-cushioned sofas and chairs; breakfast can be had here. Indoors, bright fabrics and light paintwork bring the sun into the welcoming sitting-rooms. Bedrooms are prettily sumptuous, with extravagant use of draped fabrics; furniture is in elegant 18th-century style throughout, but the decorative themes vary widely.

Light meals can be had by the hotel's pool, surrounded by trees and flowery shrubs. For more serious eating, the hotel's restaurant, the Clos de la Violette, does not let the side down, with a Michelin star and three *toques* from Gault-Millau. Not only the best hotel in Aix, but the best restaurant. No wonder the Villa Gallici offers 'courses for getting back into shape'.

Nearby Aix-en-Provence; Abbaye de Silvacane (25 km)

Avenue de la Violette 13100 Aix-en-Provence
Tel 42.23.29.23
Fax 42.96.30.45
Location just north of city centre, 500m from cathedral; in gardens with secure parking
Meals breakfast, lunch, dinner
Prices rooms 850F-2,350F; breakfast 95F, menu 300F
Rooms 19 double with bath; all rooms have central heating, air-conditioning, phone, TV, radio, minibar, hairdrier
Facilities sitting-room, bar, dining-room; terrace, swimming-pool
Credit cards AE, DC, MC, V
Children not accepted
Disabled one ground-floor bedroom
Pets accepted (50F charge)
Closed never; restaurant only, Thu
Proprietors M. Dez, M. Montemarco, M. Jouve

The South

Les Géraniums

Since its first appearance as a short entry in our 1991 edition, this three-fireplace Logis has generated a steady stream of complimentary reports – even in 1992, when M. Roux got us into hot water with some readers by leading us to advertise the existence of a new swimming-pool which failed to materialise. 'Had to go a long way to find it, but well worth the effort,' concludes the latest endorsement.

Well off the beaten track, at the edge of a small medieval village near Mont Ventoux, this is the sort of simple and peaceful *auberge* that is becoming increasingly hard to find. It is well cared for, with comfortable rustic-style bedrooms and smart bathrooms (some separating walls are rather thin), and an attractive, lofty, beamed dining-room. Cooking is uncomplicated but 'excellent', concentrating on local produce, and attracting enough custom to fill the very large terrace behind the hotel, which gives good views over unspoilt, wooded hills. There is another terrace in front of the hotel, and a sunbathing area that shares the rear views. 'Bustling', 'friendly', 'excellent service', 'good value for money' comment recent satisfied customers.

Nearby Mont Ventoux, Vaison-la-Romaine, vineyards.

Le Barroux, 84330
Tel 90.62.41.08
Fax 90.62.56.48
Location at edge of quiet old village, 12 km NE of Carpentras; with car parking (closed at night)
Meals breakfast, lunch, dinner
Prices rooms 210F-250F; breakfast 35F, menus 80F-250F
Rooms 20 double, 8 with bath, 12 with shower; 2 family rooms, both with shower; all rooms have central heating, phone
Facilities dining-room, sitting-room, bar, TV room; terrace
Credit cards AE, DC, MC, V
Children welcome
Disabled easy access to restaurant only
Pets accepted
Closed Jan and Feb
Proprietors Agnès and Jacques Roux

The South

Mas d'Aigret

Englishman Pip Phillips and his French wife Chantal took over this old farmhouse – in a fine setting with views over peaceful countryside – just in time to appear in our first edition, and have since built up a formidable reputation for their enthusiastic brand of hospitality. There is a shady dining terrace and an extraordinary restaurant carved out of the rock; all is fresh and pretty, decorated in rustic Provençal style. Some of the bedrooms are quite small, but all open out on to a terrace or balcony. Pascal Johnson is a talented chef, tipped by at least one reporter for a Michelin star before long.

Nearby Ruined fortress-village; Arles (15 km) and the Camargue.

13520 Les Baux-de-Provence
Tel 90.54.33.54
Fax 90.54.41.37
Location just below fortress, on D27A 500 m E of Les Baux; in large grounds with private car parking
Meals breakfast, lunch, dinner
Prices rooms 350F-850F; lunch 90F, dinner 180F-350F
Rooms 13 double (6 twin), 3 family rooms, all with bath; all rooms have central

heating, phone, TV, minibar
Facilities dining-room, sitting-room, bar; swimming-pool,
Credit cards AE, DC, MC, V
Children welcome
Disabled no special facilities
Pets welcome (40F), but not in restaurant
Closed Jan and Feb; restaurant only, Wed lunch
Proprietors Pip Phillips and family

The South

Converted mill, Les Beaumettes

Le Moulin Blanc

One recent report supported our continued inclusion of this ancient mill, opened as a hotel in 1981; more would be welcome. The Moulin makes an attractive (though not cheap) base for an extended stay, equipped as it is with extensive lawns and a smart pool. Bedrooms are large, with restrained decoration and handsome antiques; but those on the garden side are greatly preferable to those on the roadside, which lack sunshine and suffer from traffic noise. The main dining-room is light and lofty, the sitting-room a rough-stone vault with rugs on a polished floor. Excellent classic cooking (a *toque* from Gault-Millau), and a pretty courtyard for summer dining.

Nearby Village des Bories (5 km), Gordes (10 km).

Les Beaumettes 84220 Gordes
Tel 90.72.34.50
Fax 90.72.25.41
Location in countryside 40 km E of Avignon, on RN100; with garden and ample car parking
Meals breakfast, lunch, dinner
Prices rooms 450F-920F; breakfast 60F, menus 160F-250F
Rooms 18 double, all with bath; connecting rooms available; all rooms have phone, TV, radio alarm, minibar; some rooms have terraces
Facilities 2 dining-rooms, sitting-room; swimming-pool, tennis
Credit cards AE, DC, MC, V
Children welcome; special meals available
Disabled no special facilities
Pets dogs accepted
Closed never
Proprietor Mireille Diez

The South

La Terrasse au Soleil

This mainly modern Catalan-style hotel has gradually moved upmarket over its years in the guide, and is now of four-star status, and has now added even its own helicopter landing space. It has expanded, too, and falls outside our usual size limits. But choice in the Pyrenees-Orientales is limited, and an approving reader's report encourages us to stick to the view that this is one of the most appealing places in the region.

A key part of the appeal is the lovely setting, with the splendid Mont Canigou as backdrop on a fine day (320 days of sun per year are claimed, so you should be lucky). As you might expect, it has a terrace, where you can eat out or just observe the view (as Picasso is said to have done); and there are good facilities for the more active. Inside, a relaxed and casual atmosphere prevails despite the modern comforts. The best of the bedrooms – all of which are well equipped – are very spacious and smart.

The restaurant has recently been given a separate identity – La Cerisaie. At lunchtime there is a tempting *carte brasserie* as a lighter alternative to the more serious food that for years has merited a Gault-Millau *toque*.

Nearby Perpignan; beaches (30 km); Castelnou (30 km).

Rte de Fontfrède 66400 Céret
Tel 68.87.01.94
Fax 68.87.39.24
Location in Pyrenean foothills above town, 26 km SW of Perpignan; with gardens and car parking
Meals breakfast, lunch, dinner; room service
Prices rooms 595F-795F, suites 1,100F-1,200F; breakfast 80F
Rooms 25 double, all with bath; 1 suite, with bath; all rooms have air-conditioning, phone, TV, minibar, hairdrier
Facilities dining-room, sitting-room, bar; ping-pong, helipad, swimming-pool, tennis-court, petanque, golf practice area **Credit cards** MC, V **Children** accepted
Disabled no special facilities
Pets accepted
Closed end Oct to end Feb
Proprietor M. Leveille-Nizerolle

The South

Town inn, Château-Arnoux

La Bonne Etape

'Exceptional food, impeccable service, beautiful pool and rooms – worth every franc' says a very satisfied recent visitor to this long-established 'good stopover'.

The setting (on a busy road in an unremarkable town) is not auspicious, and the outside gives little hint of what lies within – one of the most satisfactory blends of refinement and hospitality to be found in France. Where to start? Perhaps in the kitchen, where Pierre and Jany Gleize (father and son) make innovative and stylish use of largely home-grown ingredients, earning a star from Michelin and 18/20 from Gault-Millau. Among their specialities is Sisteron lamb (raised on fragrant Provençal pastures). The light, warm dining-room is a supremely comfortable and relaxing place, with well-spaced round tables.

But this is no restaurant-with-rooms. Bedrooms are more than comfortable – beautifully decorated and furnished with a tasteful mix of modern and antique pieces; some of the bathrooms, too, are delightfully individual. Even in the corridors there is attention to decorative detail. The pool is a superb sun-trap, with an attractive terrace surround. To cap it all, the Gleize family are warmly welcoming hosts, happily committed to their work.

Nearby Les Mées (10 km); Sisteron – citadel; hill-walking.

Chemin du Lac 04160 Château-Arnoux
Tel 92.64.00.09
Fax 92.64.37.36
Location in country town, on main RN 85 14 km SE of Sisteron (motorway 3 km); with car parking, garage and garden
Meals breakfast, lunch, dinner
Prices rooms 600F-900F, suites 900F-1,300F; breakfast 85F, menus 220F-520F
Rooms 11 double, 7 suites, all with bath; all rooms have air-conditioning, phone, TV, radio, minibar
Facilities 2 dining-rooms, sitting-room, bar, conference room; heated swimming-pool
Credit cards AE, DC, MC, V
Children accepted
Disabled no special facilities
Pets accepted
Closed Jan to mid-Feb; Sun night and Mon from Nov to Mar
Proprietors Gleize family

The South

Hostellerie de Crillon le Brave

'Delightful,' enthuses one satisfied visitor to this luxurious hotel occupying the old vicarage in the hilltop village of Crillon-le-Brave. 'Very good restaurant, excellent service, a lovely setting and a charming *patron*.'

The rambling 16thC stone-built house is solid and calm, but most of the credit for the resounding success of the hotel – open only since late 1989 – must go to the aforementioned *patron*, Peter Chittick, a Canadian lawyer with exceptionally clear ideas about hotelkeeping. A considerable share goes also to the perched location, giving uninterrupted views of a heavenly landscape of olive groves and vineyards.

The central trick that Mr Chittick and his collaborator Craig Miller have pulled off is to provide luxury without erasing character. Despite the designer fabrics, fitted carpets and smart bathrooms, the exposed beams, white walls and rustic furniture dominate both in the sitting-rooms and the spacious bedrooms. You eat beneath stone vaults, or out on the pretty terrace. Chef Philippe Monti produces refined Provençale food that is in perfect harmony with this blissful setting.

Nearby Mont Ventoux; Orange (35 km); Avignon; Gordes.

Place de l'Eglise, 84410 Crillon-le-Brave
Tel 90.65.61.61
Fax 90.65.62.86
Location in hilltop village 35km NE of Avignon, on D138 off D974, with garden, private car parking and garages
Meals breakfast, lunch, dinner, snacks
Prices rooms 750F-1,250F, suites 1,450F-2,150F; breakfast 75F, dinner about 300F
Rooms 18 double (7 twin), 16 with bath, one with shower; 6 suites; all rooms have central heating, phone, minibar, hairdrier
Facilities 3 sitting-rooms, dining-room; swimming-pool
Credit cards AE, MC, V
Children welcome; babysitting available **Disabled** access difficult **Pets** accepted
Closed Jan to Mar; restaurant, lunch, Mon-Fri
Proprietors Peter Chittick and Craig Miller

The South

Converted castle, Dieulefit

Les Hospitaliers

Readers continue to be impressed by this distinctive hotel, a former stronghold in a dominating position above the perched medieval village of Le Poët-Laval. Apart from the views, especially from the terrace (where meals are served in fine weather) and pool area, the warm welcome and the comfortable top-floor sitting-room are singled out. The restaurant has an interesting collection of paintings; Yvon Morin is a former art dealer. Tables are laid with fine china, white linen or lace, and candles; service is hard to fault, and the food is excellent – the daily changing menu is particularly recommended. Bedrooms are furnished with antiques; size varies along with price.

Nearby Montélimar (20 km); Viviers (30 km) – medieval town.

Le Poët-Laval, Dieulefit 26160
La Bégude-de-Mazenc
Tel 75.46.22.32
Fax 75.46.49.99
Location at top of old village, 5 km W of Dieulefit; with gardens; car parking nearby
Meals breakfast, lunch, dinner
Prices rooms 520F-1,100F; menus 160F-450F
Rooms 21 double, 20 with bath, one with shower (8 twin); 3 family rooms, all with bath; all rooms have central heating, phone
Facilities 2 dining-rooms, 2 sitting-rooms, bar; swimming- pool
Credit cards AE, DC, MC, V
Children accepted
Disabled no special facilities
Pets cats and dogs accepted
Closed mid-Nov to Feb
Proprietors M. and Mme Yvon Morin

The South

Château hotel, Eygalières

Mas de la Brune

Stefan Gagg, who for some years devoted himself to making Mas de la Brune one of the most welcoming, comfortable and distinctive places to say in the south, has moved on. Fortunately, the new owners have changed very little.

This is your typical Provençal *mas*. It is a superb Renaissance mansion, formerly a consul's residence and now a listed historic monument. The front façade is impressively ornate, the back creeper-clad. In summer, meals are served on the terrace, overlooking the park. The dining-room and salon, which was recently redecorated, are both stone-vaulted; one has a grand open fireplace, the other houses a traditional olive press. All the bedrooms have wonderfully comfortable beds and are carefully furnished, with antiques, colourful but harmonious fabrics; fresh flowers, fruit and fluffy bath robes await your arrival.

There is a *'tout compris'* pricing formula, including an aperitif, house wine and coffee. Dinner offers no choice, and one inspector's meal, although well presented was not particularly impressive. But this was prior to new chef Olivier Boscolo's arrival at Mas de la Brune. More reports welcome.

Nearby Cavaillon (13 km); Avignon (25 km).

13810 Eygalières-en-Provence
Tel 90.95.90.77
Fax 90.95.99.21
Location near village, 8 km E of St-Rémy on D99; in grounds, with guarded car park
Meals breakfast, dinner
Prices DB&B 845F-1,025F including aperitif, house wine and coffee
Rooms 10 double, all with bath (5 twin); all rooms have central heating, phone, air-conditioning, hairdrier, TV, minibar, safe
Facilities dining-room, sitting-room, terrace; swimming-pool
Credit cards MC, V
Children accepted over 12 years
Disabled no special facilities
Pets accepted in bedrooms
Closed Nov to Mar
Manager Gilles Benedetti

The South

Country hotel, La Favède

A l'Auberge Cévenole

A trickle of encouraging feedback from readers encourages us to carry on recommending this neat country hotel, taken over by the Burlons shortly after its appearance in our first edition – more reports would be welcome.

The usual approach is through the disagreeably industrialized valley which runs north from Alès; but don't be put off. The *auberge*, set in a little circle of hills, is as peaceful and alluring as any you could wish to find. The building – a much-expanded 1950s villa, opened as a hotel in 1960 – is white, with a red-tiled roof and a shady, creeper-clad terrace. It is set in an exceptional garden: informal, full of flowers, with plenty of secluded corners in which to read, plus a fair-sized (unheated) swimming-pool. Inside the pace is slow, the atmosphere quietly old-fashioned. A rash of shepherds and shepherdesses covers many of the walls; bedrooms and bathrooms range from adequate to very comfortable without being luxurious (with the exception of the two apartments, which are).

Nearby Château de Rousson (20 km); St-Jean-du-Gard and Corniche des Cévennes (25 km); Grotte de Trabuc (25 km).

La Favède 30110 Les Salles-du-Gardon
Tel 66.34.12.13
Fax 66.34.50.50
Location in hamlet on D283 off N106 14 km N of Alès; with large garden, ample car parking
Meals breakfast, lunch, dinner
Prices rooms 300F-600F; breakfast 45F, menus 165F-265F
Rooms 19 double (6 twin), all with bath or shower; all have central heating, phone
Facilities dining-room, bar/sitting-room, TV room; swimming-pool, mini-tennis, table-tennis
Credit cards MC, V
Children accepted
Disabled 8 ground-floor rooms
Pets accepted
Closed mid-Oct to Mar
Proprietors M. and Mme Burlon

The South

Moulin de la Camandoule

We stick to this lovingly restored olive-mill through thick and thin. Some years we get complaints, some years (like this) nothing but praise for the Rillas' deeply relaxing country hotel. An inspection visit confirms that it is one of the most captivating hotels in these pages.

The mill lies in extensive private grounds divided in half by the low Roman aqueduct which used to bring water to the mill. The existing building dates from the 19th century, and was rescued from ruin some thirty years ago. Shirley and Wolf Rilla (an English/German couple) moved here in 1986.

Food is a highlight for most visitors, including our inspector. Meals are served outside in summer – on a terrace overlooking the cherry orchard, or by the pool – or in the delightfully rustic dining-room decorated with original mill trappings. Between this and the lofty, beamed sitting-room (with its adjoining 'snuggery') is the ancient water wheel, now preserved behind glass. Bedrooms differ widely in size and style, but are all charmingly done out. Books, family paintings, ornaments and fresh flowers add to the welcoming (not at all smart) atmosphere.

Nearby Grasse (30 km) – perfumes; Cannes (30 km).

Chemin Notre-Dame-des-Cyprès 83440 Fayence
Tel 94.76.00.84
Fax 94.76.10.40
Location at foot of village, 30 km NW of Cannes; in large grounds with ample car parking
Meals breakfast, lunch, dinner
Prices rooms 265F-690F, DB&B 485F-570F; breakfast 50F, menu 180F-260F
Rooms 10 double with bath (4 twin); 2 single with shower; all rooms have central heating, phone, TV
Facilities dining-room, sitting-room with bar; swimming-pool with bar, barbecue
Credit cards MC, V
Children not accepted
Disabled no special facilities
Pets accepted (40F)
Closed never
Proprietors Wolf and Shirley Rilla

The South

Converted mill, Fontvieille

La Régalido

We continue to be fond of this 19th-century oil mill, a Relais &
Chateaux place which manages to remain informal and friendly
despite its elegant furnishings and high prices – largely thanks to
the presence at all hours of the welcoming and helpful Jean-
Pierre Michel, chef-proprietor.

The Régalido has been converted into a fine auberge in a
thoroughly Provençal style, decorated with great flair by Madame
Michel. There is a charming sitting-room full of flowers, and a log
fire lit on chilly days. Tables are beautifully set in the elegant,
peaceful, stone-vaulted dining-room, and there is an atmosphere
of well-being which suits the excellent cooking of Jean-Pierre. His
style is classic, but he has a penchant for Provençal dishes
(seafood, olive oil, herbs and garlic) – and terracotta or cast iron
pots appear alongside the silver salvers.

Bedrooms are individually decorated, and very comfortable,
with lots of extras in the well equipped bathrooms. Friendly staff
and a pretty, flowery garden – with a terrace surrounded by
mimosa and shaded by fig and olive trees – complete the picture.
Nearby Montmajour Abbey; Arles; the Camargue (10 km) –
flamingoes, white horses; Tarascon (15 km) – château.

Rue Frederic-Mistral 13990
Fontvieille
Tel 90.54.60.22
Fax 90.54.64.29
Location in middle of village,
9 km NE of Arles; with
gardens and ample car
parking
Meals breakfast, lunch, dinner
Prices rooms 640F-1,420F;
breakfast 90F, menus 250F-
410F
Rooms 15 double, 12 with
bath, 2 with shower; all rooms
have central heating, air-
conditioning, phone, minibar
Facilities dining-room, 2
sitting-rooms, bar
Credit cards AE, DC, MC, V
Children accepted
Disabled one specially
equipped ground-floor
bedroom
Pets accepted (at a charge)
Closed Jan; restaurant only,
Mon and Tue lunch, Mon
dinner in low season
Proprietor Jean-Pierre Michel

The South

Relais de la Magdeleine

'If only there were more hotels like this,' begins our latest enthusiastic reader's report on this lovely old *bastide*. We share the sen-
timent: for those of us who can't or won't pay the prices (or
don't like the style) of Relais & Châteaux places, a gracious country house like this is quite a find. It is a family affair. Daniel
Marignane's mother opened the hotel in 1932, he and his wife
now run the hotel with great charm and good humour, and their
son is now in charge of the kitchen – and achieving great things.

An acid test of a hotel is visitors' reactions to flaws. When they
reveal them to us grudgingly, in a favourable light, we know we
are on to a winner. 'A touch of shabbiness here and there only
adds to the charm,' says one report otherwise full of praise.

The great trick that the Marignanes pull off is that of steering a
sensitive middle course. The public rooms are elegant, but lived-
in. The bedrooms too are home-like, but the best have posh bathrooms. The hotel pampers grown-ups, but is welcoming to
children. Prices are at exactly the level that many comfortably-
off British travellers in France will find bearable. If only there
were more like this, indeed.

Nearby Cassis (15 km) – coastal inlets; La Ste-Baume massif.

13420 Gémenos
Tel 42.32.20.16
Fax 42.32.02.26
Location on outskirts of town,
23 km E of Marseilles; with
garden and ample car
parking
Meals breakfast, lunch,
dinner
Prices rooms 395F-750F;
menu 250F
Rooms 24 double, 20 with
bath, 4 with shower (12 twin);
4 family rooms, all with bath;
all rooms have central
heating, phone, TV
Facilities sitting-rooms,
dining-rooms; swimming-pool
Credit cards MC, V
Children accepted
Disabled no special facilities
Pets not accepted
Closed Dec to mid-Mar
Proprietors M. and Mme
Marignane

The South

Village hotel, Grimaud

Le Coteau Fleuri

Our files contain a pretty solid record of support for this attractive stone house, built into the hillside at the edge of the fashionable perched village of Grimaud, and run by Jacques Minard (previously manager of the Mas de Chatelas) since 1988. Our most recent reporter had not only 'a good time' in general, but 'the best meal of the holiday.'

The house is about a hundred years old and retains a simple Provençal style. There is a rambling garden with olive trees, and a small flowery terrace in front of the hotel. The spotless bedrooms have pretty furnishings and prints, and smart tiled bathrooms; most are rather small, but many have a splendid view of vineyards and the Maures massif (others look out over the garden and the ruins of Grimaud castle and chapel). The public rooms are attractive and relaxing: there is a small bar, a dining-room in two parts (both of which extend on to the terrace and benefit from the view), and a spacious sitting-room with tiled floor and grand piano. Throughout the hotel are masses of fresh flowers. In winter there are log fires.

Food is a highlight; *nouvelle* in style but not in quantity, theatrically presented by attentive staff. The *mousse au chocolat* is acquiring cult status

Nearby St-Tropez (10 km); Pampelonne (15 km).

Place des Pénitents, Grimaud
83310 Cogolin
Tel 94.43.20.17
Fax 94.43.33.42
Location in middle of village behind chapel; with car parking in front
Meals breakfast, lunch, dinner
Prices rooms 300F-475F; breakfast 45F, menus from 190F
Rooms 13 double, 8 with bath, 5 with shower (4 twin); one family room with bath; all rooms have phone
Facilities dining-room, sitting-room, bar
Credit cards AE, DC, MC, V
Children welcome
Disabled no special facilities
Pets accepted if well behaved
Closed 3 weeks Dec, 2 weeks Jan; restaurant only, Tue (except Jul and Aug)
Proprietors Jacline and Jacques Minard

The South

Country hotel, Grimaud

Le Verger

'Glad to see Le Verger appearing in your guide,' says a reader, in response to its inclusion for the first time a few years ago. 'I've known this pleasant little spot for some years, and often thought it was your kind of hotel – that is, a very unhotel-like hotel.' Indeed: the Zacharys have kept the scale and feel of the private house they converted in 1987. It is a typical Provencal building – low, with shallow roofs of pale tiles.

'Our friends call this place 'Little Normandy' because it is so green, unlike most of the Côte d'Azur,' says Anne Zachary, highlighting just one attractive aspect of Le Verger. The 'French windows' of harmonious, freshly decorated bedrooms open directly on to the lawn, and so the pool. Meals are served outside in summer, on a partly covered terrace looking across the pool to woods and hills, or before an open fire in a large dining-room in cooler weather. M. Zachary – an experienced chef, with quite a local following – cooks varied and satisfying dishes in the Mediterranean style, with no pretensions. And while you're at dinner your bed will be turned down – one of the little things that Anne insists on, in order to make your stay entirely restful.
Nearby Provence countryside; St-Tropez (12 km).

Route de Collobrières 83360 Grimaud
Tel 94.43.25.93
Fax 94.43.33.92
Location in countryside 1 km W of Grimaud, on D14 off D558, 12 km W of St-Tropez; in spacious gardens with private car parking
Meals breakfast, lunch, dinner
Prices rooms 500F-850F; breakfast 60F, menus 100F-150F
Rooms 6 double, all with bath; 2 single, one with bath, one with shower; all rooms have central heating, phone, TV
Facilities sitting-room, dining-room; swimming-pool
Credit cards MC, V
Children accepted, but no special facilities
Disabled not very suitable
Pets welcome
Closed Nov to Easter; restaurant also Christmas and New Year
Proprietor Mme Zachary

The South

Le Cagnard

A reader's report raised some doubts about this lovely hotel, perched along the ramparts of an old hill village – specifically about standards of service in the Michelin-starred restaurant. It is far from the most expensive hotel in the Relais & Châteaux group, but it is pricey enough for expectations in this department to be high. Off went an inspector; happily, all was well.

Le Cagnard has been sensitively converted from a series of medieval houses, most with separate street entrances. In the main house there is a stunning medieval vaulted dining-room where you eat by candlelight. But the real knockout is the upper dining-room, leading out on to the terrace: its elaborate painted ceiling slides away at the touch of a button, opening the room to the sky. The bedrooms vary widely; most retain a medieval feel, thanks to the preservation of features such as stone floors, and are furnished with style, but incongruous exceptions remain. Three rooms in one house have a lovely flowery garden. Access in anything other than a small car is tricky, and getting to some rooms involves a bit of awkward suitcase-lugging.

Nearby Château Grimaldi – modern art museum, with Renaissance courtyard; Nice (15 km); Grasse (30 km) – perfumes.

Rue Pontis-Long, Haut-de-Cagnes 06800 Cagnes-sur-Mer
Tel 93.20.73.21
Fax 93.22.06.39
Location in middle of hill village, 2 km above main town of Cagnes; car parking 300m away at entrance to village
Meals breakfast, lunch, dinner
Prices rooms 400F-1,050F, suites 1,300F-1,500F; breakfast 80F, menus 300F-500F

Rooms 18 double, 10 apartments, all with bath; all rooms have central heating, phone, TV, minibar; most have air-conditioning
Facilities dining-room, bar
Credit cards AE, DC, MC, V
Children accepted
Disabled no special facilities
Pets accepted
Closed restaurant only, Thu lunch and Nov to mid-Dec
Proprietors Barel Laroche family

The South

Village inn, Llo

Auberge Atalaya

The Toussaints' delightful little rustic inn continues to impress, although recent reports are few, and more would be welcome. Llo is an attractive village high up in the Pyrenees, and is typical of the Cerdagne – a high sun-drenched plateau of pastures and pine forests, popular for summer and winter sports. The Atalaya, in a prime spot in the village, was expertly converted from an old farmhouse in 1969. The bedrooms are quiet, comfortable and intimate, with romantic fabrics and soft lighting. Local speciali-ties are served either in the rustic dining-room – gleaming antiques against stone walls – or on a charming flowery terrace.
Nearby Odeillo (10 km) – solar furnace; Font-Romeu (15 km).

Llo 66800 Saillagouse
Tel 68.04.70.04
Fax 68.04.01.29
Location in middle of village, 2 km E of Saillagouse and 10 km E of Bourg-Madame; ample car parking
Meals breakfast, lunch, dinner
Prices rooms 480F-715F; breakfast 60F, menus 155F-195F
Rooms 12 double, 10 with bath, 2 with shower (3 twin); one suite; all rooms have central heating, phone, TV, minibar
Facilities sitting-room, bar, dining-room; swimming-pool
Credit cards MC, V
Children welcome if well behaved
Disabled no special facilities
Pets accepted in bedrooms only
Closed mid-Jan to Mar
Proprietors M. and Mme H Toussaint

The South

Château hotel, Madières

Château de Madières

This magnificently sited 14th-century fortress, perched above the Vis river gorge, was upgraded a few years ago to four-star status. More importantly, the refurbishments have given the interior a new vitality, shifting the hotel from the 'historic and adequately comfortable' category to the distinctly compelling.

The château was rescued from decay by the Brucys in the mid-1980s. They opened for business in 1986, having restored it to its former glory – creating comfortable rooms within the existing framework of medieval walls and arches. No two bedrooms are alike, though all have modern bathrooms and most have good views. The best are very spacious and delightfully furnished, with bold, colourful fabrics against plain white walls and oriental rugs on tiled floors. Key attractions are the public rooms – a galleried sitting-room with a vast Renaissance fireplace, and the vaulted dining-room, jutting out of the main building, with spectacular valley views. Above it is the main terrace.

Madame's cuisine – *'très raffinée et genereuse'* – receives some good reports (and a toque from Gault Millau). More comments would be welcome.

Nearby Cirque de Navacelles; Grotte des Demoiselles; Ganges.

Madières 34190 Ganges
Tel 67.73.84.03
Fax 67.73.55.71
Location on hillside overlooking village, on crossroads of D48 and D25; with shady park and ample car parking
Meals breakfast, lunch, dinner
Prices rooms 650F-1,150F; breakfast 80F, menus 190F-380F, children's 120F
Rooms 7 double (one twin), 3 apartments, all with bath; all rooms have central heating, phone, TV, minibar
Facilities 3 sitting-rooms, bar, 2 dining-rooms, 3 terraces, swimming-pool
Credit cards AE, MC, V
Children accepted
Disabled no special facilities
Pets accepted
Closed Nov to Easter
Proprietors Bernard and Françoise Brucy

The South

Hilltop hotel, Mougins

Les Muscadins

'It's really delicious!' Our latest reporter doesn't give us any clue as to whether this endorsement is a literal verdict confined to the food, or whether it is a metaphorical verdict on the whole of this lovely place.

It certainly could be the latter; if it's the former, our reporter is at odds with our colleagues at the Guide Michelin, who have withdrawn the star Les Muscadins gained a few years ago. This is part of a gastronomic earthquake that has shaken fashionable hill-top Mougins. Michelin withdrew stars from two other restaurants as well, leaving Roger Vergé's famous Moulin sitting tight with its two stars. Meanwhile, rival guide Gault-Millau suspended Vergé's *toques*. Make of that what you will.

Star or no star, Les Muscadins – a white-washed building surrounded by tropical vegetation – is irresistible. The American owner Edward Bianchini has filled it with memorable antiques, many from the lavish homes of 18thC fops called *Muscadins*. The luxurious bedrooms are highly individual and beautifully coordinated, and have impeccable bathrooms; most also have views of the coast. Elegantly furnished terrace.

Nearby Cannes; Grasse; Vallauris (10 km) – Picasso museum.

18 Bd Courteline 06250 Mougins
Tel 93.90.00.43
Fax 92.92.88.23
Location on E road into old village, 2 km N of A8 motorway, 6 km N of Cannes; with car parking
Meals breakfast, lunch, dinner
Prices rooms 750F-950F, suite 1,200F; breakfast 60F, menus 115F-290F
Rooms 7 double, one suite; all rooms have central heating, air-conditioning, phone, TV, minibar
Facilities sitting-room, dining-room, bar
Credit cards AE, DC, MC, V
Children welcome
Disabled access difficult
Pets welcome
Closed 1 week in Dec, mid Feb to mid Mar
Proprietor Edward Bianchini

The South

Auberge de Noves

'The most relaxing hotel we visited. Yes, it's expensive, but worth every penny,' says one of the few reports we have on this luxurious and pricey hotel (nothing like an *auberge*) isolated in the Provençal countryside. Of course, there are elegant antiques throughout the splendid house, and the bedrooms are beautiful and highly individual. Of course, the cooking is exquisite (Michelin starred), and breakfast extraordinary. Of course, the service is polished to perfection. What comes as a bonus is the charming attention of the suave M. Lalleman, who displays a genuine interest in his guests despite the amounts they are paying him.

Nearby Avignon – Palais des Papes, cathedral; Nîmes (40 km).

13550 Noves
Tel 90.94.19.21
Fax 90.94.47.76
Location in countryside off D28, 2 km NW of Noves, 11 km SE of Avignon; in grounds, with car parking
Meals breakfast, lunch, dinner
Prices rooms 1,150F-1,500F, suites 1,800F; breakfast 100F, menus 210F-495F
Rooms 19 double, 4 suites, all with bath; all rooms have central heating, air-conditioning, phone, TV
Facilities dining-room, sitting-room/bar, conference room; swimming-pool, tennis, helipad
Credit cards AE, DC, V
Children welcome
Disabled 10 bedrooms accessible
Pets accepted
Closed Jan; restaurant only, Wed lunch
Proprietors Lalleman family

The South

Auberge de la Madone

'Delightful' was the one-word verdict offered by a reader report-ing on this top-of-the-range Logis, and it remains a fair summary of a hotel that happily combines a sense of special hospitality with affordable (though not low) prices.

You may think that you have taken a wrong turning as you first spy Peillon, perched impossibly above, with little sign of any road leading up. But ascent is possible, and well worthwhile. Time stands still here. The medieval village consists of a few dark cobbled alleys leading up to the church, and tall stone houses looking out over rocky crests and distant forests.

The *auberge* is set just outside the walled village itself, although it shares the views. Behind, paths lead off into the hills, past the grazing sheep with their tinkling bells; in front is the village car park and *boules* area. Within, the rather small bedrooms (with equally small balconies) were completely refurbished a few years ago, and are attractive and comfortable with stylish all-white bathrooms. Meals are served on the pretty, sunny terrace, under a large awning, or in the welcoming Provençal-style dining-room. Cooking is above average (a *toque* from Gault-Millau), and the menus are fair value. An all-weather tennis court is another of the hotel's attractions.

Nearby Monaco – Palace, museums, exotic gardens.

06440 Peillon-Village
Tel 93.79.91.17
Fax 93.79.99.36
Location on edge of perched village, 19 km NE of Nice; with ample car parking
Meals breakfast, lunch, dinner
Prices rooms 440F-780F; breakfast 55F; DB&B 450F-680F; menus 130F-360F
Rooms 20 double, 15 with bath, 5 with shower; all rooms have central heating, phone, TV
Facilities bar, 2 dining-rooms; tennis court
Credit cards MC, V
Children very welcome
Disabled no special facilities
Pets accepted by arrangement
Closed mid-Oct to mid-Dec, 2 weeks Jan
Proprietors Millo family

The South

Country guest-house, Plan-de-la-Tour

Mas des Brugassières

'Very relaxed atmosphere – an excellent place to unwind after the long drive south,' is the verdict of one visitor to this modern (1974) 'farmhouse', set in lush gardens surrounded by vineyards. Bedrooms (some non-smoking) have tiled floors and traditional furniture; some open out directly on to the garden and swimming-pool (and are ventilated only by leaving the door open). There is one public room – a sitting-room-cum-bar with simple wooden furniture and vast French windows – but from Easter to October most sitting will be done outside. Mas des Brugassières is basically a breakfast-only place, but in high season light lunches can be had by the pool.

Nearby Ste-Maxime – beach resort; Port-Grimaud (15 km)

Plan-de-la-Tour 83120
Ste-Maxime
Tel 94.43.72.42
Fax 94.43.00.20
Location in countryside 8 km NW of Ste-Maxime; with gardens and ample car parking
Meals breakfast
Prices rooms 420F-550F; breakfast 40F
Rooms 14 double, all with bath and shower (5 twin); all rooms have central heating, phone
Facilities sitting-room/bar; swimming-pool, tennis
Credit cards MC, V
Children accepted
Disabled ground-floor bedrooms
Pets dogs accepted at extra charge (60F)
Closed Nov to mid-Mar
Proprietors Steve and Annick Geffine

The South

Auberge de Cassagne

Although this Provençal-style *auberge* in a leafy suburb of Avignon
is at the top end of our size range, it is emphatically our kind of
hotel. Up to now it seems to have excited readers rather less than
it has excited us. We look forward to more reports.

The mellow 18th-century house sits in lush gardens which are
among the main attractions of the hotel. There is ample space
for relaxing – a swimming-pool, a plane-shaded terrace for
meals, manicured lawns and paved courtyards surrounded by
peaceful bungalow-style bedrooms with traditional Provençal
furniture and confidently colourful fabrics, as well as all modern
conveniences. There are some bedrooms in the main building,
along with a cosy sitting-room. The dining-room is a lofty,
spacious affair with huge exposed beams, and 'French windows'
overlooking the garden.

When chef Philippe Boucher first came to the Auberge de
Cassagne he was advertised as an ex-disciple of Paul Bocuse and
Georges Blanc; now, he has an established reputation of his own,
recognised with a star from Michelin and two *toques* from
Gault-Millau.

Nearby Avignon – Palais des Papes, Pont St-Bénèzet.

84130 Le Pontet -Avignon
Tel 90.31.04.18
Fax 90.32.25.09
Location in rural suburb of
Avignon, 4 km NW of middle,
3 km W of A7; with gardens
and ample car parking
Meals breakfast, lunch, dinner
Prices rooms 490F-1,180F;
menus 230F-460F, children's
110F
Rooms 27 double, all with
bath or shower; 5 family
rooms, all with bath; all rooms
have central heating, air-
conditioning, phone, satellite
TV, minibar, safe
Facilities dining-room,
2 sitting-rooms, bar;
swimming-pool
Credit cards AE, DC, MC, V
Children welcome
Disabled no special facilities
Pets accepted; 60F charge
Closed never
Proprietors Jean-Michel
Gallon, Philippe Boucher and
André Trestour

The South

Auberge de Reillanne

We don't get many reports on this lovely old *bastide* turned country auberge, but they are always positive, and sometimes verge on the ecstatic. Maurice Bellaiche, who took over the place just after its appearance in our first edition, is now firmly established.

Despite the grandeur of the building – mainly 18th-century, but with parts dating from the 12th – it is not a hotel of four-star sophistication. It's a peaceful place (surrounded by fields, with views towards the Lubéron massif) with a private-home feel, sparsely furnished with great style and individuality. There are seven very large bedrooms with stone walls and beamed ceilings, and rows of books take the place of the usual mod cons – there are no radios or TVs. In the dining-room, paintings and sculptures are in perfect harmony with the setting.

Maurice Bellaiche is also in charge in the kitchen and impresses visitors with his simple honest dishes. One reporter describes him as a 'brilliantly inventive self-taught cook'. More reports would be welcome.

Nearby Lubéron Park – marked trails; St-Michel observatory (10 km); Aix-en-Provence (70 km); Avignon (80 km).

04110 Reillanne
Tel 92.76.45.95
Location in countryside, 1 km from village, 19 km SW of Forcalquier; in garden, with car parking
Meals breakfast, dinner
Prices rooms 260F-360F; breakfast 45F; menus 125F-170F
Rooms 5 double, all with bath (2 twin); 2 family rooms, both with bath; all rooms have central heating, phone,

minibar
Facilities sitting-room, 2 dining-rooms
Credit cards MC, V
Children welcome
Disabled no special facilities
Pets welcome if well behaved
Closed never
Proprietor Maurice Bellaiche

The South

Auberge du Colombier

Yes, this attractive-looking hotel in Provence really does have rooms at 160F a night – but they are singles, without a garden view, in winter. Whether you'll judge the doubles with garden terraces to be good or bad value at around 600F-700F in summer will probably depend on your luck with the weather; the rooms are relatively plain, but the gardens and pool are 'wonderful' (to quote a recent reporter), which makes up for a lot.

This is an old *mas*, low and white, whose chief attraction is certainly the setting – amid tall, shady trees, with views over wooded hills towards the sea – and the outdoor facilities that go with it. There is an especially attractive terrace for summer eating, a tennis court, and plenty of space around the swimming-pool for lounging. Should the weather let you down, you'll find a pleasant dining-room with rustic furniture indoors.

We lack recent reports on the food in general, but breakfast is good, with 'some of the best pastries we've had.' This is a useful base for seeing the sights of the Côte d'Azur – though you may be tempted to stay put instead; the Wolffs and their young staff are charming hosts.

Nearby St-Paul (10 km); Grasse – perfumeries.

06330 Roquefort-les-Pins
Tel 93.77.10.27
Fax 93.77.07.03
Location in countryside off D2085, 15 km E of Grasse, 18 km N of Cannes; with large garden and car parking
Meals breakfast, lunch, dinner
Prices rooms 160F-650F, apartments 450F-800F; breakfast 50F; menus 125F-190F, children 60F
Rooms 18 double (7 twin), 2 apartments, all with bath; all rooms have phone, TV
Facilities 2 dining-rooms, sitting-room, bar, conference room; swimming-pool, tennis court, private night-club
Credit cards AE, DC, MC, V
Children accepted
Disabled no special facilities
Pets accepted
Closed Jan
Proprietor M. Wolff

The South

Country villa, Roussillon

Mas de Garrigon

'We arrived without reservation and were willingly accommodated; the Provençal-style room was very comfortable, the bathroom large and well stocked; the pool was heavenly after a long drive, and the surrounding area pleasant for strolling; dinner was wonderful, with a wide selection and large portions.' A reader reports this ideal end to a day's touring, supporting our promotion of this farmhouse-style hotel to a full entry last year.

The ochre-coloured building was purpose-built by the Rech-Druarts in the late 1970s, though you might not guess it: the traditional Provençal farmhouse style has been carefully reproduced, with a multiplicity of rough-tiled roofs facing this way and that, as if built at random over the years. The hotel stands isolated among pines and scrub, facing the Lubéron hills. In front of the house is a neat sheltered pool sharing country views with the sunny private terraces of the bedrooms – done out in restrained modern style, and thoroughly equipped.

The place is run on house-party rather than conventional hotel lines. Guests are encouraged to browse in the well-stocked library or listen to classical music in the comfortable salon – before an open fire in winter. Philippe Anzallo's cooking is ambitious and competent, and Mme Rech-Druart is much involved in the menu-planning and daily food shopping.

Nearby Gordes (7 km) – château; Village des Bories (5 km).

Rte de St-Saturnin d'Apt, Roussillon 84220 Gordes
Tel 90.05.63.22
Fax 90.05.70.01
Location in countryside, on D2 3 km N of Roussillon, 7 km E of Gordes; in grounds with ample car parking
Meals breakfast, lunch, dinner
Prices rooms 720F-960F; breakfast 75F, menus 185F-325F
Rooms 7 double (2 twin), two family rooms, all with bath; all rooms have phone, TV, minibar, terrace
Facilities 3 dining-rooms, bar, library, sitting-room; swimming-pool
Credit cards AE, DC, V
Children older ones accepted if well behaved **Disabled** ground-floor bedrooms
Pets accepted if well behaved
Closed restaurant only: Sun dinner and Mon; mid-Nov to end Dec **Manager** Mme Christiane Rech-Druart

The South

Country villa, St-Paul-de-Vence

Le Hameau

It's a standard pattern among readers reporting on Le Hameau that they stay longer than they planned to, which is about as clear a recommendation as you can get. Not only is it a captivating place, but also it offers very good value.

St-Paul-de-Vence is a perfectly preserved hill village. Its ramparts, rising above green terraces of vineyards and bougainvillea, provide panoramic views of the Alpes-Maritimes, and its old streets are lined by galleries, workshops and chic boutiques. Of the few hotels in and around the village, Le Hameau is certainly one of the most desirable – an unusually stylish and notably relaxed place run by a friendly and eager-to-please young couple.

It consists of a cluster of red-roofed Provençal villas, surrounded by orange, lemon and other fruit trees. Bedrooms are rustic in style, with beams, dark-wood furniture and rugs on red-tiled floors; they vary in size and price considerably – many have their own terrace or balcony. There is a cool, neat breakfast room, but you will be hoping to have no need of it – one of Le Hameau's great delights is breakfast (with home-made jam) taken in the large terraced garden, which accommodates a small but smart pool.

Nearby Maeght Foundation – contemporary arts; Cagnes-sur-Mer (5 km); Nice (15 km); Grasse (25 km) – perfumes.

528 Rte de la Colle 06570 St-Paul-de-Vence
Tel 93.32.80.24
Fax 93.32.55.75
Location one km outside village, 20 km from Nice; with gardens and ample car parking
Meals breakfast
Prices rooms 390F-600F, suites 700F; breakfast 52F
Rooms 11 double (5 twin), one single, 3 suites; all with bath or shower; one children's room ; all rooms have central heating, air-conditioning, phone, minibar, safe
Facilities sitting-room, dining-room; swimming-pool
Credit cards AE, MC, V
Children accepted if well behaved
Disabled no special facilities
Pets accepted if well behaved
Closed mid-Nov to 24 Dec, mid-Jan to mid-Feb
Manager Xavier Huvelin

The South

Château de Roussan

The McHugo family, who took over this beautiful country house some five years ago, are now well into their stride, with necessary upgrading (of the kitchen, for example) and a larger restaurant, now behind them. The welcoming private-home atmosphere so carefully cultivated by the original Roussel family remains intact.

The château was built by a grandson of Nostradamus (Catherine de Medici's famous astrologer) at the beginning of the 18th century. An impressive avenue of trees leads to a gracious building with a mellow exterior and fine rooms carefully and beautifully furnished with antiques. The bedrooms vary in size but are all furnished in an appropriate style (though bathrooms are modern) and are enormously atmospheric. There is a formal library/salon in the oldest part of the house, and a vaulted breakfast room.

Meals and drinks can be had on the terrace. In the delicious, informal grounds there is plenty of room to sit in perfect solitude – overlooking a fountain, or perhaps the 16th-century farmhouse which belonged to Nostradamus himself.

Nearby Tarascon (15 km) – château; Avignon (30 km); Arles (30 km) and the Camargue.

Rte de Tarascon 13210 St-Rémy-de-Provence
Tel 90.92.11.63
Fax 90.92.50.59
Location in countryside, 2 km W of town; in large park, with ample car parking
Meals breakfast, dinner
Prices rooms 360F-750F; menus 75F-135F
Rooms 21 double (7 twin), 17 with bath, 4 with shower; all rooms have central heating, phone

Facilities TV room, library
Credit cards AE, MC, V
Children welcome
Disabled 1 ground-floor bedroom
Pets accepted
Closed never
Proprietors Judy and Brian McHugo

The South

La Ponche

You might not think St-Tropez would be our kind of town, but La Ponche is our kind of hotel, at least when we're feeling like a treat. Tucked away in a tiny square overlooking the small fishing port and tiny beach of La Ponche, this cluster of 17th-century houses offers a compelling combination of sophistication and warmth. Margerite Barbier started her fishermen's bar in 1937; later her daughter, Simone Duckstein, steadily transformed it into a stylish, arty hotel, full of personal touches. Paintings by Mme Duckstein's first husband cover the walls.

You can eat on a terrace, looking across a small square to the sea, or in one of several areas indoors, including the main dining-room – small, freshly decorated, unpretentious but sophisticated. The food is memorable, particularly the seafood. Bedrooms are captivating and very comfortable. Many were very smartly revamped in 1993, with stylish colour schemes and slick bathrooms. A couple of noisier bedrooms facing the street may induce you to sleep with the double-glazed windows closed and the air-conditioning on.

Nearby Beaches: Les Graniers (100m); La Bouillabaisse (1 km); Tahiti (4 km).

3 Rue des Remparts 83990 St-Tropez
Tel 94.97.02.53
Fax 94.97.78.61
Location in heart of old town, overlooking Port des Pêcheurs; with private garage and valet parking
Meals breakfast, lunch, dinner
Prices rooms 700F-1,600F, suites 1,100F-2,200F; breakfast 60F, lunch 120F, dinner 170F

Rooms 11 double with bath; 2 family rooms with bath; 2 apartments; 3 suites; all have air-conditioning, central heating, phone, satellite TV, minibar, safe
Facilities TV room, bar, 2 dining-rooms
Credit cards AE, MC, V
Children accepted
Disabled access difficult
Pets accepted
Closed end Oct to end Mar
Proprietor Mme Barbier

The South

Mas de la Fouque

Given the prices, which are about as high as any in this guide, it's perhaps not surprising that we rarely get reports from readers on this casual but exclusive retreat in a lagoonside setting near the main resort of the Camargue. But a recent inspection visit confirms its attractions for an entirely peaceful, away-from-it-all stay – with the wildlife and famous white horses of the Camargue as an added dimension. Rooms throughout are smartly decorated – white walls, tiled floors, timbered ceilings – and the bedrooms are the epitome of comfort, with private terraces built over the lagoon. Despite the four-star luxuries, this is very much a family-run hotel with a friendly, relaxed atmosphere. Food is excellent, with regional dishes elegantly presented; many vegetables and herbs are home-grown.

Nearby The Camargue; Aigues-Mortes (25 km); Arles (38 km).

Rte du Petit Rhône 13460 Les Stes-Maries-de-la-Mer
Tel 90.97.81.02
Fax 90.97.96.84
Location in the Camargue, 4 km NW of Les Stes-Maries-de-la-Mer; with ample car parking
Meals breakfast, lunch, dinner
Prices rooms 980F-2,010F; lunch 170F-225F, dinner 225F-395F
Rooms 10 double, all with bath and terrace (4twin); 3 family rooms, with bath; 1 children's room with shower; all rooms have phone, TV, air-conditioning, minibar, fans
Facilities 2 sitting-rooms, bar, dining-room; tennis, swimming-pool, putting
Credit cards AE, DC, MC, V
Children welcome if well supervised **Disabled** access easy; all on ground floor
Pets dogs accepted
Closed Jan to mid-Mar
Proprietor Jean-Paul Cochat

The South

L'Abbaye de Sainte-Croix

For over seven hundred years, Cistercian monks were the only ones to enjoy the panoramic views of the Provençal countryside from this beautiful 12thC abbey. In 1969 the Bossard family rescued it from ruin and turned it into a luxury (four-star, Relais & Châteaux) hotel. Now, the trees they planted are maturing nicely, and the various extensions they have built blend perfectly with the mellow original buildings, which from the outside are more farm-like than ecclesiastical.

A maze of stone passageways leads through low arches to a beamed dining-room (with fabulous views), a cosy vaulted sitting-room with a huge open fireplace, and bedrooms named after saints. Some of these are cavernous, but others, originally monks' cells, are small and dark – deliciously cool in summer, perhaps less compelling in winter. Furnishings have an appropriately restrained, solid style, and decoration is tastefully muted. The pool is a good size.

Food is a highlight, with a distinct Provençal influence; Michelin awards a star, Gault-Millau two *toques*.

Nearby château, museum; Aix-en-Provence (30 km); Arles (40 km); Avignon (45 km).

Route du Val de Cuech, 13300 Salon-de-Provence
Tel 90.56.24.55
Fax 90.56.31.12
Location in sweeping countryside, 3 km NE of Salon on D16; with garden and ample car parking
Meals breakfast, lunch, dinner
Prices rooms 605F-1,275F; breakfast 100F, meals 195F-415F
Rooms 19 double, 17 with bath, 2 with shower; 5 apartments, all with bath; all rooms have central heating, air-conditioning, phone, TV, minibar **Facilities** dining-room, bar, TV room; swimming-pool (unheated), table-tennis
Credit cards AE, DC, MC, V
Children accepted
Disabled no special facilities
Pets not accepted in restaurant **Closed** Nov to Feb; restaurant only, Mon lunch
Proprietors Bossard family

The South

Hôtel des Deux Rocs

This captivating hotel in a famously captivating hill village no longer generates the reports that it did in earlier years. Perhaps this is just an indication that it has recovered from its exposure on British TV in the 1980s; but more reports would be welcome.

The hotel's setting (it is an 18th-century mansion, just outside the medieval walls) remains one of its main attractions. Parking may be awkward, but for most visitors that counts for little compared to the pleasure of breakfast or an evening drink beside the fountain on the shady little cobbled square in front, looking across the green valley.

Inside there are two inviting little *salons*, one serving as a bar, and a long wood-and-stone dining-room. The food is traditional and excellent. Bedrooms vary in size and standard. Those at the back of the house are rather cramped, while some of those at the front are marvellously spacious and light, with vigorous colour schemes. The dynamic Mme Hirsch is ever-present, overseeing the scrupulous housekeeping – first-class linen and towels – taking the orders at dinner, advising on sightseeing excursions.
Nearby Lac de Saint Cassien (15 km); Gorges du Verdon (40 km); Grasse (32 km); Cannes (47 km).

Place Font d'Amont 83440 Seillans
Tel 94.76.87.32
Fax 94.76.88.68
Location at top of small village, 30 km W of Grasse; with terrace
Meals breakfast, lunch, dinner
Prices rooms 260F-520F; breakfast 43F; DB&B 310F-440F; menus 140F-210F
Rooms 15 double (5 twin), all with bath or shower; all rooms have central heating, phone, minibar
Facilities dining-room, bar, sitting-room
Credit cards MC, V
Children accepted
Disabled no special facilities
Pets dogs accepted but not in dining-room
Closed Nov to mid-Mar
Proprietor Mme Hirsch

The South

Converted castle, Trigance

Château de Trigance

For well over 20 years now, Jean-Claude Thomas and his wife have run this characterful and comfortable hotel in the remote limestone hills that surround the dramatic Gorges du Verdon, but they show no sign of flagging. Trigance remains a welcoming port of call in a region of few villages and even fewer hotels.

On arrival, you might be taken aback. Is this fortress perched high on a rocky hilltop really your hotel? (Yes.) And if it is, how are you going to penetrate its defences? (By climbing a steep flight of rocky stairs – don't worry, your bags will be carried up.)

Once inside, you are in the Middle Ages. Stone by stone, M. Thomas has painstakingly rebuilt his 11thC castle (for many years it served as a quarry for the local villagers); he will be delighted to show you before-and-after photographs to prove it. The impressive stone-vaulted, candle-lit dining-room, and the sitting-room below, are windowless and highly atmospheric, furnished in medieval style. Most of the bedrooms (cut into the hill) are similar, with canopied beds, antique furniture, tapestries and banners – and fine views from their windows. The cooking is surprisingly good, considering the remoteness of the place.

Nearby Verdon gorge – Europe's 'Grand Canyon'.

83840 Trigance
Tel 94.76.91.18
Fax 94.85.68.99
Location overlooking tiny village, 10 km NW of Comps-sur-Artuby; with terrace, and private car parking
Meals breakfast, lunch, dinner
Prices rooms 550F-900F, suites 850F; menus 195F-360F
Rooms 8 double, all with bath; 2 suites; all rooms have central heating, phone, TV

Facilities dining-room, sitting-room
Credit cards AE, DC, MC, V
Children welcome
Disabled access very difficult
Pets accepted
Closed Nov to mid-Mar
Proprietor Jean-Claude Thomas

The South

Le Manoir du Raveyron

It sounds grand, but is nothing of the sort: this is the sort of rustic village inn that is the bedrock of French hotelkeeping – a two-fireplace Logis offering simple but satisfactory accommodation, modest prices, a warm welcome and excellent wholesome food (visit the place on a Sunday and you'll find it bursting at the seams with lunching families.) The hotel faces an ugly modern building; but the surroundings do not intrude, because the old stone building is set well back from the street, behind gates and a large and leafy courtyard-cum-garden. We get occasional reports confirming our recommendation of the Manoir, but we would welcome more.

Nearby Gorges de l'Ardèche; Pont d'Arc (5 km); Marzal (20 km)

Rue Henri Barbusse 07150 Vallon-Pont-d'Arc
Tel 75.88.03.59
Fax 75.37.11.12
Location in village on D579, 33 km S of Aubenas, 51 km NE of Alés; with garden and car parking
Meals breakfast, lunch, dinner
Prices rooms 175F-270F; menus 98F-220F, children's 42F
Rooms 15 double, one single, all with shower; all rooms have central heating
Facilities dining-room, sitting-room/bar
Credit cards MC, V
Children welcome
Disabled no special facilities
Pets accepted
Closed mid-Oct to mid-Mar
Proprietors M. Bourdat and M. Gauthier

The South

Village hotel, Villeneuve-lès-Avignon

Hostellerie la Magnaneraie

Eliane and Gérard Prayal write to tell us of the numerous improvements they are continuing to make to their friendly, mellow stone house in a well-heeled residential corner of Villeneuve-lès-Avignon. First they added entirely new bedrooms next to the magnificent swimming-pool, and renovated and enlarged the 'old' bedrooms in the main house, adding air-conditioning but retaining an elegant and refined style. Next came the sitting-room. The Prayals have now turned their hand to the lobby, hall and reception areas, Despite all this up-grading, and the sense of elegance that prevails, the easy-going atmosphere that the Prayals have prided themselves on still exists: many of the bedrooms can accommodate families (some have charming bunk beds), and (well behaved) children are much in evidence. There is a large dining-terrace as well as an elegant dining-room Their efforts have been rewarded with promotion to four-star status, and at the same time Gérard has been made a Maitre Cusinier de France. With two toques from Gault-Millau, a Michelin star (for the moment still the preserve of the nearby Prieuré) cannot be far away.

Nearby Tour Phillipe-le-Bel, Chartreuse du Val-de-Bénédiction; Avignon – Palais des Papes, cathedral, Pont St-Bénézat.

Rue du Camp-de-Bataille
30400 Villeneuve-lès-Avignon
Tel 90.25.11.11
Fax 90.25.46.37
Location in residential area on fringe of village, across the Rhône from Avignon; with garden and car parking
Meals breakfast, lunch, dinner
Prices rooms 500F-1,200F; breakfast 70F, menus 180F-350F
Rooms 25 double, all with bath; 1 suite; all rooms have central heating, phone, cable TV, minibar; many rooms have private terrace and/or air-conditioning
Facilities dining-room, sitting-room, bar, conference room; swimming-pool, tennis
Credit cards AE, DE, MC, V
Children accepted
Disabled access easy but no special facilities
Pets accepted **Closed** never
Proprietors Gérard and Eliane Prayal

The South

L'Ermitage-Meissonnier

The French gourmet guides are not impressed by the new direction of this once-famous restaurant, and the spacious rooms can disappoint in other respects, but in summer the pool and terrace are delightful. More reports, please.

■ Ave de Verdun, 30133 Les Angles (Gard) **Tel** 90.25.41.02
Fax 90.25.11.68 **Meals** breakfast, lunch, dinner **Prices** rooms 230F-480F; menus 100F-450F, children's 120F **Rooms** 16, all with bath or shower, central heating, phone **Credit cards** AE, DC, V **Closed** Jan, Feb

---

Le Logis du Guetteur

This 11thC fort still looks more or less as it must have done nine centuries ago. The modernised bedrooms are quiet, with lovely views, and there is a pleasant pool. But the main emphasis is on the medieval cellar restaurant and terrace, where satisfying classic dishes are served.

■ Place du Château, 83460 Les Arcs (Var) **Tel** 94.73.30.82
Fax 94.73.39.95 **Meals** breakfast, lunch, dinner **Prices** rooms 450F; breakfast 48F, menus 135F-280F **Rooms** 11, all with bath or shower, central heating **Credit cards** AE, DC, MC, V **Closed** mid-Jan to mid-Feb

---

Le Cottage

An enthusiastic readers' report restores the entry of this three-fireplace Logis, evidently much improved since its last appearance: 'We'd be pleased to go back. Bright, simple room; elegant, innovative and delicious dinner.' Pleasant garden, with pool.

■ 21 Rue Arthur-Rimbaud, 66700 Argelès-sur-Mer (Pyrénées-Orientales)
Tel 68.81.07.33 **Fax** 68.81.59.69 **Meals** breakfast, lunch, dinner
Prices rooms 280F-520F; breakfast 48F, lunch 80F, menu s 140F-265F
Rooms 32, all with central heating, phone, TV, hairdrier
Credit cards MC, V **Closed** Nov to end-Mar

Auberge de la Vignette Haute

This extraordinary place has been virtually rebuilt since the disastrous fire of 1986, but has the feel of a medieval farmhouse. It is filled with gleaming rustic antiques, and bedrooms are spacious, and highly individual. Pool. There is a farm menagerie nearby. Caters for parties, so you might want to avoid weekends.

■ 06810 Auribeau (Alpes-Maritimes) **Tel** 93.42.20.01 **Fax** 93.42.31.16
Meals breakfast, lunch, dinner **Prices** rooms 750F-1,900F; breakfast 80F-110F, menus 350F-500F **Rooms** 12, all with bath, central heating, phone, TV, minibar **Credit cards** AE, MC, V **Closed** never; restaurant only, mid-Nov to mid-Dec

The South

Country hotel, Baix

Hostellerie La Cardinale

The birthplace of the Relais & Châteaux chain. La Cardinale is a gloriously welcoming old house, with four beautiful bedrooms; the rest, along with a smart pool, are 3 km away at the Résidence.

■ Quai du Rhône, 07210 Baix (Ardèche) **Tel** 75.85.80.40 **Fax** 75.85.82.07 **Meals** breakfast, lunch dinner **Prices** rooms 700F-1200F, suite 1,500F-1,800F; breakfast 100F **Rooms** 14, all with bath or shower, air-conditioning, TV, phone, minibar **Credit cards** AE, DC, V **Closed** Jan to mid-Mar

---

Country inn, Les Baux-de-Provence

Auberge de la Benvengudo

The Beaupied family's creeper-clad hotel remains compelling – and much more affordable than most places in the area. Rooms have the style of a private country house: a cosy sitting-room with beams, an intimate dining-room and bedrooms with pretty patterned curtains. Pool and tennis.

■ Vallon de l'Arcoule, 13520 Les Baux-de-Provence (Bouches-du-Rhône) **Tel** 90.54.32.54 **Fax** 90.54.42.58 **Meals** breakfast, dinner **Prices** rooms 520F-670F, suites 800F-930F; menus 240F **Rooms** 20, all with bath, central heating, air-conditioning, phone, TV **Credit cards** AE, MC, V **Closed** Nov to mid-Feb; restaurant only, Sun

---

Seaside hotel, Cap d'Antibes

La Gardiole

We have conflicting reports on this unassuming, pink-washed hotel – one of the more modest places in this 'exclusive' area. It is furnished simply but effectively – dark-wood chairs and rugs on polished tiled floors – and run in friendly fashion. The regional cooking is 'not cheap but very good'. More reports, please.

■ Chemin de la Garoupe, 06600 Cap d'Antibes (Alpes-Maritimes) **Tel** 93.61.35.03 **Meals** breakfast, lunch, dinner **Prices** rooms 500F-750F; menus 120F-170F **Rooms** 21, all with bath or shower, central heating, air-conditioning, phone, minibar, safe; TV on request **Credit cards** AE, DC, MC, V **Closed** Nov to Feb

---

Country house hotel, Carcassonne

Domaine d'Auriac

A relaxing country house of which the primary attractions are outdoors: golf and tennis on the doorstep, a pool surrounded by beautifully manicured gardens and a dining terrace with a blissfully verdant view. But conditions indoors are comfortable too – this, after all, is a member of Relais & Châteaux.

■ Route de Saint-Hilaire, 11009 Carcassonne (Aude) **Tel** 68.25.72.22 **Fax** 68.47.35.54 **Meals** breakfast, lunch, dinner **Prices** rooms 700F-1,300F; breakfast 80F, menus 180F-350F **Rooms** 25, all with bath or shower, central heating, phone, TV, minibar **Credit cards** AE, DC, MC, V **Closed** 8 Jan to 2 Feb; Sun, Mon lunch out of season

The South

Country hotel, Céret

Le Mas Trilles

Two separate reports force this charming 17thC farmhouse to our attention – 'the hotel we enjoyed most in two very enjoyable weeks,' says one; 'like staying with friends, in a beautiful setting,' says the other. Simple, stylish furnishings in spacious rooms. Lush garden with a fair-sized heated pool.

■ Le Pont de Reynès, 66400 Céret (Pyrénées-Orientales) **Tel** 68.87.38.37 **Fax** 68.87.4 2.62 **Meals** breakfast, dinner **Prices** rooms 440F-975F; breakfast 65F, menus 165F-200F **Rooms** 10, all with bath, central heating, phone, TV **Credit cards** MC, V **Closed** Nov to Mar

---

Village hotel, Cotignac

Lou Calen

The shady garden, dining terrace and pool are the key attractions of this shuttered house on the occasionally noisy village square of Cotignac. The house is furnished in a home-like blend of antique and rustic styles, and bedrooms vary considerably in size, style and price. Cooking is simple but hearty.

■ 1 Cours Gambetta, 83850 Cotignac (Var) **Tel** 94.04.60.40 **Fax** 94.04.76.64 **Meals** breakfast, lunch, dinner **Prices** 290F-600F; menus 105F-245F **Rooms** 16, all with bath or shower, central heating, phone, TV **Credit cards** AE, DC, MC, V **Closed** Jan to late Mar; Wed except Jul and Aug; restaurant only Wed

---

Seaside hotel, Eze

Château Eza

Stunning views are only one attraction of this luxury hotel perched at the top of the precipitous medieval village of Eze. Bedrooms and suites are magnificent, with priceless antiques and marble bathrooms. The renowned restaurant is one of several Michelin starred places in the village.

■ Rue de la Pise, 06360 Eze (Alpes-Maritimes) **Tel** 93.41.12.24 **Fax** 93.41.16.64 **Meals** breakfast, lunch, dinner **Prices** rooms 1,500F-3,500F; menus 380F-530F **Rooms** 10, all with bath, central heating, air-conditioning, phone, TV, radio, minibar, hairdrer **Credit cards** AE, DC, MC, V **Closed** Nov to mid-Dec

---

Country inn, Gigondas

Les Florets

This small, family-run hotel is appropriately named: floral bedrooms, flowers on the tables and (at the right time of year) surrounded by a riot of blossom on the nearby hills. Food is excellent, and the patron is a winemaker.

■ Route des Dentelles, 84190 Gigondas (Vaucluse) **Tel** 90.65.85.01 **Fax** 90.65.83.80 **Meals** breakfast, lunch, dinner **Prices** rooms 345F-410F; breakfast 50F, menus 155F-210F **Rooms** 15, all with central heating, phone; some have TV **Credit cards** AE, DC, MC, V **Closed** Jan, Feb; restaurant only, Wed

The South

Farm guest-house, Gordes

La Ferme de la Huppe

'Very comfortable room in a converted stable. Beautiful pool and a lovely courtyard garden. Well run by a Dutch/Swiss family. Food very good.' So ran the reader's report that earned a place for this huddle of farm buildings. Furnishings are stylishly rustic, with some antiques and tasteful fabrics. More reports, please.

■ Les Pourquiers, 84220 Gordes (Vaucluse) **Tel** 90.72.12.25 **Fax** 90.72.01.83 **Meals** breakfast, lunch (Sun only), dinner **Prices** rooms 400F-600F with breakfast; menus 145F-200F, children's 110F **Rooms** 8, all with bath, central heating, phone, TV, minibar, hairdrier **Credit cards** MC, V **Closed** early Nov to late Mar

---

Country hotel, Gordes

Le Gordos

No restaurant, but few other drawbacks to this *mas de pierre seche*, just outside Gordes – especially if the Provençal sun shines. Most of the rooms are in outbuildings opening directly on to some part of the garden; there is tennis, as well as an attractive small pool. 'Very good' service.

■ Rte de Cavaillon, 84220 Gordes (Vaucluse) **Tel** 90.72.00.75 **Fax** 90.72.07.00 **Meals** breakfast, snacks **Prices** rooms 390F-800F; breakfast 55F **Rooms** 19, all with bath or shower, phone, TV **Credit cards** AE, V **Closed** Nov to mid-Mar

---

Château hotel, Lamastre

Château d'Urbilhac

This fairy-tale château – 19thC but in Renaissance style, with round tower and steep roof – has a peaceful, elevated setting in a large park, with a good pool. The interior is rather ponderous but does not lack character or comfort. 'Good food' but 'atmosphere a little stilted' comments a visitor.

■ 07270 Lamastre (Ardèche) **Tel** 75.06.42.11 **Fax** 75.06.52.75 **Meals** breakfast, lunch, dinner **Prices** rooms 450F-700F; menus from 200F;DB&B (obligatory in season) 500F-600F **Rooms** 13, all with bath or shower, phone **Credit cards** AE, DC, MC, V **Closed** Oct to Apr

---

Town hotel, Lamastre

Hôtel du Midi

The restaurant is the heart of this hotel, serving a very successful blend of traditional and nouvelle dishes. The dining-rooms are rather plain but intimate, service helpful and friendly. Bedrooms, in a separate building a minute's walk away, are comfortably spacious and tastefully furnished.

■ Place Seignobos, 07270 Lamastre (Ardèche) **Tel** 75.06.41.50 **Fax** 75.06.49.75 **Meals** breakfast, lunch, dinner **Prices** rooms 300F-450F; menus 195F-400F **Rooms** 13, all with bath or shower, central heating, phone; some have TV **Credit cards** AE, DC, MC, V **Closed** Sun evening, Mon; mid-Dec to Feb

The South

Seaside hotel, Le Lavandou

Auberge de la Calanque

This arcaded hotel overlooking the marina of Le Lavandou has no right to be here, but it comes strongly recommended by a reader – not only for the 'fantastic' view but also the 'very comfortable, airy' rooms and 'very helpful' manager. Restaurant in the hotel, but also lots of others nearby.

■ 62 Avenue du Général de Gaulle, 83980 Le Lavandou (Var) **Tel** 94.71.05.96 **Fax** 94.7 1.20.12 **Meals** breakfast, lunch, dinner **Prices** rooms 500F-1,050F; breakfast 55F, menu 180F **Rooms** 38, all with bath/shower, central heating, phone, TV **Credit cards** AE, DC, MC, V **Closed** Nov to mid- Mar; restaurant only, end-Oct, Wed out of season

---

Village inn, Maussane-les-Alpilles

L'Oustaloun

This village hostellerie – a cheaper alternative to staying in nearby Les Baux – has abundant old-world charm and character. The restaurant occupies three 16thC stone-vaulted rooms; food is honest, regional fare. Bedrooms are simple in style but furnished with handsome antiques. Reports welcome.

■ Place de l'Église, 13520 Maussane-les-Alpilles (Bouches-du-Rhône) **Tel** 90.54.32.19 **Fax** 90.54.45.57 **Meals** breakfast, lunch, dinner **Prices** rooms 260F-400F; breakfast 34F, menus 120F (Jan to Jun and Oct to Dec), 150F (Jun to Oct) **Rooms** 9, all with bath or shower, phone, TV **Credit cards** MC, V **Closed** Jan to mid-Feb; restaurant only, Wed, Jan to Jun, and Oct to Dec; Thu from Jun to Sep

---

Village hotel, Mirmande

La Capitelle

A rough-stone building in a backwater setting in a walled medieval village, yet only a few minutes' drive from the autoroute – La Capitelle makes an excellent stopover. It has an air of confident good taste, with a stylishly traditional feel to the individually and boldly decorated bedrooms, and the vaulted dining-room.

■ Le Rempart, 26270 Mirmande (Drôme) **Tel** 75.63.02.72 **Fax** 75.63.02.50 **Meals** breakfast, lunch, dinner **Prices** rooms 260F-550F; breakfast 45F, menus 85F-175F, children's 60F **Rooms** 11, all with bath or shower, central heating, phone **Credit cards** AE, DC, MC, V **Closed** mid-Jan to mid-Feb; T ue and Wed lunch

---

Country hotel, Montferrat

La Calanco

The proprietor of one of our Burgundian entries suggests this new hotel in a 400-year-old house, tucked away from the crowds. Six 'lovely' bedrooms, tastefully decorated and thoughtfully equipped, and 'unobtrusive and considerate hospitality'.

■ Rue du docteur Rayol, 83131 Montferrat (Var) **Tel** 94.70.93.10 **Fax** 94.70.91.49 **Meals** breakfast, dinner on request **Prices** rooms 280F-450F with breakfast; dinner 130F **Rooms** 6 , all with bath, central heating, hairdrier **Credit cards** MC, V **Closed** never

The South

Country hotel, Mougins

Le Mas Candille

A charming old farmhouse that made a brief appearance in the guide in 1991. Since then it has been smartened up, and is now one of the most compelling hotels in (just outside, in fact) fashionable Mougins. Tiles, beams, ochre walls; pretty dining-terraces by the house and one of the two pools; extensive grounds.

■ Boulevard Rebuffel, 06250 Mougins (Alpes-Maritimes) **Tel** 93.90.00.85 **Fax** 92.92.85 .56 **Meals** breakfast, lunch, dinner **Prices** rooms 680F-980F; suites 2,100F; breakfast 85F, menus 165F-280F **Rooms** 24, all with bath or shower, phone **Credit cards** AE, DC, MC, V **Closed** Nov to mid-Mar ; restaurant only, Tue, Wed lunch

---

Château hotel, Nans-les-Pins

Domaine de Chateauneuf

For golfing bon viveurs, this takes some beating – a polished little Relais & Châteaux hotel beside the golf course of Sainte-Baume. The four-square 17thC house, white-painted and red-roofed, stands surrounded by pines. Inside, the style of the public rooms is grandly traditional; bedrooms have a fresh, designer style.

■ Au Logis de Nans, 83860 Nans-les-Pins (Var) **Tel** 94.78.90.06 **Fax** 94.78.63.30 **Meals** breakfast, lunch, dinner **Prices** rooms 600F-2,250F; breakfast 70F, menus 170F-380F **Rooms** 30, all with bath or shower, phone, satellite TV, minibar, hairdrier **Credit cards** AE, DC, MC, V **Closed** Dec to Feb

---

Country hotel, Olargues

Domaine de Rieumegé

A reader alerted us to this peaceful, rustic 17thC house in the foothills of the Haut-Languedoc national park. Good food in the barn-like restaurant, antique furnishings in the cosy sitting-room and simple bedrooms. Pool and tennis in the lush grounds.

■ Rte de St-Pons, 34390 Olargues (Hérault) **Tel** 67.97.73.99 **Fax** 67.97.78.52 **Meals** breakfast, lunch, dinner, snacks **Prices** rooms 285F-510F; breakfast 55F; menus 100F-165F **Rooms** 14, all with bath or shower, central heating, phone; TV on request **Credit cards** AE, MC, V **Closed** Nov to Easter

---

Converted mill, Ornaisons

Relais du Val d'Orbieu

A carefully converted old mill encircled by trees, with simply but neatly furnished rooms, mostly at ground level and opening on to a grassy courtyard. The fixed-price menu is 'excellent', the carte 'fabulous', the welcome warm. Pool and tennis. More reports, please.

■ 11200 Ornaisons (Aude) **Tel** 68.27.10.27 **Fax** 68.27.52.44 **Meals** break fast, lunch, dinner **Prices** rooms 420F-950F; breakfast 70F, menus 195F-325F, children's 125F **Rooms** 20, all with bath, central heating, phone, TV, radio, minibar, hairdrier **Credit cards** AE, DC, MC, V **Closed** Feb; restaurant only, Sun evening Nov to Mar

The South

Country hotel, Pégomas

Le Bosquet

This modern hotel with a spacious garden but no restaurant has a special place in the affections of many British and other foreign visitors – probably due to the relaxed atmosphere, coupled with the the very un-Provençal prices. Pool, tennis. Our most recent reporter was 'very happy' here.

■ Quartier du Château, 06580 Pégomas (Alpes-Maritimes)
Tel 93.42.22.87 **Meals** break fast **Prices** rooms 160F-320F, studios 340F-430F; breakfast 30F **Rooms** 24, all with bath or shower, central heating, phone **Credit cards** not accepted **Closed** 1 Nov

---

Seaside hotel, Ile de Port-Cros

Le Manoir

This large green-shuttered 19thC manor house stands on a lush, secluded island (a nature reserve) a few km off the south coast and is run along house-party lines. White-walled bedrooms are furnished with 19thC pieces – simple but stylish and comfortable. Good seafood.

■ Ile de Port-Cros, 83400 Hyéres (Var) **Tel** 94.05.90.52
Fax 94.05.90.89 **Meals** breakfast, lunch, dinner **Prices** DB&B 700F-1,000F **Rooms** 23, all with bath or shower, central heating, phone **Credit cards** MC, V **Closed** Oct to Apr

---

Château hotel, Rochegude

Château de Rochegude

Despite the high cost of rooms here, we cannot resist including this sumptuous château because of its wonderful setting – overlooking the vineyards of the Rhône plain – and its equally wonderful food (one Michelin star). Bedrooms are palatial. Relais & Châteaux.

■ 26790 Rochegude (Drôme) **Tel** 75.04.81.88 **Fax** 75.04.89.87
Meals breakfast, lunch, dinner **Prices** rooms 500F-2,500F; breakfast 95F, menus 200F-480F **Rooms** 29, all with bath, central heating, air-conditioning, phone; most have TV, minibar **Credit cards** AE, DC, MC, V **Closed** Mid-Jan to mid-Mar

---

Seaside hotel, St-Clair

Hôtel Belle-Vue

This informal seaside hotel in lush, colourful gardens lives up to its name, with a wonderful view across the bay. It offers unpretentious but comfortable accommodation; bedrooms vary – the best are bright and spacious, with big new bathrooms; some have sea views. More reports welcome.

■ Blvd du Four des Maures, St-Clair, 83980 Le Lavandou (Var)
Tel 94.71.01.06 **Fax** 9 4.71.64.72 **Meals** breakfast, lunch, dinner
Prices rooms 350F-750F; menus 170F-250F **Rooms** 19, all with bath or shower, central heating, phone **Credit cards** AE, DC, MC, V **Closed** Nov to Mar

The South

Villa guest-house, St-Jean-Cap-Ferrat

Clair Logis

It is not easy to find such a reasonably priced hotel in such an exclusive area, let alone one which has the charm of a private villa and is set in lush, secluded gardens. Bedrooms are simple (those in the annexe are not particularly spacious) and four can accommodate families. No restaurant.

■ 12 Ave Centrale, 06230 St-Jean-Cap-Ferrat (Alpes-Maritimes) **Tel** 93.76.04.57 **Fax** 93.76.11.85 **Meals** breakfast **Prices** rooms 290F-690F; breakfast 45F **Rooms** 18, all with bath, central heating, phone; most have TV, minibar **Credit cards** AE, DC, MC, V **Closed** mid-Nov to mid-Dec

---

Village hotel, St-Paul-de-Vence

La Colombe d'Or

A famous, chic small hotel, distinguished by a collection of modern art, but also a delightful place to stay. All is simple and in exquisite 'country' taste; outside there is a creeper-surrounded terrace. The food wins no awards, but that hardly matters.

■ Place de Gaulle, 06570 St-Paul-de-Vence (Alpes-Maritimes) **Tel** 93.32.80.02 **Fax** 93 .32.77.78 **Meals** breakfast, lunch, dinner **Prices** rooms 1,150F-1,400F; breakfast 60F, menus 250F-400F **Rooms** 25, all with bath, some with spa baths, central heating, air-conditioning, phone, TV, radio **Credit cards** AE, DC, MC, V **Closed** mid-Nov to mid-Dec

---

Country villa, St-Paul-de-Vence

Les Orangers

A traditional Provençal house in a fine hillside setting (good views), furnished with simple good taste and immaculately kept. In the sitting-room there are exposed beams, solid antiques, fresh flowers; most of the bedrooms have balconies or terraces. 'A lovely hotel despite the busy street,' enthuses a visitor.

■ Chemin des Fumerates, 06570 St-Paul-de-Vence (Alpes-Maritimes) **Tel** 93.32.80.95 **Fax** 93.32.00.32 **Meals** breakfast **Prices** rooms 410F-730F; breakfast 45F **Rooms** 10, all with bath, central heating, phone **Credit cards** MC, V **Closed** never

---

Village hotel, St-Paul-de-Vence

Le Saint-Paul

If you can afford it, another exceptionally captivating place to stay in pricey St-Paul, in a beautifully restored 16thC house. Bedrooms are done out with real panache, and the public areas are equally welcoming; there is small dining terrace. Above-average cooking.

■ 86 Rue Grande, 06570 St-Paul-de-Vence (Alpes-Maritimes) **Tel** 93.32.65.25 **Fax** 93.3 2.52.94 **Meals** breakfast, lunch, dinner **Prices** rooms 700f-1,700F; breakfast 90F, menus 185F-290F **Rooms** 18, all with bath, air-conditioning, satellite TV, minibar, safe **Credit cards** AE, DC, MC, V **Closed** 8 Jan to 16 Feb

The South

Country hotel, St-Pierre-dels-Forcats

Mouli del Riu

St-Pierre is in one of the Pyrenees' major ski areas, around Font-Romeu. The Mouli – a modern and undistinguished house, despite the traditional-sounding name – is a simple and rather quirky place, in the guide since 1989 but in new hands since 1992. More reports please.

■ St-Pierre-dels-Forcats, 66210 Mont-Louis (Pyrénées-Orientales) **Tel** 68.04.20.36 **Fax** 68.04.20.25 **Meals** breakfast, lunch, dinner **Prices** rooms 230F-280F; menus 85F-145F **Rooms** 15, all with bath, central heating **Credit cards** AE, MC, V **Closed** Wed; Nov to mid-Dec

---

Town hotel, St-Rémy-de-Provence

Hôtel des Arts

The shady pavement tables of this unpretentious place have long been a happy spot to sit and watch the Provençal world go by. The restaurant serves well cooked, reasonably priced, simple food (liberally laced with the region's herbs). Bedrooms seem secondary but are neatly done out in rustic style.

■ 30 Blvd Victor-Hugo, 13210 St-Rémy-de-Provence (Bouches-du-Rhône) **Tel** 90.92.08.50 **Fax** 90.92.55.09 **Meals** breakfast, lunch, dinner **Prices** rooms 185F-328F; menus 95F-160F **Rooms** 17, all with central heating, phone **Credit cards** AE, MC, V **Closed** Feb; restaurant, Tues

---

Château hotel, St-Rémy-de-Provence

Château des Alpilles

An elegant, upright 19thC manor house offering an atmosphere of gracious living combined with the facilities of a modern luxury hotel. Bedrooms are spacious and furnished with antiques, the bathrooms marble and modern. Food is served by the swimming-pool in summer.

■ Route Départementale 31, 13210 St-Rémy-de-Provence (Bouches-du Rhône) **Tel** 90.92.03.33 **Fax** 90.92.45.17 **Meals** breakfast **Prices** rooms 860F-1,080F; suite 1,290F-1,660F; breakfast 74F, menus 180F-250F **Rooms** 20, all with bath, central heating, phone, satellite TV, radio, minibar **Credit cards** AE , DC, MC, V **Closed** Jan to Mar

---

Country hotel, St-Rémy-de-Provence

Domaine de Valmouraine

The McHugos, who now manage the Château de Roussan, offer a rather more indulgent experience at their own charming farmhouse, stylishly converted into a hotel in the late 1980s. It is beautifully furnished in rustic style, and the flowery gardens contain a smart pool. Good, inventive food.

■ Petite Route des Baux, 13210 St-Rémy-de-Provence (Bouches-du-Rhône) **Tel** 90.92.44.62 **Fax** 90.92.37.32 **Meals** breakfast, lunch, dinner **Prices** rooms 590F-1,310F; breakfast 65F, menus 220F-3 30F **Rooms** 14, all with bath, central heating, air-conditioning, phone, TV, minibar, hairdrier **Credit cards** AE, DC, MC, V **Closed** never

The South

Farm guest-house, St-Rémy-de-Provence

Mas des Carassins

One of the few hotels occupying an authentic mas: a farmhouse built in 1854, mellow and peaceful, set in large and rambling gardens. Almost all the bedrooms have views of the rocky Alpilles and there is a cosy sitting-room with books and plenty of local information.

■ 1 Chemin Gaulois, 13210 St-Rémy-de-Provence (Bouches-du-Rhône) **Tel** 90.92.15.48 **Fax** 90.92.63.47 **Meals** breakfast; simple evening meal on request **Prices** rooms 370F-520F **Rooms** 15, all with bath, central heating, phone **Credit cards** MC, V **Closed** mid-Nov to mid-Mar

---

Village inn, St-Restitut

Auberge des Quatres Saisons

The vine-clad auberge is a fascinating conversion of ancient houses in a backwater perched village, preserving many of the old stone walls. Bedrooms are quiet, rather dark and cosy – with heavy patterns and furniture, in Provençal style. Good regional fare.

■ Place de l'Eglise, 26130 St-Restitut (Drôme) **Tel** 75.04.71.88 **Fax** 75.04.70.88 **Meals** breakfast, lunch, dinner **Prices** rooms 325F-450F; menus 130F-195F **Rooms** 10, all with bath or shower, phone **Credit cards** AE, DC, MC, V **Closed** Jan; Sat lunch

---

Seaside villa, St-Tropez

Le Yaca

This smart little hotel has been cleverly converted from three 200-year-old buildings, using a confusing mix of styles, but with 'rustic-chic' predominating. Bedrooms are furnished with antiques, simply decorated in a typical southern style, but with all the comforts.

■ 1 Blvd d'Aumale, 83990 St-Tropez (Var) **Tel** 94.97.11.79 **Fax** 94.97.58.50 **Meals** breakfast **Prices** rooms 1,200F-2,300F, suite 3,400F; breakfast 85F **Rooms** 23, all with bath, central heating, air-conditioning, phone, TV, radio, minibar **Credit cards** AE, DC, MC, V **Closed** mid-Oct to Easter

---

Village hotel, Séguret

Table du Comtat

Built against the hillside above a tiny, unspoilt medieval village, this hotel enjoys wonderful views. The much modernized interior is light, airy and spacious, with attractive fabrics and furniture. Excellent, eclectic food, Michelin-starred. Pool.

■ Séguret, 84110 Vaison-la-Romaine (Vaucluse) **Tel** 90.46.91.49 **Fax** 90.46.94.27 **Meals** breakfast, lunch, dinner **Prices** rooms 420F-600F; menus 250F-450F **Rooms** 8, all with bath, central heating, phone, TV **Credit cards** AE, DC, MC, V **Closed** Tue and Wed, except Jul, Aug, Easter and Christmas

The South

Restaurant with rooms, Tavel

Hostellerie du Seigneur

This congenial little restaurant-with-rooms is a cosy place, with a pleasant little terrace overlooking a square. Inside a bar-cum-reception area leads into the hotel's hub: an intimate stone-vaulted dining-room where cuisine bourgeoise is offered. Bedrooms are old-fashioned but entirely adequate.

■ Place du Seigneur, 30126 Tavel (Gard) **Tel** 66.50.04.26
Meals breakfast, lunch, di nner **Prices** rooms 170F-280F; menus 95F-136F **Rooms** 7, all with central heating **Credit cards** MC, V
Closed mid-Dec to mid-Jan

Country hotel, Tourtour

La Bastide de Tourtour

This modern but traditional-style hotel offers comfort and attentive service (it is in the Relais & Châteaux group), and the food is excellent, if not in the first rank. For many, the key attraction is the secluded setting, high up amid pine forests. Swimming-pool.

■ Rte de Draguignan, Tourtour, 83690 Salernes (Var) **Tel** 94.70.57.30
Fax 94.70.54.9 0 **Meals** breakfast, lunch, dinner **Prices** rooms 420F-1,400F; lunch 160F, menus 290F-360F **Rooms** 25, all with bath, central heating, phone, TV, minibar **Credit cards** AE, DC, V **Closed** Nov to mid-Mar

---

Manor house hotel, Tourtour

L'Auberge Saint-Pierre

This 16thC manor house is a peaceful, unpretentious retreat run as a welcoming hotel by the helpful Marcellins. The public rooms preserve something of a medieval feel; the spacious bedrooms are newly refurbished. Food relies heavily on produce of the home farm. Pool.

■ Tourtour, 83690 Salernes (Var) **Tel** 94.70.57.17 **Fax** 94.70.59.04
Meals breakfast, lunch, dinner **Prices** rooms 400F-520F; breakfast 50F, menus 170F-200F **Rooms** 18, all with bath or shower, central heating, phone **Credit cards** V **Closed** Oct to end Mar; restaurant only, Wed

---

Restaurant with rooms, Valence

Pic

The food's the thing. Despite the death in 1992 of Jacques Pic, this remains (under son Alain) one of the best restaurants in the country – yet it is delightfully free of any snobby atmosphere. Comfortable bedrooms, newly decorated and rarely vacant. Be aware that the 'cheap' menu is only for weekday lunchtimes.

■ 285 Ave Victor-Hugo, 26001 Valence (Drôme) **Tel** 75.44.15.32
Fax 75.40.96.03 **Meals** breakfast, lunch, dinner **Prices** rooms 700F-1,000F; breakfast 100F, menus 280F-650F **Rooms** 5, all with bath, central heating, phone, TV **Credit cards** AE, DC, MC, V **Closed** Sun evening; 3 weeks Aug

The South

Village hotel, Vénasque

Auberge la Fontaine

First an excellent restaurant, then five lovely suites, then in 1993 an alternative 'bistro' – the Soelkes show no sign of flagging. The rooms in this 18thC village house are decorated in rustic style – stone-flagged floors, wooden furniture, dried flowers.

■ Place de la Fontaine, Vénasque, 84210 Carpentras (Vaucluse) **Tel** 90.66.02.96 **Fax** 90.66.13.14 **Meals** breakfast, lunch (in bistro), dinner **Prices** rooms 700F; breakfast from 50F, lunch 80F, dinner 200F **Rooms** 5, all with bath, central heating, air-conditioning, phone, TV, radio, minibar, hairdrier **Credit cards** MC, V **Closed** restaurant and bistro only, mid-Nov to mid-Dec

---

Town villa, Vence

La Roseraie

This 'belle époque' villa has undergone considerable refurbishment over the past few years. Enthusiastic visitors describe the owners as 'gracious and accommodating', the bedrooms, decorated in Provençal style, as 'rather small but comfortable'. Splendid views, and the place itelf is 'an oasis of peace'. Pool.

■ Ave Henri Giraud, 06140 Vence (Alpes-Maritimes) **Tel** 93.58.02.20 **Fax** 93.58.99.31 **Meals** breakfast **Prices** rooms 380F-480F; breakfast 45F **Rooms** 12, all with bath, central heating, phone, TV, radio, minibar, hairdrier **Credit cards** AE, MC, V **Closed** never

---

Town hotel, Villeneuve-lès-Avignon

Hôtel de l'Atelier

This old town house has been sympathetically restored – original stone walls much in evidence – with careful attention to detail. There is a picturesque courtyard at the back, enclosed by a jumble of old buildings – an ideal place in which to sit and drink muscat before dinner.

■ 5 Rue de la Foire, 30400 Villeneuve-lès-Avignon (Gard) **Tel** 90.25.01.84 **Fax** 90.25 .80.06 **Meals** breakfast **Prices** rooms 220F-450F; breakfast 38F-42F **Rooms** 19, all with bath or shower, central heating, phone; some have TV **Credit cards** AE, DC, MC, V **Closed** Nov to Dec

Corsica

Corsica isn't our strong point. The reports we get from readers on Corsican hotels can be counted on the fingers of one hand.

Contenders in Corsica
Pioggiola, Auberge de l'Aghjola 95.61.90.48 Family-run creeper-clad inn; beams and painted furniture.
Porticcio, Le Maquis 95.25.05.55 Sophisticated fairly pricey (but special) hotel by water's edge.
St-Florent, Hôtel Bellevue 95.37.00.06 Chic, freshly decorated modern hotel with sea views and ambitious food.

Seaside hotel, Barcaggio

La Giraglia

The rooms in this simple creeper-covered stone building are no more than adequate, but the position overlooking the sea is superb and the atmosphere is relaxed and welcoming. This is a lovely and wild part of Corsica, well off the beaten tourist track. We would welcome more reports.

■ Barcaggio, 20275 Essa (Corse) **Tel** 95.35.60.54 **Fax** 95.35.65.92 **Meals** breakfast **Prices** rooms 320F-420F with breakfast **Rooms** 14, all with central heating, phone **Credit cards** not accepted **Closed** late Sep to mid-Apr

---

Country hotel, Calvi

La Signoria

A very welcome addition to our thin Corsica section – a 17thC country house in lush grounds, furnished and decorated with stylish simplicity. Inventive and excellent food is served in a beamed, ochre-washed room or beneath palms on the terrace overlooking the smart pool. There is also tennis and a steam room.

■ Route de la Forêt de Bonifato, 20260 Calvi (Corse) **Tel** 95.65.23.73 **Fax** 95.65.38.77 **Meals** breakfast, lunch (except Jul/Aug), dinner **Prices** rooms 450F-2000F; breakfast 70F; meals 300F-350F **Rooms** 10, all with bath, air-conditioning, phone, hairdrier, TV, minibar, safe **Credit cards** AE, MC, V **Closed** Nov to Mar

---

Village inn, Monticell

A Pasturella

Recent reports confirm the attractions of this modest little 'gem' on the square of a sleepy hill village, its bar at the very heart of local life. Bedrooms are pretty and mostly spacious, with terraces and balconies giving views. Food is wholesome and generous.

■ Monticello, 20220 l'Ile-Rousse (Corse) **Tel** 95.60.05.65 **Fax** 95.60.21.78 **Meals** breakfast, lunch, dinner **Prices** rooms 300F-320F; menu 140F **Rooms** 19, all with bath or shower, phone **Credit cards** DC , MC, V **Closed** Nov; restaurant only, Sun dinner Dec to Mar

Index of hotel names

In this index, hotels are arranged in order of the most distinctive part of their name; very common prefixes such as 'Auberge', 'Hôtel', 'Hostellerie' and 'Le/La/Les' are omitted, but more significant elements such as 'Château' are retained.

Index of hotel names

Index of hotel names

Index of hotel names

Index of hotel locations

In this index, hotels are arranged by the name of the city, town or village they are in or near. Hotels located in a very small village may be indexed under the name of a larger place nearby.

Index of hotel locations

221

Index of hotel locations

Index of hotel locations